# Pitt Series in Policy and Institutional Studies

Bo Rothstein

# The Social Democratic State

The Swedish Model and the Bureaucratic Problem
of Social Reforms

University of Pittsburgh Press
Pittsburgh and London

Published by the University of Pittsburgh Press, Pittsburgh, Pa. 15261
Copyright © 1996, University of Pittsburgh Press
Manufactured in the United States of America
Printed on acid-free paper

10   9   8   7   6   5   4   3   2   1

LIBRARY OF CONGRESS CATALOGING-IN-PUBLICATION DATA
Rothstein, Bo, 1954–
     The social democratic state : the Swedish model and the bureaucratic problem of
social reform / Bo Rothstein.
          p.   cm.—(Pitt series in policy and institutional studies)
          Includes bibliographical references and index.
          ISBN 0-8229-3881-2 (alk. paper). — ISBN 0-8229-5674-8 (pbk.:alk.paper)
          1. Sveriges socialdemokratiska arbetareparti. 2. Sweden—Politics and government—
1905–1950.   3. Sweden—Politics and government—1950–1973.   4.Sweden—Social policy
5. Bureaucracy—Sweden.   I. Title.   II. Series.
JN7995.S86R68   1995
324.2485'072—dc20                                                           95-2869
                                                                            CIP

A CIP catalogue record for this book is available from the British Library.
Eurospan, London

# Contents

# Abbreviations

AK    The Unemployment Commission (Sw. Statens
      Arbetslöshetskommission)
AK    Swedish Parliament, Second Chamber (Sw. Riksdagens
      andra kammare)
AMK   The Labor Market Commission (Sw. Statens
      Arbetsmarknadskommission)
AMS   The National Labor Market Board (Sw.
      Arbetsmarknadsstyrelsen)
ATR   The National Association of Employment Service Officers
      (Sw. Arbetsförmedingstjänstemännen riksförbund)
Ds    Reports from the Ministries (sw. Departementsserien)
FK    Swedish Parliament, First Chamber (Sw. Riksdagens
      första kammare)
KÖY   The National Board for Vocational Training (Sw. Kungl.
      Överstyrelsen för yrkesutbildning)

LO        The Swedish Confederation of (blue collar) Unions
          (Sw. Landsorganisationen)

Prop.     Government Bill (Sw. Riksdagsproposition)

RD        Swedish Parliament (Sw. Riksdagen)

RRV       The National Audit Bureau (Sw. Riksrevisionsverket)

SACO      Swedish Confederation of Professional Associations
          (Sw. Sveriges Akademikers Centralorganisation)

SAF       The Swedish Employers' Federation (Sw. Svenska
          arbetsgivareförening)

SAP       The Swedish Social Democratic Party

SCB       The Swedish National Bureau of Statistics (Sw. Statistiska
          centralbyrån)

SOU       Government Reports (Sw. Statens offentliga utredningar)

SÖ        The National Board of Education (Sw. Skolöverstyrelsen)

TCO       The Swedish Federation of Salaried Employees (Sw.
          Tjänstemännens Centralorganisation)

# Preface

This book has a long and somewhat winding history. It began in 1979 when I started working as a research assistant in a project entitled Sweden Under Social Democracy 1932–1976. The project was based at the Department of Sociology at the University of Lund and financed by the Swedish Research Council for the Humanities and Social Sciences.

During the project, I realized there was something strange about how the relation between the ruling Social Democratic party (SAP) and the Swedish bureaucracy had been commonly portrayed. In brief, the picture painted in textbooks and in research made this relationship appear unproblematic. Social Democratic governments, which had then ruled Sweden for forty-four years, had enacted many new laws and social reforms, and the existing bureaucratic state machinery had faithfully carried them out. This simply could not be true, I thought, and so I started searching for the flaws in this pretty picture.

This research issued in my dissertation in political science, which was published (in Swedish) and defended at the University of Lund in 1986. This book is a revised version of that dissertation. In 1991, owing to unexpected lucky circumstances, I got the chance to start work on revising this dissertation. Since it was written for a Swedish audience, however, and as I have come upon some new ideas about how to structure my argument, this revision became a much more complicated affair than I had expected. While the empirical chapters (4–7) have been left largely intact, the theoretical and concluding chapters (1–3, 8–9) have been rewritten from start to finish.

It is a pleasure to acknowledge the assistance I received in the course of researching and writing this manuscript. I am deeply indebted especially to the following three persons (in order of appearance). Göran Therborn invited me to participate in the Sweden Under Social Democracy 1932–76 project and gave me both the inspiration and opportunity to take on this research. Lennart Lundquist was for me the perfect thesis adviser, always supportive without ever loosing his critical edge. He read and commented upon more drafts than I want to remember—a man with great patience. Gunnar Olofsson shared generously his abundance of ideas and introduced me to what social science research is all about.

Several other persons read and commented upon drafts that eventually did, or did not, become parts of this book, or gave me valuable help and advice. I want to thank Göran Arnman, Torben Beck-Jørgensen, Tomas Bergström, Boel Berner, Hans Blomkvist, Bengt Gesser, Jörgen Hermansson, Magnus Jerneck, Anders Kjellberg, Staffan Marklund, Tommy Nilsson, Per Nyström, Johan P. Olsen, AnnChristin Rothstein, Mats Sjölin, Lars-Göran Stenelo, Nils Stjernquist, and the participants in Torbjörn Vallinder's seminar at the Department of Political Science at the University of Lund. Special thanks also to Rolf Torstendahl for inviting me to present my ideas to his research group at the Department of History at Uppsala University.

I would also like to thank the many persons I interviewed for this book. Especially Bertil Olsson, Nils-Gustav Rosén, and Ove Jönsson who gave me invaluable information about sensitive issues.

I would never have started rewriting the book for an English edition without encouragement from Jonas Pontusson. When it comes to understanding the "limits of reformism" in general, and the Swedish Social Democrats in particular, he is the person whom I like most to disagree with. And if Sven Steinmo had not invited me to Colorado (where he almost outskied me), the idea that I could make the argument understandable for a non-Scandinavian audience would never have come to my mind.

Lastly, I would like to thank Patrik Hort who made the original translation of chapters 4 through 7, and Christine Ingebritsen and Peter Mayers who checked my efforts to write the rest of the book in English. Peter also gave the last version of the manuscript a final check and at the same time gave me much valuable advice about the substance and presentation of the argument.

I am grateful for the financial support for the project from the Swedish Council for Research in the Humanities and Social Sciences. Parts of the original research as well as the translation of chapters 4 through 7 were financed by the council.

# The Social Democratic State

# 1. Understanding Social Democracy

## The Problem

This book began as an effort to understand the political logic of Swedish social democracy (henceforth SAP, Sw. Socialdemokratiska Arbetarpartiet). As the world's most successful social democratic party (at least in electoral terms), the SAP seemed to merit study. It has led the government for fifty-two of the last sixty-two years, and indeed its success must be reckoned outstanding among all Western political parties, social democratic or otherwise.

The party participated in every government from 1932 to 1976, either alone or as the dominant force in a coalition government. The SAP has worked closely, moreover, with a trade union movement organizing about 85 percent of the labor force (the highest rate among the advanced industrial democracies). Even when the bourgeois parties ruled Sweden from 1976 to 1982 (in five different combinations during those six years), they neither challenged social democratic hegemony nor altered any established government programs (Bergström 1991; Heclo and Madsen 1987). Sweden remained a social democratic polity.

In 1982, moreover, the Social Democrats returned to power for a nine-year period, and they have held more seats than any other party in the Swedish Parliament (Riksdag) since 1919. If one wants to know if politics, and most especially reformist politics, matters—if, that is, political mobilization can change democratic capitalist societies—then Sweden under the Social Democrats is clearly one of the best empirical cases to study (Korpi 1983; Pontusson 1992, 1–2; cf. Therborn et al. 1978).

This raises the fundamental question of the true significance of electoral and governmental powers in capitalist societies. These two types of power resource are not the only ones of importance in a capitalist society. Other power resources include organized class movements, interest organizations, bureaucracies, and the mass media as well as groups formed along ethnic, religious, and cultural lines. Traditional Marxian state theory holds that parliamentary power is rather negligible and that reformist governments' freedom of action is severely limited by various structurally embedded, extrapolitical class forces (Carnoy 1984; Isaac 1987; Lindbom 1977; Poulantzas 1968, 1978).

I will argue that some important lessons can be drawn from the Swedish case regarding the possibility for political reformism in other democratic capitalist countries. For more than any other political party in the Western world, the Swedish Social Democrats have been granted the chance to change their society through parliamentary means.

To what degree, then, has the labor movement enjoyed success in its efforts to change Swedish society? As might be expected, social scientists have ventured greatly differing assessments of the impact of the long era of social democratic rule in Sweden. The two extremes in this debate may be summarized as follows: one side argues that, despite their long hold on governmental power, the Social Democrats have succeeded only in making rather marginal changes. After all, Sweden is still basically a capitalist society, and the Social Democrats have neither changed the underlying capitalist economic structure nor gained control over investments. Furthermore, the SAP has succeeded neither in altering the essential structure of power in the production process (Pontusson 1992) nor in producing significant social structural changes (Olofsson 1979; Therborn et al.

1978). Sweden remains, in sum, very much a capitalist class society, and economic and social power rest firmly in the hands of big capital. Moreover, efforts on the part of the labor movement to replace the capitalist logic of economic power have come to nought; ideological defeat and the political strength of Swedish capital have dictated retreat (Gough 1979; Pontusson 1992). By this line of reasoning, which stresses the production side of the economy, the impact of the long period of social democratic political dominance must be considered rather small, perhaps negligible.

The other extreme in this debate highlights the fact that the Social Democrats have established an exceptionally generous and comprehensive welfare state in Sweden. Analysts in this tradition argue that Swedish wage earners have, to a greater extent than workers in any other industrialized democracy, attained relief from being solely dependent on their prospects for selling labor power. Social protection has been established as a universal right of citizenship, moreover, which has enhanced the position of wage earners in a way that means-tested and other stigmatizing social programs cannot (Esping-Andersen 1990; cf. S. E. Olsson 1990; Stephens 1979).

Sweden leads among welfare states in many areas, and has often been considered a model for other countries, not least when it comes to policies for combating unemployment (Mucciaroni 1992, 245–54; Weir 1992; Wilensky 1990). Writers in this tradition argue that the social democratic party, and the labor movement it represents, have been the most important forces behind this development; reformism, therefore, is a viable political option (Esping-Andersen 1985; Korpi 1983; S. E. Olsson 1990).[1] Another distinctive feature of Swedish society is the considerable influence of trade unions, both at the plant level and in national policy making (Heclo and Madsen 1987; Kjellberg 1983; Rothstein 1990).

Persuasive theoretical arguments and empirical evidence can, in my view, be marshaled in support of both these views. How one evaluates Swedish social democracy and, more generally, the possibility of reformism, depends very much on the questions one raises, as well as on the standards one selects for measuring the success of reformism. Yet the possibilities and limits of reformism cannot, for methodological reasons, be judged in this way.

Different authors have chosen different measures for assessing the impact of Swedish social democracy, but these measures have been designed not to confront their main hypotheses but rather to illustrate them. These authors seem, in other words, to have chosen empirical cases that they knew beforehand would prove their theory. These studies have thus aimed mainly at illustrating, rather than challenging or proving, the theories lying behind them (cf. Pedersen 1977).

I shall argue that our understanding of the limits of political reformism ought not be limited by these methodological problems. On the one hand, these theory-illustrating studies do provide a great deal of information about the areas in which reformism in general and the SAP in particular have been successful; they illuminate as well the respects in which they have failed. On the other hand, because of their lack of systematic, theory-challenging comparisons of policies or policy areas, these studies fail to tell us much about the more general conditions under which reformist political strategies are likely to succeed or fail.[2]

One obvious but important conclusion to be drawn from the debate touched on above is that the Swedish Social Democrats have been highly successful in some areas and not so successful in others. In my view, however, if one is to say anything important about the possibilities of reformism, Swedish-style or other, one cannot select such cases as one knows beforehand will tend to support one's hypotheses (George 1979; Pedersen 1977). A more fruitful approach would be to compare successful reformist policies with those which have failed (cf. Pontusson 1993). The major goal of this book is to explain the prospects and limits of reformism by means of such a comparative policy study.

Two problems in particular facing social democratic political strategy have received attention in the social sciences. One is the electoral question—what kinds of policies and political strategies should social democratic parties adopt in order to obtain electoral support sufficient for achieving and holding governmental power? Some have argued that social democracy faces a problematic trade-off in this area (Przeworski 1985; Przeworski and Sprague 1986; Svensson 1994).

The party can either restrict itself to traditional industrial working-class questions, which will make it harder to attain the requisite numbers of supporters (given the existing class structure); in compensation, however, it will be easier to keep the party ideologically and politically united. Or the party can try to broaden its electoral base by adopting policies attractive to white-collar employees and the middle class; this approach might well help the party achieve power, but the dilution of working-class ideology and policy entailed will tend to create strong tensions within the party.

The steepness of this trade-off varies across countries, however, depending on the class structure and the organization of the labor movement; this explains the variable success of different social democratic parties. Some writers have also argued that the steepness of this trade-off can be changed by the specific ways in which social democratic policies are modeled, i.e., some policies create class divisions detrimental to the party, while others serve to unite different groups (e.g., blue- and white-collar workers) behind the party (Davidson 1989; Esping-Andersen 1985; Marklund 1982; Svensson 1994).

The other major problem facing a reformist politics which has attracted attention in the social sciences has to do with social democratic macroeconomic management. Social democratic parties usually rely on a strong union movement, with the consequence that, when in government, these parties must bestow advantages on the unions in the form of wage increases, laws strengthening unions' bargaining position, social policy measures, and, above all, policies to keep unemployment low. This creates a serious problem, however, for a social democratic government must simultaneously keep capitalists contented enough (i.e., confident that money-making prospects are good) to continue investing in the country. Union demands must be balanced, in other words, with the interests of capital. Social democratic governments have usually sought to manage this conflict by introducing various corporatist arrangements; the result has been a range of economic, industrial, and employment policies designed to satisfy both labor and capital (Cameron 1984; Hall 1986; Garrett and Lange 1989, 1991; Hibbs 1977; Katzenstein 1985; Lange 1984, 1987; Scharpf 1991; Shonfield 1965).

Both of these research programs have contributed substantially to our understanding of the problems faced by political reformism. This book, however, addresses a third and often neglected obstacle to the achievement of reformist aspirations. There are, according to classical Marxian state theory, not one but two types of structural hindrance to reformism. One was mentioned above: the structural power embodied in capitalists' control over investments. The other, with which I deal in this study, is the bureaucratic bourgeois state apparatus.

Briefly, I argue the following: even if the electoral problem has been solved, and even if corporatist macroeconomic agreements are in place, a social democratic government must make sure its policies are implemented by the state machinery in accordance with the political intentions and goals of the party. If the policies are not carried out in the way the party has intended, or are not implemented at all, the electorate will respond negatively no matter how clever the party's strategy to incorporate different social classes has been.

The same may be said of any macroeconomic corporatist agreements by social democratic governments. They can "be expected to pursue active labor market policies that facilitate rapid and positive adjustment to changes in international market conditions by the work force" (Garrett and Lange 1991, 546). In theory this is certainly true, but I argue that these policies will be of no value in securing economic balance and growth, not to mention the electoral prospects for the government, if not implemented in accordance with the government's intent.

The basic premise of reformist politics is that, in order to govern, a social democratic party must be able to direct the state machinery. The question dividing Marxist thinkers is whether this "committee for managing the common affairs for the whole bourgeoisie" (to use the classical formulation of Marx and Engels) can be a viable instrument for implementing socialist policies (Carnoy 1984, 50–55; Pierson 1986). For just as battle is what armies are about, policy is what political parties are about. One might say, quoting Engels, that the effort to implement policy is to politics "what cash payment is to trade, for however rarely it may be necessary for it actually to occur, everything is directed towards it, and eventually it must take place all the same and must be decisive" (quoted in Keegan 1976, 28).

The problem of governance, then—of the character of the bureaucratic bourgeois state—is a critical third "limit of reformism" faced by social democratic parties, in addition to the electoral and macroeconomic problems mentioned above. If one wishes to understand social democracy one cannot, in my view, ignore this problem. Indeed, effective governance has historically posed a major problem for social democratic governments.

This third problem has been well documented, in the British case, by the former minister of housing, Richard Crossman, in his recollections of his dealings with the "mandarins" of Westminster (Crossman 1975). Seymour Martin Lipset, moreover, wrote a fascinating account of this problem in his study of a local branch of the Canadian social democracy (Lipset 1950). Another telling example can be taken from the history of the German Social Democratic Party. The famous German Social Democrat and economist, Rudolf Hilferding, took office as the minister of finance in 1923. The leading bureaucrats in the ministry decided, however, to run the ministry without taking any notice of their new minister. After a short while, Hilferding suffered a nervous breakdown. When he returned upon recovering, he had to promise the mandarins not to interfere further with the operations of the Prussian ministerial bureaucracy (Beetham 1985, 12–14). Aside from this and many other similar stories, in any case, it is obvious that, if a social democratic government cannot get the state machinery to implement its policies in accordance with its intentions, every electoral and macroeconomic strategy of the type mentioned above will be invalid, for the simple reason that it will not be implemented. The general theme of this study may therefore be stated as follows:

*What limits does a social democratic government labor under, and what possibilities does it enjoy, in using the state to implement large-scale social change?*

This theme implies we must explore yet another classical question in political science—the control and direction of public bureaucracies. There are several reasons for this. For one thing, almost all governments, social democratic or other, are dependent on the state machinery to implement their policies. For another, it was in their view of the state, among other things, that the reformist and revolutionary branches of the labor movement diverged so markedly. The revolutionary section of the labor movement, in both its Leninist and syndicalist versions, viewed the existing capitalist state (democratic or not) with great suspicion and argued the labor movement could not turn the state to its own interests. Instead, the Leninists argued, the state must be "smashed" and replaced by a new type of state organization; the syndicalists, for their part, opposed using the state in any possible form. The reformist wing of the labor movement, on the other hand, came to accept the existing state apparatus (after voting rights had been extended) and argued the labor movement could and should use the state to improve the standing of the working class (Bernstein [1899] 1965; Lenin [1907] 1967; Luxemburg [1899] 1972; cf. Pierson 1986).

Both Karl Marx and Max Weber, it should be noted, took a stand in this debate concerning the character of the capitalist state and its use for reformist purposes. After the fall of the Paris Commune in 1871, for example, Marx wrote that it had become obvious to him that the working class could not simply take over the existing state apparatus and use it for its own purposes; rather, thorough changes in the structure of the state would be necessary first (Therborn 1980). Just what changes would be needed he never specified, for no fourth volume of *Das Kapital* (which was meant to be about the state) was ever written. Yet it seems clear that, while Marx held reformist views in some respects—after all, the *Communist Manifesto* is a rather reformist document in the specific changes it demands—he nonetheless perceived the discrepancy between the interests of the working class and the capabilities of the existing bureaucratic bourgeois state machinery.

Max Weber, the founder of the theory of modern bureaucracy, actually held almost the same view as Marx. At a meeting in Mannheim in 1907 with the German Society for Social Policy (the Verein für Sozialpolitik), he entered into a debate with some conservative older scholars—the so-called Katheder-sozialisten—about extending the suffrage to the working class. The conservatives feared that, if parliamentary democracy were introduced, the Social Democrats would capture the state and use it to pursue their own narrow class interests (i.e., confiscate capital, etc.). Haunted by this "red spectre," they warned furiously against such a development, considering it contrary to their view of the state bureaucracy's mission, which was to serve no particular political group but rather, in Hegelian fashion, to pursue the "general interest" of society (cf. Vincent 1987). Weber rudely dismissed this argument, however. If the Social Democrats gained political power by democratic means, he averred, it would not be they who conquered the bureaucratic state. Quite the contrary. The bureaucracy, in the long term, would conquer the Social Democrats; he could see no reason, furthermore, why a bourgeois society should fear such a development (Beetham 1985, 166).

He based this argument on the experience of some large European cities in which Social Democrats had been elected to run the city government. He showed how they had been unable to use this position, and the formal control it conferred over municipal administration, to enact the changes feared by the conservative antidemocrats. The Social Democrats had instead been forced to adopt very cautious policies, on account of the incapacity of city administrations to serve as revolutionary instruments. Thus, two major classical writers in the social sciences pointed out the problematic relation between the labor movement and the bureaucratically organized state; both argued the latter is best seen as a hindrance to achieving the goals of the former. Among the many limits to reformism, therefore, it is clear that—from *both* a Marxian and a Weberian standpoint—the bureaucratic state deserves especially close scrutiny.

The bureaucratic phenomenon has, of course, attracted a great deal of attention in the social sciences. Samuel Eisenstadt beautifully captured the problem of politics and organization in a sentence both short and simple: the question is "whether bureaucracy is master or servant, an independent body or a tool, and if a tool, whose interests it can be made to serve" (Eisenstadt 1965, 179). Any inquiry into the limits of reformism must confront the problem of bureaucracy and implementation, since, as adumbrated above, a reformist government bent on achieving social change is dependent on the state administration's willingness and ability to perform in accordance with government intention (cf. Skocpol and Finegold 1982). Yet when it comes to evaluating the impact of the SAP on Swedish society, this aspect of Marxian state theory—concerning the party's relationship to the Swedish state apparatus—has been almost completely neglected. Neither those affirming nor those denying the possibility of reform from above have investigated this question.

This is more than passing strange, since bureaucratic inertia is generally considered a highly significant obstacle to implementing policies for social change (Ripley and Franklin 1982). It is well known, of course, that the study of public administration and public policy has often been restricted to narrow questions of administrative efficiency, due process, and technical rationality (Fesler 1990). Let me state here that I do not share this apolitical view of the administrative question. On the contrary, a central aim of this study is to demonstrate that, behind seemingly apolitical administrative problems, questions of the greatest political importance lie hidden. The British author, Malcolm Muggeridge, has in my view captured this problem most precisely, albeit in an area other (and more interesting) than politics:

I have always been deeply interested in the administrative side of love, which I find more absorbing than its purely erotic aspects. What Lady Chatterly and her gamekeeper did in the woods is, to me, of only passing interest, compared with how they got there, what arrangements were made for shelter in the case of inclement weather, and for refreshments, how they accounted for their absence, whether either party could recover incidental expenses and if so, how. This attitude is, after all, not so unreasonable. Most great generals have admitted that planning campaigns and winning victories in the field is relatively easy compared with arranging transport and supplies. An army, Napoleon said, in one of his most celebrated remarks, marches on its stomach. So do lovers. If the administrative arrangements are faulty, the campaign which follows cannot be but laborious, and even victory brings little satisfaction. (Muggeridge 1961, 61)

The intent of this study is thus to reintroduce the state machinery as an important factor in explaining the success or failure of reformism. I write "*re*introduce," since I mean to refer back to the writings of Max Weber and, though he did not elaborate on the matter of administration in detail, of Karl Marx. More recently, the complexity of the relationship between the state and the labor movement has been underlined by those attempting to "bring the state back in" (Block 1987; Crouch 1986; Heclo 1974; Lembruch 1991; Skocpol 1985; Weir and Skocpol 1985). As Theda Skocpol and Kenneth Finegold (1982) stated in one of the earliest works in this approach, no guarantee exists that governments will command the organizational capacity to implement the policies they set forth. I am very sympathetic to this line of reasoning, as will become clear below, but for my purposes I pose the question a bit differently.

Theda Skocpol and her colleagues, who have renewed interest in the relation between the state and the development of social policies, have argued that one reason for the highly variable success of Western labor parties in executing social policies may be found in the structure and capacity of the state, rather than in such socially structured variables as the political mobilization of the working class. Some types of state administration and/or administrators have at certain critical historical moments been more favorable to the introduction of social policies than others, and this has had long-term effects on the development of both social policies and labor parties.

My argument in this study is, however, a bit different. First, I contend that state structure does not just facilitate or hinder the initial translation of social demands into operative public policies. The role of the public administration is critical also (negatively or positively) *after such policies* are introduced. Once introduced, some reformist policies fail and others succeed on account of how the administrative apparatuses responsible for implementing them are organized. Thus, whether state structure has its effect before or after the introduction of a policy (or at both times) should be considered an open question.

A second and more significant difference I have with the "state capacity" school is that, while they view the structure of the state as a given—which politicians and parties must accept as objective—I argue this is not always the case. On the contrary, the organization (and reorganization) of the state is at certain times within the power of political parties—that is, they can refashion it into a more suitable instrument for pursuing their objectives. The same argument can be made against such notions as "policy legacies" and "path dependency" (David 1985; cf. North 1990, chap. 11).

I do not propose, however, to add yet another argument to the debate about the relative importance of societal versus state forces (Noble 1988; Skocpol and Finegold vs. Goldfield 1991). I intend, rather, to demonstrate the importance of explaining the varying logic of the interaction between social forces and state structures at different points in history (Birnbaum 1988; Lembruch 1991). The state should be seen, in sum, both as a structure and as an object for political structuration (Giddens 1984).

Several quite different schools of thought converge in analyzing the relation between reformist policies and public administration. One such school is the structural variant of Marxism, which became prominent in Western Europe and the United States in the 1960s (Poulantzas 1968, 1978; cf. Block 1987; Carnoy 1984). Structural Marxism aims to establish, on a macrotheoretical level, the structural limits to state action in democratic capitalist societies (e.g., Carnoy 1984; Jessop 1982). This school sought to develop a new Marxian theory of the state's relation to various class-based political forces.

Another approach, somewhat similar to the foregoing, may be found in neoinstitutional theory. This approach focuses on political institutions as key to explaining the variation in, among other things, social policies. Neoinstitutionalists portray political institutions as not merely the outcome of political struggles, but also as an important cause of variation in the formation and impact of policies, as well as in the influence of different class-based political movements drawing strength from such policies. Political institutions, such as government organizations, are thus seen as intermediate variables, located between deeper social and economic structures on the one hand, and political behavior on the other (Hall 1986; Immergut 1992; Olsen 1983; Rothstein 1990; Steinmo and Thelen 1992).

Interest in the possibility of politically imposed social change has also arisen in an intellectual tradition altogether different from the two mentioned above. Since the early 1970s, a growing number of public policy studies have focused on problems of implementation. These studies examine primarily the microlevel of the policy process—the behavior of individual bureaucrats, professional groups, and public organizations. An interesting feature of this research is the close study of how political intentions, as expressed in policy goals at the central level, are translated into actual practice on the local level (see Lipsky 1980; Mazmanian and Sabatier 1983; Palumbo and Calista 1990; Scharpf 1977). In his classical study, *The Forest Ranger*, Herbert Kaufman stated that "policy is enunciated in rhetoric; it is realized in action" (1960, 3).

Thanks to these case studies, we now know much more about the conditions under which particular policy goals are likely to succeed or fail. Implementation research may be thought of as research in "empirical state theory," because it entails examining what the democratic capitalist state can and, most importantly, cannot do (Rothstein 1992b, 109).

Even if these research traditions vary greatly in intellectual origins and theoretical ambitions, they do have some common attributes. One is their main object of study: *state interventionism* in its various forms. It is not legalistic, rule-governed policies that are in question, nor are such social policies as social insurance the object of attention. Socially invasive policies, rather, which aim to achieve social change by means of direct state intervention in markets and other social relations, are the focus of study. Richard Elmore has stressed, from an implementation perspective, the difficulty of achieving changes in such areas as education, employment, housing, and regional economic growth (1978, 186). Writing from a Marxist viewpoint, Claus Offe has argued that an inherent weaknesses of the Keynesian welfare state "resides in the limits of its legal-bureaucratic, monetarized and professional mode of intervention," which is especially problematic in personal services and "people-processing" areas such as education, health care, employment, and social work (1983, 242–43; cf. Mayntz 1978, 633).

Another common feature of these research programs is their focus on the organizational structure of the state as an important limit to successful political intervention. Marxian state theory, the neoinstitutional school, and implementation research have all heightened interest in peering inside "the black box"—the organizational processes and institutions which transform centrally enunciated policy goals into concrete results (Clarke and Dear 1984; Offe 1984; Olsen 1983; Palumbo and Calista 1990).

In this study, I do not opt for one of these three approaches as the best suited for solving the question of the limits of reformism. Instead, I adopt a conscious eclecticism aimed at integrating findings from all three research programs. I argue that each approach aids us significantly in understanding the problem of reformism; all three have limited application, however, on account of their restriction to a single level of analysis. For while these approaches all deal with essentially the same problem, they operate on different analytical levels.

An adequate explanation of reformism's limits must link these levels. Any explanation limited to a single level must remain incomplete. As Peter Hall has argued, it is necessary to connect the study of ideas and policies with the study of administration (1989; cf. Scharpf 1977). Therefore, one aim of this study is to combine approaches from these disparate theoretical traditions.

## The Empirical Cases

I submit my basic argument, and substantiating empirical cases as well, in chapters 3 and 4. I also explain the logic of my case selection in these chapters. To anticipate briefly here: in order to cast light on the limits of reformism problem, I propose to compare a successful reformist policy with one that has failed. One way to do this would be to compare results when the same policy was launched by social democratic parties in different countries. This strategy holds the advantage that the specific policy can be held constant, thus enhancing the value of the comparison. Against this, however, one could argue that social democratic parties employ varying strategies to cope with obstacles to reform, and that these strategies are what matter (Scharpf 1991).

Other points against such a choice of empirical cases are obvious: no two similar policies in different nations are quite the same, nor are any two social democratic parties perfectly alike in character or objectives; furthermore, class structure, policy styles, political institutions, and political culture all vary greatly between countries (cf. King and Rothstein 1993). A comparison of educational policy in different countries, for example, might tell us a lot about cross-national variations in school systems but rather less about the limits of reformism, since the surrounding circumstances may be too dissimilar.

Comparing different policies in one country has the advantage that one can hold other possible variables explaining the success or failure of a given reformist policy—social democratic electoral strategies, capitalist investment patterns, national political culture, etc.—constant (cf. George 1979; Skocpol 1988; cf. Pontusson 1993). This frees us to examine the structure of the different state apparatuses—precisely the variable of importance for the theoretical questions addressed in this study. It is this variation which might increase our understanding about how different organizational settings condition the possibility for politically imposed social change.

The choice of cases is of course critical for a study of this kind, and one can argue at length for various choices. The policy success I have chosen is the Swedish active labor market policy, while the Swedish comprehensive school reform serves as the policy failure. The reasons for these choices are several. First, these two cases are indeed clear examples of policy success and failure respectively, as will be shown in chapter 4. Success and failure are of course problematic notions, and I do not argue the former policy was an unblemished success nor the latter an unmitigated failure. I do stress, however, that the variation in success between these two policies has been considerable, when measured against the political intentions behind them.

Secondly, both policies have been central to the SAP's long-term political strategy for changing Swedish society. It would be misleading, of course, to compare two policies varying greatly in the importance attached to them by the leadership of the labor movement.

Both of the policies considered here, however, have been central to the SAP, both for their own merits and, more importantly, for their instrumental value in creating a more egalitarian society.

Thirdly, both policies (the active labor market policy especially) have played a critical role in "the Swedish Model" (Heclo and Madsen 1987; Katzenstein 1985, 119; Tilton 1990; 193–214). Both, moreover, are typical instances of the type of state interventionism, or socially invasive policy, described above.

Finally, both policies entail massive organizational efforts at the stage of implementation. This feature enables us to study the role and importance of state apparatuses in regard to interventionist policies. If the bureaucratic organization of the capitalist state hinders the successful implementation of reformist policies, this should be plainly visible in these two cases. For the structure of state agencies may well determine the fortunes of policies; Mucciaroni furnishes an example of this when, contrasting the failure of efforts to establish an active labor market policy in the U.S. with the policy's success in Sweden, he writes that "employment programs can contribute to the attainment of economic policy goals only if they are carried out by an administrative apparatus with sufficient resources at its disposal and if it has the ability to intervene flexibly in the labor market" (1992, 226). As I show below, however, the construction of such an administrative apparatus is more easily said than done.

There is, furthermore, a crucial temporal similarity between these two policies. Roughly speaking, they were both planned during the late 1940s, put to a large-scale test during the 1950s, and implemented on a full scale during the 1960s and 1970s. The overarching political, social, cultural, and economic background can thus be held constant by examining these two cases of Social Democratic reformism.

The success of the labor market policy can be measured not least in the great international interest it has aroused since the mid-1960s, both among policy makers and among scholars in comparative public policy. Many OECD countries tried similar policies during the 1960s and 1970s but with meager results. Harold Wilensky and Lowell Turner conclude that, "in sophistication, resource commitment and policy continuity, as well as success in reducing unemployment, Sweden is unrivalled" (1987, 26; cf. Scharpf 1991).

In the last three years, moreover, no less than three scholarly studies have been published analyzing the failure of employment policy in the U.S., with all three pointing to Sweden as the opposite, successful case (Janoski 1990; Mucciaroni 1992; Weir 1992). However, while these authors all stress institutional features, such as government capacity, in explaining differences between Sweden and the U.S. in this area, they have not, as I show below, grasped fully the underlying institutional factors behind this policy's success in Sweden.

In summary, we can study here two important cases of interventionist reforms while holding constant such critical variables as the major political force sponsoring the reform, prevailing national political values, the political and constitutional systems, the time at which the reform was introduced, and the overall social and economic structure. The reason we can hold all these variables constant is, of course, that the two policies were applied within the same country at the same time. It is true that substantial differences between these two policies create difficulties of comparability, but much the same problem would arise were we to compare similar policies in different countries, for there is really no such thing as identical policies in different countries.

## The Organization of the Book

The following chapter is devoted to presenting the theoretical project of this study. It also includes a more specific argument for the choice of method than presented hitherto. Chapter 3 is meant to serve as the bridge between the theoretical construction and the empirical cases. I present two theoretical ideal types of government organization—the well-known Weberian bureaucracy, on the one hand, and the cadre organization, on the other. I employ these two ideal types in comparing the state apparatuses enjoined with accomplishing the labor market and school reforms. These ideal types serve to highlight the problem posed by the bureaucratically organized state for implementing reformist policies. I present the two policies themselves in chapter 4, including the political intentions behind them and the results to which they have given rise. Chapters 5, 6, and 7 are the empirical core of the book. I describe the organizational and historical background of the two reforms, as well as their institutional setting, in chapter 5, and I attempt to answer the following question: when the SAP's reformist policies and the Swedish state encountered each other in the early postwar years, what did they look like? Chapters 6 and 7 analyze the organizational structure of the state agencies charged with implementing the two policies. Chapter 8 summarizes the findings and seeks to elucidate the relationship between the bureaucratic state apparatus and the implementation—successful or otherwise—of reformist policies.

The empirical study is restricted largely to the period of uninterrupted Social Democratic governance in Sweden (1932–1976). I have, however, added an epilogue updating the empirical data. This concluding chapter serves to strengthen the conclusions reached earlier, for the fortunes of the two policies and their associated agencies during the 1980s and early 1990s have been very much in congruity with the argument here put forward.

# 2. State, Class, and Organization

## Linking Levels of Analysis

The relation between political reformism and the state may be studied at many different levels. A reformist movement must define its strategy toward the state—both as a whole and in its various parts—and toward political opponents as well. Social democratic reformism is interventionist by its very nature, moreover, which means it must find a way to cope not only with parliamentary problems and macroeconomic strategy, but also with the administrative and bureaucratic side of the political system, for it is the latter part of the system which must actually carry out its reforms.

As indicated in the introduction, the administrative and organizational problems confronting reformism can be studied at several different analytical levels, from the macro- to the microlevel. At least three such levels may be found in the relevant literature (Giddens 1981, 54; Ham and Hill 1984, 17–18; Lundquist 1985; Offe 1985, 221):

1. The relation between state and society

2. The relation between the general character of the state and the organization of specific state apparatuses

3. The relation between the organization of specific state apparatuses and the implementation of policy

One encounters a range of theories and intellectual traditions pertaining to each of these levels. Theories addressing the relation between state and society will be called state theories in this study. This concept has been used mainly in Marxist theory, but other theoretical traditions take up this matter as well, such as corporatist and (in principle) various pluralist approaches (Ham and Hill 1984, 22–44). One reason why the term "state theory" has been used primarily in Marxist analysis may be that the state seemed to have disappeared as a theoretical problem in pluralist theory from the 1960s on (Olsen 1983; Skocpol 1985). As Alan Wolfe put it, "political science became the study, not of the state, but of something at a less rarefied level called government" (1977, xii).

Institutional theory (or organization theory) and implementation theory pertain to the other two levels listed above. As with theories addressing the state/society relation, fundamentally contradictory approaches are taken toward the study of levels two and three. Regarding the institutional level, for instance, not just neoinstitutionalism (March and Olsen 1989; Steinmo and Thelen 1992) but also more traditional organization theories are on offer (Mintzberg 1983; Pfeffer 1982). State apparatuses are, after all, first and foremost organizations, and organizations are among the most important institutions treated in neoinstitutional analysis (cf. March and Olsen 1989). This "organizational link" serves also as a necessary bridge between individual action and the social structure, that is, the micro-macro link. I tend to agree with Göran Ahrne when he writes that "there is no macrostructure above organizations. Individual actors confront 'society' in the form of organizations" (1990, 51). Theories of policy implementation, finally, may in this context be considered microlevel approaches within organization theory. They examine the compatibility between a given policy and the specific state organization responsible for implementing it.[1]

I want to stress that I use the word theory very loosely here. These "theories" are not usually scientific theories proper but rather "approaches," "analytical frameworks," etc. The character of specific theories varies, but one may say that, as a rule, those frameworks usually termed theories are actually loose analytical and intellectual traditions sharing some basic concepts and identifying more or less the same problems. Clearly, the limits of reformism problem has attracted interest from highly various theoretical traditions operating on different levels of analysis.

The usual way of handling this problem is to confine the analysis either to a single analytical level or to a specific theoretical tradition. Scholars tend to identify very strongly with specific levels of analysis (to say nothing of theoretical traditions) and to make only a few loose assumptions (if they make any at all) about problems pertaining to other levels. The major drawback with such a research strategy is its partiality: the analysis remains too narrow to contribute significantly to our understanding of such a complex problem as the limits of politically enforced social change. The main theoretical claim I launch in this book, then, is that multilevel analysis is necessary in studies of this problem.

One frequently encounters calls, on the other hand, for a more comprehensive analysis in this field. Researchers in public policy and administration have emphasized the need to connect the study of administrative institutions to a broader analysis of the state/society relation (Ham and Hill 1984, 17; Lundquist 1985, chap. 2). Eric Wright has written that "Marxists have generally continued to focus on the dynamics and contradictions of capitalist society seen as a total system, while paying relatively little attention to the organizational dynamics of the state." He argues further that scholars in organization theory analyze organizations "in isolation from the social contradictions in which they are embedded" (Wright 1978, 102; cf. Therborn 1980, 37–38). And regarding the level of policy implementation, Fudge and Barrett contend that "the study of implementation at this time needs to consider a linking of levels of analysis" (1981, 250; cf. Wolman 1980, 33–39).

A theme common to the above-mentioned research traditions is the quest for more dynamic and historical analyses of the relation between public policy, politics, and the bureaucracy (Hall 1986; Ham and Hill 1984, 17; Wittrock 1983). I therefore agree with Sven Steinmo and Kathleen Thelen (1992, 3) when they argue that "institutional analyses do not deny the broad political forces that animate various theories of politics: class structure in Marxism, group dynamics in pluralism. Instead, they point to the ways that institutions structure these battles and in so doing, influence their outcomes."

How, then, does one set about this ambitious task of linking analytical levels? Can one combine such very different theoretical traditions as, for example, Marxian state theory and implementation research without falling into a fundamentally contradictory theoretical eclecticism? In my view, it is not fruitful to restrict one's analysis just because of the pejorative sound of the word eclecticism. An approach should not be dismissed as inappropriately eclectic merely because it contains insights from different schools of thought. Eclecticism is inappropriate only insofar as insights from different theories are joined in a logically contradictory and/or analytically inconsistent manner (Giddens 1984, xxii; cf. Offe 1984, 257–60). In fact, combining levels of analysis is necessary, because the empirical object under study is, in fact, multileveled.

The starting point for this journey is a variant of the Marxist theory of the state which, I will argue, is possible to combine with certain features of institutional and organizational theory. These two approaches may in turn incorporate some of the insights of implementation research. My main theoretical goal in this study is to demonstrate that such a theoretical construction is possible, and indeed that it can form the basis for empirical analysis. To accomplish this, I address one of the oldest and most significant theoretical discourses in the social sciences, the agency/structure debate. I draw my basic approach from the organization theorist John K. Benson, who has argued the following:

The policy sector is multi-levelled in the sense that its patterned practices may be divided into several partially autonomous levels, which are related to each other as limits within limits. At each succeeding level, using a metaphor of depth, we encounter a set of limits upon the level just above. Thus the practices at the surface level follow a set of rules to that level and are limited by sets of rules at deeper levels. (1982, 149; cf. Wright 1978, 230)

For example, the behavior of an individual bureaucrat must be understood against the background of his or her local organization, which in turn must be seen in its broader context of the national agency of which it forms a part; this agency, furthermore, must be analyzed in relation to the national state apparatus as a whole (Ahrne 1990, 109). Agency and structure intertwine at all of these levels. What room does such an analysis leave for political actors in bringing about social change? As Anthony Giddens has argued, social scientific approaches concentrating on action have typically accommodated structural variables only with difficulty, and they have failed to relate theories of action to institutional change (1979, 49).

This study, on the other hand, addresses the problems and possibilities of institutional change (cf. Levi 1990). The possible limits to reformism are structural variables such as, in this case, the bureaucratic character of the capitalist state. Structural variables are therefore central to this analysis. But, and I want to underline this point, this furnishes no grounds for dismissing the importance of political action. Quite the contrary. The very purpose of analyzing structural variables *at different levels of analysis* is to make possible a deeper understanding of the possibilities for, and limits to, politically imposed social change.

The questions are therefore: first, if the bureaucratic nature of the capitalist state hinders the successful implementation of reformist policies, can the nature of the state be changed? Second, if the bureaucratic mode of organization is the problem, what is the alternative? In the chapter that follows, I will show that such an alternative exists, namely the cadre organization.

If it is not just necessary but also possible to change state organizations in this manner, can such change be propelled by concrete political actors such as, in this case, a social democratic political party? The relation between the agency/structure and limits of reformism debates should be clear: structural constraints are a matter both of political strategy (i.e., the limits inherent to the political agent, in this case, the Social Democratic government) and of organizational structure (in this case, the bureaucratic bourgeois state); these constraints may, or may not, render politically enforced social change impossible (Grafstein 1988). As one writer has recently argued, the "tension between convictions that politics, and human agency in politics, really *matter,* and desires to *explain* politics and political decisions, almost inevitably in terms of exogenous, impersonal forces" has been a fundamental problem in political science since its inception (Smith 1991, 3).

This study proceeds on the view, articulated by Steven Lukes, that a dialectical view of the agency/structure problem is in order:

Any stand-point or methodology which reduces that dialectic to a one-sided consideration of agents without . . . structural limits, or structures without agents, or which does not address the problem of their interrelations, will be unsatisfactory. No social theory merits serious attention that fails to retain an ever present sense of the dialectic between power and structure. (1977, 29; cf. Giddens 1981, 53–54)

However, incorporating this dialectic of "agency within structure" into concrete empirical studies is a rather complicated matter (Lundquist 1985, chap. 2; Smith 1991). Different structures operate on different levels, and their effect on agents is difficult to determine. Structures change over time, moreover, and so any dialectical effort of the kind proposed above renders causal analysis extremely complicated. Therefore, the methodological strategy we select to address these difficulties is vitally important.

If we wish to isolate the impact of the public bureaucracy's structure on the prospects for politically imposed social change, then we must adopt a comparative research design in which as many as possible of the other structural variables can be held constant. This means that, if we wish to proceed according to the agency within structure dialectic (which is the metaproblem of this study), we must find a minimum of two different but comparable political processes in which the same political agent has had to confront the same structural conditions.

I have chosen here the "method of structured, focused comparison" of historical cases, originally developed by Alexander George (1979, 61; cf. George and McKeown 1985). The term "focused" means that one limits the collection of data to particular aspects of the historical cases used, while "structured" implies that the questions identified as theoretically crucial control the collection and analysis in the historical cases.[2]

Steven Lukes's and Anthony Giddens's approach to structural analysis is especially interesting, because they work with a definition of agents which assumes a moment of decision and a space for action. Agents are those who can "act otherwise" (Giddens 1979, 56; cf. Elster 1985, 5–8; Lukes 1977). This implies that agents, whether individuals or organizations, enjoy at least some room for maneuver; or as Marx said, they make history, but under circumstances not of their own choosing (Marx [1852] 1979, 103–104). An "agent" totally dominated by surrounding structural factors is thus not an agent in Lukes's and Giddens's sense, but rather a part of the structure.

Structures are here defined as "patterned regularities" (Ranson et al. 1980, 3; cf. Giddens 1979, 65). They consist of organized rules and recourses which endure over time (Giddens 1981, 35–36; cf. Levi 1990).

Structures, according to this loose definition, may thus include a wide range of phenomena, from the basic economic system to political institutions (such as a newly established government agency).

Political institutions are of special interest here, since at a particular moment they are created by political agents in pursuit of a goal. However, because they are relatively durable (or "sticky"), they become structural factors at a later stage, furnishing some agents with greater room for maneuver than others, mobilizing some interests but not others, facilitating some kinds of preference formation but not others, etc. (Hall 1986, 19; Mouzelis 1984; Steinmo and Thelen 1992).

Yet despite this durability, political institutions are not everlasting, unchangeable entities. On the contrary, their "stickiness" is relative. At particular points in time, and by specific political agents, they can be deliberately changed, and indeed changed rapidly (Krasner 1984). I mean in this investigation, then, to throw some light on a general problem in social science, namely: "how individuals under given conditions produce new conditions" (Przeworski 1985b, 404).

This agency within structures approach raises another methodological problem. What is the status of counterfactual explanations in the social sciences? If one assumes that agents can always "act otherwise," then one runs up against the very complex problem of how to describe and account for the actions that could "otherwise" have been taken.

How can one prove, for instance, that despite an actor's actual nonaction, various other courses of *potential* action in fact stood open to him or her? How can one know, in other words, when a situation was structurally open? And is it possible, furthermore, to launch a persuasive argument to the effect that, if a certain type of action were taken (e.g., if an institutional framework were changed) then the following sequence of events (e.g., policy effects of a certain sort) would have occurred? Can one say with any confidence that such results *would* have occurred, even though they did not in fact?

Such counterfactual if-then questions are clearly very problematic, methodologically speaking (Gustafsson 1976). If rigorous scientific standards are to be met, such questions can only be answered in a truly experimental situation. Since such conditions are obviously unavailable, the best we can do is examine historically comparable cases (cf. George 1979).

To find as comparable cases as possible—with respect both to structural factors and political agency—is thus the only available way to tackle the counterfactual problem. This method yields no definite answer, of course, but one should at least be able to conclude that an otherwise type of action was possible at a particular time, since the background structural factors were, if not identical, then at least very similar.

## State and Society

When a parliamentary majority has taken the formal decision to launch a policy aimed at some form of social change, its primary instrument for achieving the desired impact is a specific network of state apparatuses. Whether the specific policy and the organization chosen to implement it are mutually compatible is, however, an open question. The contribution of Marxian state theory is to give us a better understanding of why a particular socioeconomic order gives rise to a specific type of state apparatus. Or to be more specific, why Western style capitalism *and* the legally oriented, bureaucratically organized state?

Since the late 1960s, Marxists have moved away from the traditional static view of this relation, in which the state was seen as a mere reflection of the economy, as scarcely more than the instrument capitalists used to manage their common affairs. They developed instead a more dynamic theory of the state/class interrelation; the result was a number of remarkable historical works (e.g., Anderson 1979; Hobsbawn 1976; cf. Hilton 1984). This neo-Marxist theory, as I shall here refer to it, invented such concepts as the "relative autonomy" of the state from the underlying economic structure (Poulantzas 1968; cf. Carnoy 1984). This theory contested the instrumental view of the state as a mere reflection of extrapolitical forces (Poulantzas 1978; cf. Therborn 1980).

The problem with this theory, however, lies in its basic concept, the relative autonomy of the state. Neo-Marxist state theorists have not been able to answer the following questions: how relative is relative, and can a concept like "autonomy" be relative? (Block 1987, 51–68). Even in his last work, Poulantzas upheld the notion that the economy, in the "last instance," had precedence over the state, and argued that all measures undertaken by a capitalist state—even those resulting from the mobilization of the oppressed masses—in the long run become subsumed in a procapitalist strategy by the state and its ally, the dominant hegemonic bourgeois bloc (Poulantzas 1968, 183–84).

The problem with this approach is its functionalism: the very way in which the theory defines the problem it sets out to solve excludes from consideration many outcomes which ought to be treated as empirical possibilities (cf. Elster 1982). There is thus no way to test such a theory empirically, for such an explanatory approach

becomes tautological, for anything that happens in the concrete situation can be linked ex post facto, to the functional requirements of the system. . . . Every event becomes a victory for the system, another demonstration of the eternal character of bourgeois relations of production. (Clarke 1977, 20; cf. Jessop 1982, 183; Elster 1982)

Theories at this very high level of generality cannot explain the enormous variations in policy and state organization within the advanced capitalist world (Hall 1986; Steinmo and Thelen 1992). Moreover, political agency (such as class struggle) seems in this theory to have no significance for changing capitalist society or the state. The theory furnishes, furthermore, no reason to test any limits of reformism empirically, since the answer is already supplied by the theory.

The fundamental question we must pose to this functionalist variant of Marxian state theory is, of course, how does it do it? How are the functional requirements of the capitalist economy translated into actual state policies? If every explanation based on agency is dismissed, then what is the specific mechanism by which the state ensures the long-term protection of the capitalist accumulation process? It is one thing to identify a general societal function and quite another to identify the specific mechanism guaranteeing the accomplishment of this function (Dearlove and Saunders 1984, 241).

Clearly, a still more dynamic view of the state/society relation is necessary. Such a perspective would replace the static instrumentalist view of the state with a more dynamic portrayal of the state as an arena, or terrain, for class conflict (Przeworski and Wallerstein 1982). On a national level, for example, organized class interests engage each other in an ongoing contest.

These class struggles are genuine conflicts, yet they are at the same time structured by the existing state (Birnbaum 1988; Lipset 1983). The outcomes of class conflict can vary greatly across states, depending on how the contests are structured by these states. The manner and means by which class conflict is conducted also range greatly, from extreme violence to a peaceful disposition to compromise (Lipset 1983; cf. Rothstein 1991). Whether class conflict issues in a stable compromise is, in this perspective, dependent not only on the strategy of parties or the economic conditions of classes, but also on how the state has historically managed such conflict.

In this more dynamic approach, the specific historical development of the relations between the state and social classes in particular countries is of vital importance to answering the limits of reformism question. To clarify this point, we may contrast my argument to that put forth by Adam Przeworski and Michael Wallerstein. They contend that the policies pursued by capitalist states to ensure the capitalist system's reproduction do not result from a confrontation between a repressive state and a revolutionary working class. Instead, they argue, state policy, and indeed the state as such, result from a compromise serving the interests of both capitalists and workers (Przeworski and Wallerstein 1982, 236).

The very generalized notion of the state underlying this reasoning is inadequate, however. Such an approach, although probably correct in portraying state policy as resulting from some sort of compromise (or stalemate) between organized class interests, nevertheless cannot explain the enormous variation in state/society relations among capitalist countries (cf. Birnbaum 1988). As early as 1979, Ian Gough criticized the various Marxist state theories for not viewing the state as an independent political subject capable of choosing, posing alternative strategies, taking initiatives, and even making mistakes (1979, 157; cf. Esping-Andersen et al. 1976, 190–91). This line of reasoning has been followed up and strengthened by, among others, Pierre Birnbaum (1988) and Margaret Weir and Theda Skocpol (1985), who have shown that the state is a critical independent variable, capable of contributing in its own right to explaining cross-national variations in social policy and the structuring of class conflict.

Why then not abandon the Marxist theory altogether and replace it with (let us say) interest group theory? One reason not to adopt such a course is furnished by the notion of class conflict as the most critical source of political conflict (Elster 1985). I find persuasive Nicos Mouzelis's claim that social historians working in the Marxian tradition have produced more interesting accounts of long-term social change than have historians influenced by, for example, Parsonian functionalism. This is because Marxian theory allows for viewing society "both in terms of actors' collective strategies and in terms of institutional systems *and* their reproductive requirements" (Mouzelis 1990, 26).

The weakness of mainstream Marxist analysis, on the other hand, arises from its lack of any concept similar to that of relations of production for use in analyzing political institutions. Some Marxists would consider such a theory a logical contradiction: if one abandons the premise that the economy in some manner dominates the polity, one abandons Marxism. But if it is possible to speak of a mode of (economic) production, it should also then be possible to speak of a mode of (administrative) domination.

There is no reason why structural explanations should be limited to the economic or material world, or why explanations highlighting agency and strategy should be reserved to the political world. On the contrary, it is obvious that structural constraints and opportunities, and strategically acting human beings as well, exist in both realms:

> In what sense, for instance, are military or administrative technologies less material or less limiting than economic ones? Or in what sense are structural tendencies towards state expansion or the concentration of the "means of administration" at the top less constraining than tendencies towards the concentration of the means of production? Do not the former constrain, set limits on agents as much as the latter? Any attempt to restrict the idea of structural tendencies or constraints to the level of the economy is unacceptable. . . . In all institutional spheres, one can identify structural tendencies setting more or less strict limits on agents' strategies and projects. (Mouzelis 1984, 115)

Although many Marxist theories of the capitalist state (and some pluralist theories too) can be criticized for understating the role played by specific national state apparatuses and for putting undue weight on societal factors, one should not conclude from this that the state should be seen as the most important explanatory factor (Birnbaum 1988; cf. Skocpol 1985). The critical thing is to appreciate the variation in how different national states and organized class interests have engaged each other in ongoing struggles and compromises and to recognize the important cross-national and cross-agency differences in the configuration of the state/class relationship.

The main weakness of purely institutional (in this case state-centered) analyses lies in their lack of connection to a substantive political theory. After all, the number of political institutions is so great (consider how many laws each state has), that without a substantive theory of politics, one cannot discern why some institutions are more important than others. Institutions indeed matter, but they matter *for* something—what is important is how the various institutional patterns reflect the variation in the overall balance of social and political power (Rothstein 1990). The problem with implementation analysis, on the other hand, is its myopic view of the organizational problem and, more specifically, its failure to address more general questions of the configuration of political power and social structure in capitalist societies (Fudge and Barrett 1981, 250; Ham and Hill 1984; Pressman and Wildavsky 1979, xi–xii).[3]

Both Marxist and state-centered analyses of the relation between state and society have usually dealt with the state *in toto,* as a single, largely undifferentiated institution. The ambition to devise a theory of *the* (capitalist) state accounts for this, I believe. One of the aims of this study is to contest the view that the state is a unified entity marked by an even distribution of class and organizational features throughout its various agencies. I proceed in this study on the assumption that state policies and organization can be explained as largely the result of the interplay between the historical legacy of the state, on the one hand, and conflicts between major social classes, on the other.

But I see no reason to assume further that the contending classes direct their best efforts toward controlling or influencing the very same state apparatuses. On the contrary, it seems far more plausible to assume that some state agencies are more important for some social classes than for others. I argue, to borrow a metaphor from Nicos Poulantzas, that different social classes seek to dominate different parts of the terrain of the state (Poulantzas 1978, 256–57). As Göran Therborn has argued:

Although the state is, in a fundamental sense, always one, the level of integration of its apparatuses varies considerably, and it should not be taken for granted that they share a common class character. For the state is the concentrated expression of a highly complex set of class relations, which are refracted in disjunctures of varying profundity between different apparatuses. Within limits imposed by the general nature of the state, it is especially probable that the class character of its diverse apparatuses will vary with the link between the tasks of the apparatuses and the concerns of classes rooted in the mode of production. (Therborn 1980, 41; cf. Skocpol and Finegold 1982)

This means that, in a society where the subordinate class can effectively challenge the political position of the dominant class, the result could be that some state apparatuses are strongly influenced, or even captured, by the subordinate class. Other agencies may constitute a more contested terrain. The challenge is to ascertain which state apparatuses are most important for a labor movement to control in a capitalist society.

Many writers concerned with the relation between class formation and public policy have argued that the design of welfare policies directly affects the organization and political power resources of the labor movement (Esping-Andersen 1990; Przeworski 1985; for an overview of this literature see Rothstein 1990). They assert that, the more social programs are organized on a universal and all-encompassing basis, and the less they are means-tested, oriented to "self-help," and directed to marginal groups, the stronger the labor movement will be. These authors have, however, ignored the question of organizational control, i.e., the control of day-to-day operations and case-by-case policy implementation.

I argue here that, while the modeling of welfare policies is important, the most important policies for a labor movement to control are those pertaining to the labor market. This is because labor's basic power resource is its organization, and the basic organization for labor is the union. While the exploitation of labor takes many forms in a capitalist society, the most important is in the production process (Marks 1989; Olofsson 1979). Unions confront this primary form of capitalist exploitation directly and are therefore the most important organizational resource for labor. Other organizational resources, such as housing cooperatives, consumer cooperatives, leisure organizations, and the like are of course also important for improving labor's condition, but not so important as the union (Korpi 1985; Offe and Wiesenthal 1980).

Now then, as is true with any producer organization, a union's strength derives essentially from its ability to control the market in which it operates, in this case the labor market. Such control entails two things. One is that the union should be the only "provider" of labor power, i.e., no labor power should be available for hire other than that controlled by the union. Second, it should not be possible to hire workers at a wage rate below that agreed to by the union. A scab-free labor market, in other words—in which wages are under the control of unions—leads to a strong union movement, which in turn is the basis for a strong labor movement. British trade unionists showed a clear understanding of this point when, in order to stop the import of cheap foreign labor, they took the initiative to organize the First International (Collins and Abramsky 1965; cf. Marx quoted in Elster 1985, 369).

If this line of reasoning is correct, the most important governmental agency for a labor movement to control is the labor market authority. Such an authority may cover many different fields—employment services, labor courts, vocational training agencies, and unemployment insurance programs, to name a few. All these agencies affect conditions on the labor market in a direct or indirect manner. In a country such as Sweden—with its uniquely strong labor movement—we might therefore expect a strong union influence over the state apparatuses operating on the labor market.

In respect to the educational sector, this approach would predict that the labor movement would be much less interested in exerting direct influence or control. The school system affects the standing of unions only very indirectly. While children from working class backgrounds have, for various reasons, a more difficult passage through the schools, this does not affect unions' bargaining position or their overall relation to capital (Olofsson 1979).

I shall seek, then, to cast light on the relation between social classes and the state by analyzing the role of specific state apparatuses in the overall national spectrum of class conflicts. If basic Marxian concepts about the interplay of class conflict and the state explain the administrative structure and capacity of the state, then this should be visible in the patterns and behavior of specific state apparatuses.

The important question is: how have such differences in organizational structure influenced the fortunes of policies? (cf. Benson 1982; Therborn 1980, 29–33). This can be divided into three more specific questions, each deriving from the three theoretical approaches identified above:

1. From Marxian state theory: Have the National Labor Market Board and the National School Board been differently situated in the field of class conflicts in Sweden?

2. From organization theory: If so, have these differences influenced the organization of these two state apparatuses?

3. From theories of public policy implementation: If so, have these differences in organization affected the implementation of the two policies in such a way as to explain success or failure?

## State Theory and Organization Theory

Let us begin with institutional and organizational theory. Most organization theories have an apolitical and functionalist character, rendering them less than useful for a study like this one (Ahrne 1990, 29–30). Studies in this field have been devoted largely to questions of administrative efficiency and have portrayed organizations as only loosely linked to the overall structure of political and social power (Therborn 1980, 37–38). These studies have tended therefore to be static, ahistorical, and apolitical (Colignon and Cray 1981, 101–04). Mayntz, for example, has argued that a discrepancy exists between the historical nature of the subject (organizations) and the ahistorical orientation of research in this field (1972, 44).

The same may be said of most work in the area of public administration (Fesler 1990). While interest among political scientists in the administrative and organizational aspect of politics has greatly increased (as with the "new institutionalism" and the efforts to "bring the state back in"), this has not issued in any cross-fertilization with organization analysis or research in public administration. Both subdisciplines suffer from this mutual neglect, in my view. As Fesler has argued, the "rediscovery" of the state and the "new institutionalism" are "scarcely conceivable as enterprises without incorporation of the administrative operations of government" (1990, 93–94).

It is unfortunate that scarcely any books about organization theory have been written from a political science perspective. Instead, approaches drawn from business administration, economics, and sociology dominate the field (Waldo 1990, 80). The political nature of government organizations (what they do, why they do it, and what difference it makes) and the apolitical nature of organization theory stand therefore in tension with each other.

Such a political and "critical" theory would treat organizations (1) as wholes—organizations must be seen in their historical and social context which gives them a distinctive set of values, (2) as structures—organizations should be understood as structures embedded within wider societal structures, (3) as arenas of conflict—organizations should not be regarded as having unified goals by definition; rather, internal organizational conflicts over goals and different power structures should be held as an open possibility (Burrell and Morgan 1979, 358–59; cf. Fesler 1990, 87; Colignon and Gray 1981).

On a metascientific level, organization theory shares with state theory the problem concerning the relation of agency and structure. Astley and Van der Ven (1983) have argued that organizations are neither objective structures nor subjective phenomena. Rather, organizations are on the one hand objective systems, because their structure can only be partly changed by their members. These structures contain human beings, on the other hand, who act according to their own beliefs in ways sometimes predictable, sometimes not. Organizations are thus both producers and products of social change (Gabriel 1981, 276; Giddens 1982, 10).

In his study of the establishment of a bureaucratically organized public administration in the U.S. in the late nineteenth century, Roy argues it was the interaction between the workers, the farmers, the merchants, the industrial capitalists, and the financial capitalists (all of them seeking to further their interests through the political structure) that produced the change in the character of the state. Marx probably had such actors in mind when he wrote about "men creating their own history but under circumstances not of their own choosing." The outcome, however, was foreseen and intended by none of these social groups, and it set the stage for further strife among them in the future (Roy 1981, 197; cf. Skowronek 1982, 4–51).

A critical conclusion of this study is that one should not regard the structure of government organizations as the result solely of the rational choices of leaders seeking to match structure with task, but as the result also of the historical legacy of the state, of the particular state apparatus in its social setting, and of policy legacies (King and Rothstein 1993; cf. Lipset 1950, 272). Organizations are not purely rational structures designed to maximize administrative efficiency. On the contrary, their specific historical legacies endow them with various cultures, meaning systems, and norms (March and Olsen 1989, 126).

As with other institutions, organizations may be viewed as "frozen ideologies." The norms, meanings, and goals which at one time had furnished the reasons for establishing them remain embedded in the organization long after these reasons have vanished. Organizations, as other institutional arrangements, tend thus to a certain stickiness (March and Olsen 1989; cf. Shepsle 1989). When an organization is established, then, it is endowed with certain values, norms, repertoires, standard operating procedures, etc., which will be very difficult to change in the future (Jelinek et al. 1983; Olsen 1983; Selznick 1949, 10).

This has important implications for organizational performance, for as Lindblom has argued, each bureaucracy tends to develop its own style and repertoire and can thereafter be directed only in accordance with these. A bureaucracy can therefore only partly and with difficulty be used for different purposes than those it was originally established to serve (Lindblom 1977, 28). The result is a "structural conservatism" within state agencies: certain solutions and policies are regarded simply as impossible (Häusserman 1977, 42–50; cf. March and Olsen 1989).

## Government Organizations and Policy Implementation

I cannot here review the enormous literature on the problems of policy implementation that has emerged since the pioneering work of Pressman and Wildavsky in 1973, *Implementation—Or How Great Expectations in Washington are Dashed Out in Oakland*. But, in my view, the research in this field has much to contribute, not just for understanding matters of administrative efficiency and other technical problems in public administration, but also more generally for understanding the limits of the modern capitalist state (cf. Palumbo and Calista 1990).

It is true that many of these studies, on account of their narrow focus on detailed problems of bureaucratic efficiency, offer rather little use for an analysis of the more general problems of state theory. But from another angle, the bulk of these studies may be regarded as studies in *empirical state theory*. By this I mean that they constitute knowledge about problems of state capacity, i.e., which factors are important for understanding the causes of policy success and failure. For a study such as this one, which seeks to explain the limits of political reformism by focusing on the relation between the labor movement and the state, this literature contains some important lessons.

Implementation research may be seen therefore as filling the empirical black hole which has so long existed in state theory. In a retrospective foreword to the book he coauthored with Pressman,

Wildavsky wrote that it was necessary to begin combining detailed field analyses of policy failure with work addressing broader social and economic matters and questions of political and social cleavages (Pressman and Wildavsky 1979, xi–xii). While most implementation research is ahistorical, many writers have called attention to the need for studies analyzing the relation between general societal factors and the variation in implementation structures (Benson 1982; Ingram 1990, 470–71; Lipsky 1980, 180–91). Some results of policy implementation research of importance for this study include the following:

## Implementation and Legitimacy

The capacity to implement policies may also be determined by whether or not the agency in question is considered legitimate by the "policy takers"—the group to which the policy is directed (Offe 1985, 286; Selznick 1949, 11). This problem should not be viewed just in technical terms, as how to maximize goal achievement. The very process of implementation can be the critical question, especially if the policy takers are an organized interest group whose participation is needed for successful implementation. One way of achieving this legitimacy is to grant such groups semiofficial status (and not merely in policy formulation, but also in implementation). The advantage of so doing is that interest organizations

are closer to the target group (their members) than state bureaucracies, and they have more intimate knowledge of its situation and concerns. It is likely that this enables them to apply rules less formalistically and to take the specific conditions of individual cases better into account—which, in turn, tend to increase the acceptance of regulation by those affected by it. (Streeck and Schmitter 1985, 22)

As Philip Selznick has shown, if the content of a policy is determined by the way in which it is implemented at the local level, the target group must participate at this level if its influence is to be more than formal (Selznick 1949, 224). A corporatist system emerges thereby. This in turn leads to tensions between implementation as administrative corporatism and implementation as rule of law (Brand 1988; cf. Blankenburg 1978). These tensions arise because the former type of implementation is directed toward the specific needs of the target group and its organization; implementation as rule of law, by contrast, is supposed to be universal and impartial.

## Organizational Tasks and Organizational Structure

The growth of research on the implementation process was in large part a reaction to the failure of some of the social programs launched during the heyday of welfare state expansion in the United States during the 1960s, employment programs not least among them (Rein 1983, 113–14). The failure to achieve the ambitious goals of many of these programs led to disillusionment and disbelief in the capacity of governments to effect social change. Of course, these failures have been attributed to many different causes, such as lack of funding, unrealistic goals, a flawed policy theory (right ends but wrong means), a hostile social environment, etc. One major reason for policy failure, according to scholars working in this field, was administrative incapacity (Rein 1983, 114). These programs typically involved massive administrative intervention into highly changeable areas, such as job creation and training, education, housing, and environmental problems (Sabatier and Mazmanian 1983, 3; cf. Weir 1992; Yin 1982;).

An extremely flexible administration is needed to cope with such policy areas as these. In order to achieve change in these areas, the government must intervene to change the character of interactions between actors in markets or other social networks. We must distinguish here between static and dynamic types of intervention. The more a policy depends on an in-depth penetration into the society with bureaucratic procedures, the less likely it is to be easily accomplished. It is a rather simple matter to change the sum on a pension check; the computer formula just has to be changed. It is far harder to change the attitudes and behavior of such field workers as social workers, teachers, policemen, and the like (Zald 1981, 102).

Many scholars have called attention to the difficulty of changing the operations of government bureaucracies and, especially, the behavior of field workers (Barrett and Fudge 1981, 4; Mayntz 1978, 635). This bureaucratic rigidity corresponds to the stickiness of political institutions identified by institutionalists. If we aim to explain policy failures with reference to the varying rigidity of government agencies, we must analyze the relation between the historical legacy of a given agency and the character of the policy it has been called upon to implement (Offe 1975; Scharpf 1977, 346).

Wolman has argued, for example, that a policy assigned to a new agency expressly established to implement it stands a much better

chance of succeeding than does a policy assigned to an already existing agency. Using an established agency is especially difficult if the
policy in question diverges markedly from those the agency has previously been accustomed to carrying out, and which requires it to alter its view of its mission or its traditional client groups (Wolman
1981, 446). Implementation theory predicts, then, that the likelihood
of policy failure at the implementation stage increases the higher the
interventionist ambitions and the greater the policy's deviation from
the agency's traditional task.

*The State Personnel*

Implementation studies have also focused on the ideological orientation and professional norms of the bureaucratic staff. Policies
aimed at changing the behavior of a specific target group are likely
to succeed only if the staff of the responsible agencies are strongly
committed to the cause, and are considered legitimate by the target
group as well (Sabatier and Mazmanian 1981, 13; cf. Kaufman 1973,
4). This is one of the lessons of Selznick's classic study of the New
Deal administration—*TVA and the Grass Roots* (1949). This applies
not just to top-level civil servants but to midlevel and field personnel as well. Lipsky has, moreover, emphasized the critical role of the
last-mentioned group—the bureaucrats in direct contact with
clients.

One may say, in fact, that the decisions and routines of these
"street-level bureaucrats" *are* the policy that is actually implemented. Public policy, as clients encounter and experience it, does not issue from parliaments or cabinets or the boardrooms of public agencies. "Really existing" public policy is, rather, the sum of the actions
and decisions of the "street-level bureaucrats" (Lipsky 1980, xii).
This insight improves upon the traditional understanding of public
policy in political science in two ways. First, it complements the traditional focus on the relation between politicians and top-level civil
servants with an orientation to the management process within government organizations. Second, viewing matters from the street level underlines the importance of bureaucratic organization for policy
success or failure. An example of such an organizational feature is
the type of staff recruited to run the organization (Rein and
Rabinovitz 1978, 310).

This also raises the question of the role played by professional
and related norms (Lipsky 1978, 399). One oft-cited reason for policy

failure is the difficulty of directing the professionals participating in the implementation process. As Mintzberg writes of organizations strongly dependent on professionals (such as schools), "since their output is difficult to measure, their goals cannot easily be agreed upon. So *the notion of strategy—a single, integrated pattern of decisions common to the entire organization—loses a good deal of its meaning*" (Mintzberg 1983, 200).

What distinguishes the interventionist policies discussed here is that they all involve discretionary behavior on the part of the street-level staff delivering the service. This arises from the changeability and complexity of the policy area, which requires adaptation to the circumstances of each and every case (Rothstein 1992, chap. 3). Any change in policy must therefore be expressed in changed attitudes, behavior, and decisions on the part of the people on the front line, for without this, no change in policy can occur. The staff's behavior is only partly shaped, however, by the requirements of the policy in question. The agency's structure and culture are also important. It is extremely important therefore to discover what determines the attitudes and behavior of the field personal. The orientation of public officials has usually been thought explicable in terms of their social background and/or political orientation.

An altogether different picture emerges from a study of the Norwegian central bureaucracy, however. This study, conducted by Johan P. Olsen, found that each government agency and ministry socialized the individual into its own infrastructure and organizational culture. Such variables as birthplace, social class, sex, geographical ties, and political orientation did not seem to affect in any profound manner the way in which civil servants acted or thought. Professional function and government agency, rather, were the most influential factors (Olsen 1983b, 2; cf. Lagreid and Olsen 1978). This study conforms well with recent developments in organization and institutional theory stressing the strong socialization effects of organizations (Pfeffer 1982, 92–96).

We cannot therefore explain a policy failure simply in terms of the social background or professional or ideological orientation of the personnel responsible for carrying out the policy. The ideological and professional orientation of the staff must itself be understood in terms of the organizational context (cf. Murphy 1976, 100), which in turn must be explained by reference to the organization's place in the overall political and social landscape. This is how the "levels within levels" metaphor cited above is meant to work (Benson 1982).

If we wish to move beyond a superficial explanation of the limits of reformism, we must on the one hand show that class forces are not metaphysical entities, but may be discerned in the concrete daily operations of the state. A purely microlevel analysis of policy failure, on the other hand, is too narrow. For street-level bureaucrats both explain a great deal and must themselves be explained. Putting the same point differently, we must link levels of analysis.

# 3. Comparing State Apparatuses

## The Bureaucracy Versus the Cadre Organization

The Social Democratic policies examined in this study—the active labor market and comprehensive school policies—are both interventionist programs aimed at changing social processes deeply embedded in capitalist society. The implementation of these policies entails a great deal more than the mere issuance of central rules and regulations by cabinet members or top-level bureaucrats. Rather, street-level public officials (teachers and employment exchange officers in particular) implement these policies in the course of their continuous interchange with citizens and clients. The actual political outcome of these two reforms is therefore very much in the hands of the state agencies responsible for implementing them. This means that, if we wish to understand the importance of the state as an institutional factor, we must specify how and why it is important for the successful implementation of reformist policies.

Since the eve of the socialist labor movement in Europe, the character of the capitalist state has been at issue in discussions of socialist strategy. Should the state "be considered an essentially *neutral apparatus* that merely needs to be 'captured' by a working-class political party for it to serve the interests of the working class, or is the apparatus of the state in capitalist society a distinctively *capitalist apparatus* that cannot possibly be used by the working class, and as a result must be destroyed and replaced by a radically different form of the state?" (Wright 1978, 195).

The Marxian theory of the capitalist state stresses the "bureaucratic nature" of its organization (Poulantzas 1968; Therborn 1980). But if this characterization is to qualify as substantive and not merely pejorative, we must spell out in greater detail what, in the internal dynamics and processes of this type of state, prevents the successful implementation of interventionist reforms (Wright 1978, 213; cf. Scott 1981, 23–24).

The same may be said from an institutional perspective. In the words of Johan P. Olsen, "Each organizational form mobilizes a certain bias—each constrains, channels and provides incentives for various behaviors . . . a task for students of organization is to specify the biases which different organizational forms mobilize and to test predictions about the conditions under which different forms will be used" (1983, 9–10). This means we must be precise when discussing the organizational form of each state apparatus.

If it is true, as Eric Wright has argued, that "state interventions are *structurally limited* by the underlying class structure of the society *and selected* by the structure of the state apparatuses" (italics mine), then our first priority must be to discover how this selection mechanism works (1978, 230). As Jon Elster has eloquently argued, methodological rigor requires us to specify the explanatory link—or feedback mechanism—connecting the two structural phenomena in question (1982, 1985). How and why does a bureaucratic type of state administration (structure I) limit the implementation of Social Democratic policies (structure II)?

The second question is whether a solution to the administrative problem can be found which avoids the drawbacks imputed to the bureaucratic mode of organization. And if such an organizational type exists, what are its characteristics? In this chapter, I shall explain why the bureaucratic type of organization is indeed a hindrance to the successful implementation of socialist policies (of the socially invasive type, at any rate).

I also present an alternative organizational form—the cadre organization—and argue it is better suited than the bureaucracy for implementing Social Democratic policies of an interventionist nature. I hope in the course of this to answer the question posed by Eric Wright, as to whether a Left government "can potentially enact certain reforms . . . which have the effect of changing the structure of the state itself in ways which erode the class selectivity of the state apparatuses" (1978, 232).

Few studies of the relation between politics and administration can surpass Max Weber's work on bureaucracy (1968). Of course, "bureaucracy" may be defined in a variety of ways: from a political system dominated by civil servants to a specific organizational technology (Albrow 1970, 91–116; cf. Ahrne 1990, 42–44). In this study, I employ the concept of bureaucracy as a theoretically informed *ideal type* for organizations featuring certain characteristics. I then contrast this with the ideal type of the cadre organization. In addition, I relate these two organizational ideal types to the main questions of this study (as specified above for each of the three levels of analysis).

The justification for using ideal types as analytical instruments is to strengthen the theoretical implications of the two empirical cases. As Edwin Amenta has pointed out, one way to enhance the value of generalizations from case studies is to use theoretically informed ideal types (1991, 173). In short, ideal types enable us to see empirical cases as something more than just unique historical events.

Even though Weber's ideal typical bureaucracy is not an empirical object, it is constructed nonetheless from empirical observations (Cawson and Saunders 1983, 14). It is important to emphasize that the use of ideal types implies no normative standpoint. As Göran Ahrne (1990, 43) has argued, Max Weber "was no organization consultant." "Ideal" here does not mean good; an empirical, "real" object may be closer to or further from a specific ideal type, but is not by virtue of that better or worse. Of course, no analytical instruments are theoretically neutral, be they ideal types, multivariate regressions, game analyses, or what have you. The variables highlighted by ideal types are not chosen at random, but rather because they identify what the analyst considers to be the *differentia specifica* of the object under study (Weber [1922] 1971, 199).

It may seem odd, for a study proceeding on the basis of a Marxian theory of the state, to use a Weberian definition of bureaucracy as one of its central analytical instruments. Yet there is no alternative, for Marxian state theory does not operate on the level of organization analysis. No fourth volume of *Das Kapital*, which was to deal with the state, ever was written.

Many scholars have argued for combining Marxian analysis of production relations (i.e., class conflicts) with Weberian concepts of relations of administration (i.e., organizational and hierarchical conflicts) (Katznelson 1981; Mouzelis 1990; Wright 1978, chap. 4;). This study is conducted therefore in the unexplored terrain between Marx's analysis of class conflicts and Weber's analysis of administrative structures.

## The Bureaucratic Organization

What follows is a description of the well-known Weberian model of bureaucratic organization. There are innumerable works on this topic, and only a few can be cited here. Unfortunately, the word itself poses a problem for clarity on account of its negative connotation; as one prominent organization theorist has written, the terms implies "accusations connoting rule-encumbered inefficiency and mindless overconformity" (Scott 1981, 23; cf. Selznick 1949, 9). Others have pointed out that, in ordinary language, bureaucracy calls to mind "inefficient, inhuman, and inaccessible" (Katz and Danet 1973, 3). Finally, bureaucracy for many is simply a synonym for organization. Following Max Weber, I use the term here to describe a particular type of administrative structure without connoting any normative ideals—positive or negative.[1]

The most ideal typical feature of a bureaucratic organization is its adherence to precise and explicit rules codified in a set of laws and regulations (Weber [1922] 1947, 330–31; 1968, 958–65). The legitimacy of bureaucratic organizations derives from "rational-legal" authority (Scott 1981, 32). The bureaucrat implements laws and regulations in a neutral and universal manner, without letting his or her personal interests interfere and without considering such particulars of each individual case as are not defined by the rules as relevant to the matter at hand (Katz and Danet 1973, 4–5). The citizen can thus *foresee* the actions of the state.

The Latin words Weber used to characterize bureaucratic behavior were *sine ira et studio* (without passion or gain). Bureaucrats are not supposed to be ideologically engaged in the performance of their tasks. They should not be recruited for their commitment to the mission of the agency they serve or because they share the ideological orientation of the ruling political party (Weber 1968, 958–65). Recruitment and promotion are instead to proceed strictly according to a codified system of formal merits linked to academic training and documented experience. The bureaucracy is hierarchically organized to achieve central coordination (Scott 1981, 32–33).

The inner drive of the bureaucracy is to strive for formal rationality, which entails the handling of tasks according to a codified set of rules and regulations. Goal-oriented rationality—the effort to ensure that substantive outcomes accord with the law's intentions—is of secondary importance. The formal rationality of the bureaucracy is expressed in the legally correct and ideologically impartial handling of tasks (Beetham 1985).

Weber did not, however, consider this organizational model an apolitical entity, as do many organization theorists today. On the contrary, Weber viewed the rise of modern bureaucracy as a distinctively political event linked directly to the rise of modern capitalism and expressive of its need for a professional, uncorrupted, rational, and above all predictable state. The functional relationship between modern capitalism and the bureaucratic, rule-governed state lay in the capitalist's need to be able to calculate the costs of his interaction with the state in regard to taxes, customs, and the like. Without this calculability, the basic requirements for a capitalist economy are not fulfilled, i.e., one cannot make contracts based on any reliable calculus of profit and risk (Ahrne 1990, 43–44). This connection between the rise of modern capitalism and the establishment of the rule-governed state is largely confirmed by a number of historical studies in "state-building" (Anderson 1979, 16–42).[2]

In respect to implementation, the strength of the bureaucracy lies precisely in its predictability. This makes it an excellent instrument for carrying out policies capable of standardization and routinization—policies, that is, in which the need to adjust measures to the specific circumstances of particular cases is limited (Perrow 1979, 4; cf. Mintzberg 1979, 333–37). "Bureaucratic work," writes Mintzberg, "is found, above all, in environments that are simple and stable" (1983, 171).[3]

An example of a welfare state program well suited to bureaucratic organization is a universal pension scheme. However, the very predictability of bureaucracies is also their Achilles' heel, for it creates difficulties in handling policy areas requiring flexible adjustment to the specific and varying circumstances of individual cases. We may refer to such policy areas as "dynamic." The more dynamic the policy area, and the greater the consequent need for "flexible adaptation" of policy measures at the local level, the more problematic the bureaucratic mode of implementation (Ripley and Franklin 1982; Robbins 1983; 200–207). As Charles Perrow has argued:

the ideal form also falls short of realization when rapid changes in some of the organizational tasks are required. *Bureaucracies are set up to deal with stable, routine tasks; that is the basis of organizational efficiency.* Without stable tasks there cannot be stable division of labor, a prescribed acquisition of skills and experience, formal planning, and so on. (1979, 4)

Another analyst who has pointed at this problem is Claus Offe, who argues that one of the inherent weaknesses of the welfare state lies in the limits of its legal-bureaucratic mode of intervention; this is especially obvious in the areas of human services and "human-processing" (1883, 242–43; cf. Offe 1985, chap. 10). In sum, the problems of bureaucracy here identified have little to do with the everyday negative connotations of the term. Rather, the very strength of bureaucratic organization in some areas causes its weakness in others. As with any other tool, it can be used only for a limited number of purposes.

## The Cadre Organization

The organization literature abounds with alternative models of bureaucracy. Unfortunately, however, most of these models have an apolitical character; they stress matters of administrative efficiency and/or due process (cf. Mintzberg 1983). Most contributions to the literature therefore explore minor aspects of the general bureaucratic theme—hierarchy, rules, formal rationality, meritocratic recruitment, etc. If one examines the literature closely, however, one finds delineated an ideal type which may be considered the polar opposite of the bureaucratic organization, namely the cadre organization. It is distinguished from the bureaucracy in setting *goal* or *substantive rationality* before formal rationality.

The cadre organization is founded neither on the staff's expert knowledge nor on their efficiency in applying formal rules to specific cases, but rather on their "*commitment* to the aims and 'line' of the organization and on experience of its struggles" (Therborn 1980, 59;

cf. Schurman 1970). The cadre can be recognized by his or her loyalty to the ideological goals and aims of the organization; formal regulations, by contrast, play a very subordinate role. Unlike the bureaucrat, moreover, the cadre does not legitimize his or her decisions with reference to a codified system of rules. Finally, the cadre organization is directed by means of ideological persuasion, mediation, and the like, rather than by regulation (Therborn 1980, 58; cf. Lipp 1978).

The cadre is recruited, then, on the basis of ideological orientation. The ideological socialization of new personnel is also very important. Formal merits play no role in the cadre's recruitment or promotion. The cadre's key skill is his or her ability to understand and embrace the organization's ideological goals and to implement them in varying circumstances. From a Weberian perspective, Balint Balla describes the differences between bureaucratic and cadre organizations as follows:

While bureaucracy is characterized by reliability, continuity, efficacy, precise application of prevailing instructions—yet also by pedantry, formalism, red tape and Veblen's "trained incapacity"—cadre administration is marked on the one hand by flexible, immediate "line-oriented" dynamism, by superiority over formalities and pragmatic ability to adjust to changing situations, yet on the other hand by diffuse unreliability and dilettantism, amorphus aversion to responsibility, rigid authoritarianism, rule-resistant incompetence and emotional paternalism. (1972; 203–04; quoted in Therborn 1980, 58–59)

A cadre organizational structure is especially typical of working-class institutions, such as unions and working-class political parties. The typical union official is a cadre, and both communist and social democratic parties are usually organized on a cadre basis (Schurman 1970; Therborn 1980, 58–59). This is immensely important to the matter here at issue, namely the limits of reformism, because one may reasonably expect that, when a working-class party tries to use the state machinery to further its constituents' interests, the result is not merely a conflict with the ideology of the traditional civil servants, but *a clash between two fundamentally different organizational principles as well.* For if the capitalist state's typical mode of organization is the bureaucracy (on account of the need for neutral competence and predictability), and if the dominant working-class organizational form is the cadre organization (because of the need for ideological motivation and flexible adaptation), we may expect—

when Social Democrats pursue socially invasive reforms—a conflict not just of ideology but also of organization.

The literature treating the cadre organization is much less developed than that about the bureaucracy. One classical study is Frank Schurman's book about the Chinese Communist Party, in which he stresses the conflict between party cadres and bureaucrats in the Chinese communist system (1970). In Western capitalist democracies, cadre organizational forms typically characterize blue-collar unions, radical political parties, and voluntary groups (Mintzberg 1983, 280; Therborn 1980, 60–61). This type of organization has, however, seldom attracted the attention of organization theorists.[4]

Nevertheless, some analysts of modern management and organization have recognized the cadre organization as a distinctive type. William Ouchi, for example, distinguishes between the bureaucracy and the clan organization; the latter's features coincide almost perfectly with those of the cadre organization. Japanese manufacturing firms are typically structured as clan organizations, in Ouchi's view. This organizational type is characterized by a strong socialization process, which trains the staff to identify the goals of the organization with their personal interests. Clan organizations are much more efficient than bureaucracies, according to Ouchi, because managers in such organizations need not rely heavily on supervision and control, for the strong socialization process inspires the staff to act according to the ideology and aims of the organization (1980, 139–40).

The clan organization enjoys the advantage, according to Ouchi, that its field personnel can adapt to changing local conditions without challenging or breaking existing rules and without seeking the permission of higher-level officials. Yet management's intentions are implemented nevertheless, on account of the ideological commitment and thorough socialization of the field personnel. In contrast to the rigidity of the bureaucracy, in other words, the operations of the clan or cadre organization can be adjusted to the varying requirements of specific cases *and still be in line* with the intentions of management. This feature is particularly important if the organization must confront a dynamic and changeable environment.

Another prominent student of organization, Henry Mintzberg, has identified this type of organization as well. After having spent 478 pages describing five traditional types of bureaucratic organization, Mintzberg concludes his book by arguing that a sixth type of organization may also be discerned: the "missionary" organization.

Typical missionary organizations are, according to Mintzberg, radical political parties, social activist groups, and revolutionary movements (cf. Etzioni 1961, 12–14).

Like the clan and cadre organizations, the missionary organization strongly emphasizes common ideology and the internalization of organizational norms and goals by the staff; it is characterized also by a concomitant lack of specific rules, formality, and direct supervision. Indeed, such organizations can be highly decentralized; coordination is accomplished not by rules or professional norms but by the thorough socialization of the field personnel, which ensures that they think and act as the leadership of the organization would if confronted with the same situation or case (Mintzberg 1979, 479–80). In addition, the cadre/missionary organization is strongly engaged in altering the norms and behavior of its environment; "rather than respond to outsiders, it seeks to have outsiders respond to it" (Mintzberg 1983, 315, 376). As for the internal power structure of such organizations, Mintzberg writes:

The strong ideology . . . allows the members to be trusted to make decisions, since each shares the tradition and beliefs—indeed embraces them through natural or selected identifications, or by virtue of being socialized and indoctrinated. Hence political games are hardly played at all in this configuration. All efforts are devoted to pursuing to the maximum the goal of preserving, extending, and/or perfecting the mission of the organization. (1983, 313).

Thus, even some mainstream organization theorists acknowledge that a type of organization exists which is the functional opposite of the bureaucratic organization.[5] This line of reasoning is echoed in institutional analysis, which stresses the explanatory importance of norms, ideology, and commitment to established institutions. Writers in this field argue that the behavior of an organization's members cannot be wholly explained in terms of instrumental rationality. Instead, they argue, institutions give rise to specific meaning systems and interpretations, which strongly influence the worldview and consequent behavior of actors operating within them (Douglas 1987, chap. 5–6; March and Olsen 1989, chap. 2).

When it comes to policy implementation, we may expect the cadre organization to encounter problems of an opposite nature to those met by the bureaucracy. Cadre organizations are not suited for handling routine tasks or standard operations, but they can effectively implement policies requiring flexible adaptation to vary-

TABLE 1. Characteristic Features of Bureaucratic and Cadre Organizations.

| Characteristics | Bureaucracy | Cadre Organization |
|---|---|---|
| Recruitment/ promotion criteria | Formal merits | Ideological commitment |
| Internal direction | Universal rules | Explicit ideology |
| Formal control | Substantial | Negligible |
| Operational logic | Formal rationality | Substantive rationality |
| External relations | Predictable | Change-oriented |
| Internal cohesion | Weak | Strong |
| Leadership style | Impersonal | Charismatic |
| Relation to clients | Neutral | Persuasive |
| Rewards to personnel | Instrumental | Goal fulfilment |
| Preferred tasks | Routine | Nonroutine |

ing cases. This type of organization might, however, be more resistant to change than a bureaucracy, inasmuch as changing rules is easier than changing deeply rooted belief systems and organizational cultures. The impact of these organizational factors is difficult to overstate. Whether the street-level officials perceive their task as the routine and impartial application of general rules, on the one hand, or the accomplishment of a specific political mission, on the other, will greatly influence the results the organization produces. The success or failure of an interventionist policy will be to a large extent determined by these features attending its implementation.[6] Some *differentia specifica* between bureaucratic and cadre organizations are specified in table 1.

In the following chapter, I present an empirical account of the two reformist policies under study, along with an argument that one reform must be considered a failure and the other a success. In the chapter succeeding, I explain the historical background and legacy of the state apparatuses responsible for each of the reforms. Chapters 6 and 7, finally, provide an empirical analysis—modeled on the table above—of the two agencies.

# 4. Reformist Policies: Success and Failure

## Introduction

The comparative design of this study is focused on the success and failure of Swedish social democracy's reforms in employment and education, respectively. The labor market policy may be regarded as an instance of "policy success," and the school policy as one of "policy failure" (Lane 1983; cf. George 1979). We have thus one case in which the structural limits of reformism were overcome by the political agent, and one in which they were not. As stated above, it is hypothesized here that the cause of success in the one case and failure in the other lies, to a considerable extent, in the institutional arrangements whereby the reformist policy intentions were converted into social change. Policy in this context can be said to consist of three components: intentions, administration, and results. Before assessing the impact of the administrative arrangements, we must establish more precisely the relation between intentions and results for the policies in question. This chapter marshals empirical evidence in support of the view that, in fact, the one policy succeeded and the other failed.

Some of the problems involved in comparing policy intentions with results are as follows: How are the policy intentions to be determined and interpreted? After how long an interval may one reasonably compare intentions with results? How are results to be measured and interpreted? At what level of congruency between intentions and results can a policy be said to have succeeded or failed? (Lundquist 1985, chap. 8; cf. Lane 1983). The evaluation of public policy is of course a full-fledged academic discipline in itself, and I do not pretend here to present an overview of the innumerable methods of assessment which have been proposed (cf. Vedung 1991). My ambitions are much more modest—to use a few insights from this literature to bring some analytical order into the discussion of the results of the two policies under study.

## Political Intentions: Analytical Problems

In a rationalist view of politics, the intentions of political actors are taken as an unproblematic given. Upon leaving the safe world of elegant but possibly superficial models of political behavior, however, we encounter numerous problems in empirically establishing the intentions behind political decisions. Due to the inevitable uncertainty about the motives of those involved, and the sheer number of individuals influencing the decision, we must settle for an approximation.

Moreover, in the case of social reforms of the magnitude considered here, political intentions tend to find expression not in a single decision but in a series of decisions spanning a considerable period of time. Intentions may be modified during this period as regards both policy direction and the degree of detail. Furthermore, the intentions expressed in such a series of decisions vary widely with respect to means and ends; that is, it is often unclear which results policy makers regard as intrinsically good and which as merely instrumentally advantageous (Lane 1983; Lundquist 1975, 25).

Policy programs of this kind do not usually present any clear and consistent hierarchy of primary objectives, secondary aims, and instruments. Due to this element of ambiguity, policy intentions cannot be elucidated as a rule from a literal interpretation of a particular document. Instead, intentions must be ascertained (approximately) from a freer interpretation of a wealth of material, of which decision documents are just a part. Thus, even if preferences are taken as a "given" in this study, detecting them is no small problem.

I have sought nevertheless to discover the strategic political model behind the Swedish Social Democrats' actions in these two policy areas. I have assumed social reforms of such import spring from general ideological tenets, from which primary policy objectives can be derived. The reconstruction and interpretation of policy intentions must therefore be undertaken in a broad social and ideological context. Another major problem in interpreting policy intentions arises from the fact that only some intentions are relevant in a comparison with results. A political party may, for instance, harbor intentions not directly related to the area of a specific policy decision. The party may aim instead to achieve or maintain a coalition, cement good relations with particular interest groups, strengthen party cohesion, or pursue other strategic or tactical objectives (cf. Sjöblom 1968). Such intentions seldom figure explicitly in policy decisions, and are not in any case pertinent in a comparison with policy results in the sense meant here. Policy intentions thus cover only part of the spectrum of intentions motivating a political agent's policy decision, and only they should be compared with policy results.

Thus, even if policy results in a particular case differ greatly from intentions, the political agent in question may not perceive the policy as a failure. The agent may be perfectly satisfied with the decision because it realized intentions in quite another field. The opposite also applies. Moreover, the intentions behind a policy decision may have nothing to do with realizing any policy result; the policy may rather have a symbolic function. In certain political situations it may, for example, be important for political agents to appear resolute, regardless of whether their decisions have any practical consequence (cf. Ingram and Mann 1980). In any case, I discuss the success or failure of policies here solely with reference to the substance of policy decisions.

Both policy areas considered here unquestionably possess high symbolic value; they confer political weight regardless of the practical outcome. In postwar Sweden, the symbolic value of defending such concepts as "full employment" and "a school for equality" has been considerable (Heclo and Madsen 1987). Yet more than symbolism has been at issue here. The Social Democrats' school policy should be regarded as more than merely symbolic, because the party has invested a large part of its political prestige in this field. The crucial importance of school reform would hardly have been emphasized in countless public documents from congresses and other party assemblies had it been just a matter of symbolism, particularly as intentions could be so easily tested in reality. Another indication of the centrality of school policy is that some of the party's leading postwar figures (e.g., Prime Ministers Tage Erlander, Olof Palme, and Ingvar Carlsson, and Alva Myrdal as well) have been directly involved in designing or implementing the party's education policy.

Another difficulty arises in interpreting policy intentions when a compromise is reached between two or more parties. While such compromises sometimes reflect a genuine interest in reaching agreement, they may in other cases be designed simply to conceal differences or to postpone a decision until more favorable circumstances arise. It may be impossible, then, to distinguish the policy intentions for the simple reason that they are buried in a mound of formulations defying analytical interpretation. Such compromises may, for example, combine intentions that are too incongruous to be achieved simultaneously.

In parliamentary terms, labor market policy has been a field in which Social Democratic policy proposals have been adopted with only minor amendments (Furåker 1976; Hedborg and Meidner 1984; Öhman 1974), whereas education policy has required numerous interparty compromises. The basic decisions proposed in the public inquiry of 1948 (SOU 1948, no. 27), and then taken in the Swedish Parliament (Riksdag) in 1950, elicited general agreement (Marklund 1980, 76–82 and 216–30; cf. Richardson 1967). Yet there are grounds for regarding the Social Democratic party as the principal agent behind the educational reforms. Besides dominating the Riksdag and government during this period, the Social Democrats held the policy initiative in the sense that their intentions formed the basis upon which compromises, resistance, and agreements focused (Richardson 1983, 36, 401–10).

Confirmation of the party's role as the primary articulator of educational policy aims can be found in many major contributions to the education literature.[1] That the party attached great importance to educational issues is also evident from the unusual arrangement whereby the two public inquiries into the reform of compulsory education (the 1946 School Commission and the 1957 School Committee) were chaired by the minister of education in person

(Erlander and Ragnar Edenman, respectively). Such an appraisal can also be found in the party's own perception of the policy process; concerning the 1946 School Commission, for example, former Prime Minister Tage Erlander wrote that "the responsibility for deriving something from the work of the Commission rested, in our assessment, with us, the Social Democrats" (1973, 240).

At the 1968 party congress, moreover, Education Minister Olof Palme declared that "Social democracy has been the force behind the reform and development of compulsory education" (SAP-protokoll 1968, 288). The role of the Liberal party is also mentioned, however, in a booklet on the reform of compulsory education published by the Social Democratic party executive:

Even though Gunnar Helen (leader of the Liberals) had rejected a comprehensive senior level as recently as 1959, the Liberals capitulated and were a party to the 1962 decision on compulsory education. . . . The achievement of this reform—one of the major social reforms—was crucially dependent on the existence of a definite Social Democratic line based on conscious values and a firm social philosophy. (*Skola för jämlikhet* 1971, 8)

While this may be a somewhat incomplete account of the contributions of the leading opposition party, it is clear that the Liberals did not hold the initiative in the area of school reform, but rather sought to compromise with Social Democratic policy initiatives (Richardson 1984).[2]

## Policy Intentions: Labor Market Policy

The Social Democrats regarded the active labor market policy as an endeavor to combine four economic policy objectives: high employment, low inflation, wage solidarity in the trade union movement, and the promotion of economic growth. The doctrine inspiring this policy is known commonly as the Rehn-Meidner (or sometimes just the Rehn) model, named after the two trade union economists who shaped it, Gösta Rehn and Rudolf Meidner (Hedborg and Meidner 1984, 72–85; Tilton 1990, 193–209).

We must, if we wish to understand the genesis of this policy, bear in mind the very high level of union membership in Sweden, as well as the uniform organization of the working class (Kjellberg 1983). A trade union movement's strength depends on its ability to maintain a monopoly over the supply of labor (Rothstein 1990); this in turn depends on two factors. One is that the reserve of unemployed workers can be reduced virtually to nil. Wage competition is accentuated when many workers are jobless, and this weakens the negotiating strength of unions. The success of a strike, the principal union weapon, requires an effective control over the supply of labor. The objective of full employment—the primary postwar aim of Swedish social democracy, as expressed for instance in the 1944 party program—is grounded partly in these organizational needs (Hedborg and Meidner 1984, 197).

The second organizational imperative for a trade union movement concerns wage policy. In the case of the Swedish Trade Union Confederation (LO), with its uniform nationwide organization and internationally unrivaled membership level, the problem is accentuated by the wide range of economic activities and occupations represented. The drive for a concerted wage policy has been of central importance for the cohesion of the organization and thereby for its strength. In the late 1950s, accordingly, the LO adopted a policy of wage solidarity, which represented an attempt to narrow the gap between low- and high-income earners among its members. This meant that, instead of adjusting wage rates to the profitability of the individual firm, national average rates would be established for the various occupational groups. Two trade union economists, Anna Hedborg and Rudolf Meidner, go so far as to assert that "for a union movement of the Swedish kind with . . . such a high membership the emergence of the two-tiered labor market . . . is a mortal threat" (Hedborg and Meidner 1984, 102; cf. Öhman 1974; Meidner 1969).

These two objectives—full employment and wage solidarity—can be justified with a variety of ideological arguments about equality and justice. Such arguments may indeed have been decisive for this choice of strategy. My search has been confined, however, to arguments reflecting a rational endeavor to strengthen the trade union movement. I assume that the course chosen by the unions reflected the essential conditions on which union activity is founded—or, as Hedborg and Meidner put it, "the endeavor inherent in any organization to keep its own organization intact" (1984, 104). Seen from the trade union standpoint, the strategic aims—very high national employment and wage solidarity—must be regarded as rational in relation to the unique characteristics of the Swedish trade union movement, its links with the Social Democrats as the party of government, and its position vis-a-vis capital (cf. Offe and Wiesenthal 1980; Olson 1982, 99; Przeworski and Wallerstein 1982). This was clearly expressed at the 1975 party congress by the LO chairman, Gunnar Nilsson:

Wage policy is the primary concern of the trade union movement. The policy of wage solidarity which the movement supports presupposes strong labor market and industrial policies. In addition to our self-evident social commitment, we are thus directly linked by common interests. (SAP-protokoll 1975, 960; cf. Hedborg and Meidner 1984, 99–100)

The simultaneous realization of these two objectives raises the problem of how they are to be combined with economic stability. This is a classic problem in economics. Full employment can be attained by means of general fiscal measures that raise domestic demand. In conjunction with wage solidarity and the strength of the Swedish trade union movement, however, this tends to result in economic disequilibrium—high inflation, for instance. Coping with this dilemma must therefore be a primary concern for a Social Democratic government responsible for the national economy (Hedborg and Meidner 1984, 104).

In the years after World War II, the Swedish Social Democrats had to face this problem not only in theory but also in practice. In order to achieve economic balance during the postwar boom, the government repeatedly persuaded the trade union movement to accept wage freezes. Prime Minister Erlander was seriously concerned with the conflicts these unpopular measures created between the party and the LO (Erlander 1974, 40–48; 1976, 37–39; cf. Elvander 1972, 186). The LO chairman, Axel Strand, in fact strongly criticized the minister of finance, Pär-Edvin Sköld, in the Riksdag in 1955 (Erlander 1976, 37; Rehn 1977; Öhman 1974, 20).

Besides posing political problems, wage freezes and other government restrictions thwart trade unions in one of their primary activities—promoting better wages for their members. This obviously lessens their ability to recruit and retain the members upon which their strength ultimately depends (Meidner 1948; Öhman 1974, 20). Since the wage freezes led to increased wage drift outside the collective bargaining system, moreover, the LO's hold on wage formation tended to diminish (Rehn 1977). In the mid-1950s, then, the Swedish union movement was squeezed between what appeared to be incompatible demands—stabilizing the economy and promoting its members' interests (Tilton 1990, 194).

It was at this point that the active labor market policy was proposed—as a way of reconciling the demands for full employment and economic balance. As one of the union economists who shaped the policy during the late 1940s put it:

We claim that full employment and reasonable economic stability are not incompatible, that it is labor market policy which can make a crucial contribution to the solution of this apparent dilemma. We have therefore developed an economic policy around the kernel of a selective labor market policy. Sometimes referred to as "the Swedish model," this has worked quite well for many years. (Meidner 1978, 3)

The main features of the model were as follows: Inflationary demand would be restricted by a tight fiscal stance; in conjunction with the unions' policy of wage solidarity, this would tend to weed out the least efficient and competitive firms in low-wage sectors, as they would not be able to afford the negotiated national wage rates. At the same time, profitable enterprises could expand because the negotiated rates would leave them a fairly large margin. Labor market policy would answer for the critical double task of facilitating the geographic and occupational migration of labor to expanding sectors, and boosting labor demand *selectively* by means of relief work and government orders (Furåker 1976, 97; Rehn 1977, 212; Tilton 1990, 194–95).

The basic difference from earlier policy lies in the *selective* element. Instead of sustaining employment in a traditional Keynesian manner by stimulating demand with *general* economic instruments (which tends to be inflationary and destabilizing), the new labor market policy would operate selectively, by actively intervening with the many and diverse instruments (removal support, government orders, vocational training, extensive employment services, and so on) deemed appropriate for each instance of local or sectoral unemployment.

The model would also give the trade unions more room in which to negotiate wage rates, for this would be done "in a situation of real resistance from employers on account of narrow profit margins" (Rehn 1977, 214; cf. Rehn 1957). Such an approach would also favor the Social Democratic government, inasmuch as it would relieve it of the necessity of intervening in collective bargaining to enforce wage restraint. The model would also enhance economic efficiency by speeding up structural adjustment: capital and labor would be transferred more rapidly to expanding sectors of the economy.

The rationalization of the industrial structure would then enhance the potential for improving real wages. Yet this rationalization would also take place in forms acceptable to the trade union movement, for those workers made redundant by the closure of unprofitable firms would, unlike in the interwar years, have access to generous support in the form of relief work at market rates, removal grants, well-equipped labor exchanges, and good retraining facilities. The transition could also be eased by government orders and industrial subsidies.

It is the provision of all these instruments, which in each case could be used in a specific mix, that constitutes the *active* element of the "active labor market policy" for which Sweden has been so internationally renowned (Katzenstein 1985, 119; Mucciaroni 1992, 224–27; Weir 1992, 8; Wilensky and Turner 1987, 26). Swedish active labor market policy has been exceptional not only in being part of a sophisticated macroeconomic model created and launched by the union movement, Swedish exceptionalness in this area can also be shown in figures.

In the late 1980s, for instance, the OECD for the first time made an effort to compare costs for labor market policies, active as well as passive (i.e., unemployment benefits). Strikingly, the Swedish costs as a percentage of GNP were not exceptionally high—among the fifteen OECD countries, Sweden ranked seventh, with costs just slightly above the average (2.91 percent compared to 2.67 percent of GNP). Where Sweden stood out was in the proportion of labor market funds spent on *active* measures. In Sweden, this proportion was 71 percent, while the average for the other fourteen OCED countries was 32 percent. Except for Norway (58 percent, but which in absolute terms was far less than Sweden—0.93 percent of GNP compared to 2.91 percent), no other OECD country spent more than 44 percent on active labor market measures as compared to passive (figures calculated from OECD Employment Outlook 1989). Both in terms of resources and political commitment, then, the Swedish active labor market policy is truly a "deviant case."[3]

Certainly the sheer amount of money spent does not say anything about the success or failure of a policy, but the figures do show the indisputable weight the Swedish Social Democrats have put on the establishment of this policy. An active labor market policy is organizationally complicated to implement, moreover, so the figures also indicate the weight of the administrative effort. It should be noted as well that neither of Sweden's neighbors, Norway and Denmark—countries very similar to Sweden in both politics and culture—have come close to emphasizing active labor market policy in the degree that Sweden has (OECD 1989; Therborn 1986).

In sum, the Rehn-Meidner model was a combination of three *different* policies: (1) a general economic policy—fiscal restraint—conducted centrally by the ministry of finance, (2) wage solidarity, a policy pursued by the trade unions, and (3) the active labor market policy, a selective and interventionist government policy requiring a strong *and* flexible administrative apparatus. Many accounts have been written on how the ideas behind the model took shape among LO economists in the late 1940s, gained acceptance at the top of the LO and the Social Democratic party in the mid-1950s, were introduced in the late 1950s, and then implemented in full in the 1960s and afterward.

The active labor market policy must be seen in the context of this model in order to appreciate that it was an instrument for implementing the more comprehensive policy embodied in the Rehn-Meidner model. When comparing intentions with results, therefore, it is essential to examine the intentions behind labor market policy in terms of that policy's function in the larger model. To confine the comparison to labor market policy alone would be to confuse means with ends. The intentions behind labor market policy have not been to achieve a certain volume of job referral activities, relief work, government orders, and so on. These are instead means for carrying out a larger policy model; the analysis needs therefore to focus on the general intentions behind that model.

I shall focus nevertheless on the labor market aspect of this model, as this is the only component with any significant element of administration and implementation. This seems a fitting approach in view of the purposes of this study. Labor market policy is the operative element in the model, and the one that involves, by virtue of its selective nature, direct government intervention. The men behind the model, moreover, considered the active labor market policy to be the vital component; the tight fiscal stance and wage solidarity, on the other hand, were merely its prerequisites (Hjern 1982, 68).

Another reason for concentrating on the organizational aspect is that several studies have shown that, in other countries, active labor market programs have often broken down and lost legitimacy in the course of being implemented (for a British example, see King and

Rothstein 1993). One of the most noteworthy examples is the Comprehensive Employment and Training Act (CETA), launched in the United States during the 1960s. The Reagan administration could close down the CETA program with almost no political opposition, because the program had become discredited in the process of implementation (Weir 1992). By the time it was discontinued, the CETA had almost become "a four letter word" in the public debate (Donahue 1989, 181).

This ignominious end can be compared to recent developments in Sweden, where the conservative-led nonsocialist government (which replaced the Social Democrats in 1991) sought to counter rising unemployment by massively increasing the resources devoted to the active labor market policy (Prop. 1991–92, no. 100, bil. 11). Support for this policy transcends party differences in Sweden (cf. Therborn 1986).

It is indeed puzzling, as Margaret Weir has pointed out, that there is so little in the way of active labor market policy in the U.S., a country in which, normatively speaking, the work ethic is very strong. It would be reasonable to assume, she writes, that Americans' strong work ethic would encourage them to offer unemployed citizens training or relief work rather than cash benefits. I agree with her argument that one answer lies in the U.S. government's historically determined disposition towards graft; the success of an active labor market policy, it is important to remember, depends crucially on the avoidance of corruption, patronage, and waste (Weir 1992; cf. Mucciaroni 1992). Thus, while active labor market policies seem rather simple on a programmatic level, they have proven very difficult to implement.

I argued above that the two reforms compared in this study have held a central position in the postwar policy of Swedish social democracy. This is evident, in the case of labor market policy, from its crucial function in what has come to be known as the "Swedish model," and from the fact that the primary objective of this policy— full employment—has featured prominently in Social Democratic party programs (Hedborg and Meidner 1984). This demand was printed in italics, for instance, in the labor movement's famous postwar program, which was published in 1944 and proclaimed as the platform of Erlander's first cabinet in 1945, "Our principal demand for the postwar era was thus the demand for full employment. Our principal task is now to plan a program for full employment and then achieve this in practice" (Arbetarrörelsens efterkrigsprogram 1946, 42).

It bears mentioning that the father of the model, Gösta Rehn, was one of the figures behind the 1944 program's section on full employment, in which the embryo of the model can be discerned. As a member of the program committee, he pointed to the inflationary risks of a full employment policy and began to discuss ways to solve this problem through various types of selective state intervention in the economy (Ohlson 1958, 55).

In his memoirs, Erlander described the Social Democratic conference in 1955—between the leaders of the party and the LO, at which it was finally agreed to launch the active labor market policy—as possibly the most important of the decade (Erlander 1976, 38–39). The aim of the conference went beyond resolving the conflict with the trade unions arising from the government's call for wage restraint:

For the first time I declared my adherence to the Meidner-Rehn labor market policy. Previously I had been worried that it would accelerate the company closures that are part of the free market economy. But my misgivings disappeared if the policy for promoting mobility, besides augmenting labor mobility, would lead to a more social utilization of our capital assets; in other words if labor market policy became more selective. (Erlander 1976, 41)

In practice as well as proclamation, then, active labor market policy has played a central role in Swedish society.[4]

My earlier assertion—that the reforms compared in this study were promoted primarily by the Social Democrats—referred to initiatives taken in the Riksdag. This assertion requires qualification as regards labor market policy, however, at least if one has in mind a broader political arena than merely the Riksdag. For in the intricate postwar interaction between the Social Democratic party and the LO, it is evident that the ideas and initiatives regarding labor market policy came entirely from the latter (Hedborg and Meidner 1984, 18; Rehn 1977; Tilton 1990).

According to Leif Lewin, the LO's 1961 program served in practice as the party's action program, as far as industrial policy is concerned (1967, 426, 440–44). At the 1961 LO congress, Erlander mentioned that many of the LO's ideas about labor market policy "had seemed novel and disquieting at first," but that the implementation of the program had now begun. He also underscored the role of the LO as a source of ideas (Öhman 1974, 72; cf. Erlander 1976, 41). In a volume published in honor of Tage Erlander in 1969, the year he resigned as prime minister, the LO chairman, Arne Geijer, cited the new labor market policy as a typical example of how union ideas could be translated via the party into practical politics (1969, 57).

## Policy Intentions: Education Policy

One of the obstacles facing postwar Social Democratic education policy was the organizational diversity of primary and secondary education. At the end of World War II, those who continued their education beyond the six compulsory years did so in no less than nineteen different types of schools (Marklund 1980, 32–36). For social democracy, however, this was only one aspect of the problem. Looking back on his experience as the new minister of education in 1945, Tage Erlander writes:

The serious aspect of this organizational diversity was that it concealed the common factor that the school system largely functioned as a class society in miniature. The different types of school recruited their pupils from fairly specific social strata. (Erlander 1973, 233)

The embryo of Social Democratic postwar school policy was likewise formulated in the 1944 postwar program. The main objectives were to replace the existing types of schools with a single comprehensive school for nine or ten years of compulsory education and to eliminate the financial obstacles to secondary and higher education. An outline had been presented in 1943 by Alva Myrdal, who promoted education issues in the group drafting the party program (Ohlson 1958, 46; cf. Richardson 1978, 226–27, 230).

The objectives of Social Democratic education policy were to achieve greater social equality, not just in the educational system but also, and more importantly, in society as a whole. The concept of equality is of course somewhat diffuse, particularly in the context of school policy. It refers in this context to an endeavor to overcome differences in individuals' social and economic conditions, insofar as these are a product of social class. Educational research confirms that this was an aim of Social Democratic education policy (Husén 1977, 12; Marklund 1982, 409). This research is open to the criticism, however, that it seldom places postwar Social Democratic school policy in its overriding strategic context. As I see it, school policy, just as labor market policy, was a component of a comprehensive political model for social change. Educational reform was merely an instrument in this model (albeit strategically one of the most important, and operationally possibly the most central).

The most detailed description and reconstruction of the model may be found in Leif Lewin's analysis of the political debate over economic planning in postwar Sweden (1967). The model, labeled by Lewin the "Social Democratic model for equality," is distinctive in that it did not focus on individual ability and opportunity in an *otherwise equal* society. According to Lewin, the liberal concept of equality was based on such an individual approach—equality of opportunity (1967, 69, 77, 447–48). In the Social Democratic model, it was instead the *initial conditions* for individuals that should be made more equal by the use of interventionist policies:

The Social Democrats call for the same freedom for everyone, "equality in freedom," which presupposes that the coercive power of the State is used to alter the structure of society. The ideological boundary between socialism and liberalism lies in this view of the power *as well as the capability* of the State. (Lewin 1967, 77; italics mine)

While Lewin takes a certain amount of state capacity for granted, I treat this matter—the ability of the state to induce social change through interventionist policies—as an open question. Indeed, it is the central question of this book. In any event, the Social Democratic model for equality, so eloquently summarized by Lewin, implies a political refusal to accept the varying conditions imposed on individuals as a result of social class, as for instance in the educational system. The Social Democrats' equality model called instead for a policy of state intervention, whereby inequalities in individuals' conditions and prospects would be overcome as much as possible (Lewin 1967, 77).

In his interpretation of the postwar Social Democratic equality model, Lewin underscores the efforts to achieve an overarching political control over economic life. As Lewin mentions in passing (1967, 77), the model he reconstructs could be applied to the party's education policy as well. My hypothesis is that the Social Democratic party regarded the reform of education as a central (and in some respects strategic) instrument for the implementation of a more general reformist objective, namely the alteration of the distribution of opportunities in society by means of state intervention. One important goal of the reform was to change the traditional elitist recruitment not only to higher education, but thereby also to key positions in the state.

Lewin argues that the Rehn-Meidner model was also designed to further this egalitarian objective (1967, 412–42). This was clearly true at the level of political rhetoric. It seems reasonable that the concept of equality should also include jobs for everyone, coupled with government support for geographical and occupational mobility and for vulnerable groups in the labor market (cf. Hedborg and Meidner 1984). It seems to me, however, that Lewin misses a great deal in interpreting the model solely in terms of the flow of ideas in the labor movement. He pays insufficient attention to the LO's institutional and organizational reasons for pursuing such a policy—reasons founded in the endeavor (which trade unions share with other institutions) to sustain the reproduction and strength of the organization (cf. Rothstein 1987).

This criticism applies as well to those who have analyzed the active labor market policy in terms of Marxian structural functionalism (Berntson and Persson 1979; Furåker 1976). The active labor market policy is, in their view, the fruit not of the contest of ideas but of the capitalist economy's unyielding demands. In addition to disregarding the LO's organizational motives, however, these authors omit to note that a great many national economies of the capitalist type have managed very well without any active labor market policy on the Swedish scale, albeit in some instances with disastrous consequences for employment (cf. Therborn 1986).

As regards the intentions behind education policy, there is less evidence of such material motives of an organizational nature. On the contrary, working-class organizations risked being drained of talent as a result of educational reform (Murray 1988). As shown by Richardson (1983, 401–10), the architects of the Social Democratic education policy thought rather along predominantly *idealistic* lines. It should be added that some Social Democrats argued for incorporating the education policy into the long-term political strategy for equality. For instance, the Social Democratic party executive, in an affirmative response to a 1948 congress motion calling for an inquiry into democracy in state administration, ventured the following observations:

Many Social Democratic representatives in central and local government have no doubt experienced how easily a strong political position in the decision-making fora may be neutralized via the influence over the administrative apparatus which is exerted by officials with a very different attitude to social policy. While it is true that competence and loyalty have been and still are characteristic features of Swedish civil servants, the pattern of recruitment up to now may lead to a lack of understanding of the practical and psychological nature of the problem. Greater congruence can no doubt be achieved when the educational facilities for our nation have become truly democratic, thereby establishing a broader base for the recruitment of public servants. With the educational monopoly that still exists in our country, recruitment is too one-sided at present. Our school system has led an excessively isolated existence. If it is given a content that aims, not so much at inculcating idle encyclopedic facts and learning by rote, as at providing a thorough introduction to the society in which we are all involved, one can certainly expect that members of the civil service will ultimately receive a better schooling for their tasks than at present. (*Demokrati inom statsförvaltningen* 1952, 7)

At the time, then, the Social Democratic party analyzed education policy in terms of a somewhat crude Marxian state theory. According to the Social Democratic leadership, the bourgeois imprint on the state was a strategic problem for reformism and one that the communist labor movement, inspired by Lenin, intended to resolve by "crushing" the state (Therborn 1980, 122–235; Wright 1978, chap. 3). But instead of requiring such drastic methods, the Social Democrats argued that the bourgeois character of the capitalist state could be educated away with the help of the new comprehensive school policy.

Prime Minister Tage Erlander is reported to have harbored serious misgivings in the mid-1960s that the professional groups working for the state, such as civil servants and teachers, would with their bourgeois political orientation pose a major problem for the successful implementation of the party's policies (Ruin 1990, 213). At the same time, Erlander's political vision called for the creation of a "strong society," which was not merely a matter of expanding the public sector. Rather, as Timothy Tilton has put it, the concept entailed "a mystical merging and identification of state and society." This idea was founded on the notion that the state was a neutral "tool" which could be used as a transmission belt for the realization of politicians' wishes (Tilton 1990, 177).

In any event, central party statements and documents provide plenty of evidence for the role of education policy in the equality model. Alva Myrdal, for instance, told the party congress in 1944: "It is becoming generally known that in Sweden we are beginning to lag behind in the elimination of class conflicts as regards education. . . . The educational monopoly is the strongest class privilege that remains to be overcome" (SAP-protokoll 1944, 426). A quarter of a century later, addressing the 1969 congress as chairperson of the party's "equality group," she had this to say:

Education policy has been regarded by the equality group as the primary strategic instrument for abolishing class barriers. . . . The most strategic element, our real spearhead for the future, is unquestionably education policy. This represents a gigantic step away from the old class society, where class divisions were such an inevitable consequence of differences in education. (SAP-protokoll 1969, 167)

That these ideas had also prevailed in the interval is evident from an address by Olof Palme (who was then minister of education) to the 1968 congress: "The school system is and will continue to be a key to the abolition of the class society" (SAP-protokoll 1968, 294; cf. an interview with Olof Palme in Hildebrand 1969, 10–16). Olof Palme had argued against the liberal concept of equality in education policy as early as 1953 in an article in *Tiden*, the party's theoretical journal—with the significant title "Obstacles at the Starting Line." Social Democratic education policy, he averred, was "an important feature of the struggle against class society," thus confirming Lewin's conception of the inner logic of the Social Democratic view of politics and the state (Palme 1953, 479; cf. Lewin 1967).[5]

In education, the counterpart of the *selective* nature of labor market policy came to be known as *individualized* instruction. Instead of the earlier practice of matching pupils with different types of schools according to their purported ability to learn, in the new policy the annual intake would not be differentiated. The requisite differentiation of teaching would be achieved by providing individualized *instruction within each class* (Isling 1980, 308–10; Marklund 1980, 87, 91–92, 143; Richardson 1983, 153–59; cf. SOU 1948, no. 27, 71). Inasmuch as pupils with very different qualifications would be taught together, new forms of instruction were clearly required. The established practice in Swedish schools until then had been that teachers addressed their classes as a single entity.

The government commission that launched the comprehensive

school reform in 1948 argued that, if the reform were to succeed, a radical change in classroom practice—in the direction of more individualized teaching—would be absolutely necessary (SOU 1948, no. 27; cf. Rothstein 1991b). As Karin Hadenius has shown, the idea of individualized teaching had become the single most important element in Social Democratic argumentation by the time the comprehensive school reform was finally introduced in 1960 (1990, 201).

## Policy Intentions: Conclusions

Considerable similarities thus characterize the Social Democrats' intentions regarding education and labor market policy. Both were strategic elements in a macropolitical social model. Both entailed considerable state intervention, and the proposed methods for implementation were similar as well, based as they were on individualization and selectivity, respectively. A clear difference remained in one respect—the source of the initiative *inside* the Social Democratic movement.

In the case of labor market policy, the Social Democratic party was scarcely more than the parliamentary executor of a policy initiated by the LO. The opposite was true in the case of education policy; none of the Social Democrats identified by Richardson as having inspired and initiated the reform in this field (Stellan Arvidson, Alva Myrdal, Oscar Olsson, Josef Weijene) were directly involved in the LO (1983, 401–10; cf. Isling 1980, 296–304). Alva Myrdal was an academic, and the other three had been teachers. Nor did two other central figures in educational reform, Tage Erlander and Adolf Wallentheim, have political roots in the trade union movement. Possible sources must be sought elsewhere. For example, the party's education policy around 1945 bore a striking resemblance to the line promoted by the Association of Primary School Teachers in the 1940 School Commission (Isling 1980, 229; Richardson 1978, 258).

## Policy Results: Analytical Problems

The analytical problems involved in measuring policy results are no less complex than those involved in determining policy intentions. The first issue concerns what to measure, i.e., what constitutes a result. It is up to each analyst to select criteria for policy evaluation. Analyses of general economic efficiency constitute one type;

evaluations of social and ideological policy effects another. In evaluative research of this kind, it is the analyst who chooses the yardstick for judging results; it is his or her model that underlies the evaluation of policy. This does not in itself diminish the value of the exercise, but clearly a great deal depends on whether or not one accepts the criteria selected (cf. Premfors 1989 chap. 6).

The present approach has a different point of departure. In keeping with the focus on policy implementation, it seeks criteria for success and failure in the political process. The results of a given policy are thus measured against the intentions behind the political model into which that policy has been incorporated. This seems to me the only conceivably objective way of assessing whether a parliamentary majority has succeeded or failed in bringing about social change by means of its control of the state apparatus (cf. Berman 1978; Lane 1983).

Inquiring into whether the results of a social reform correspond to the intentions behind it may seem straightforward and simple. Yet it often proves to be a political mine field. As Premfors argues, the Swedish model for political decision making attaches disproportionate weight to the preparation of decisions and their formal procedure at the expense of their execution, evaluation, and feedback. Any discussion of whether social reforms of the magnitude considered here have been successfully completed (and if not, then which groups intervened in the political process so as to thwart them) constitutes a challenge to strong party and professional interests (Premfors 1989).

The time dimension presents another problem. How much time must pass before one can reasonably compare policy intentions with results? There is no simple answer. Policy intentions seldom provide any indication of when the reform is expected to be completed. Moreover, any reform produces results both immediately and afterward into the indeterminate future.

The two reforms considered here had their beginnings in the Social Democrats' postwar planning efforts in the mid-1940s. They were tested in practical politics in the 1950s and implemented in full in the 1960s and 1970s. The unique duration of Social Democratic governmental dominance in Sweden surely provides a reasonable interval for the evaluation of intentions in relation to results.

If social changes of the type discussed here could not be achieved by parliamentary means even in Sweden, reformism may well never be feasible. This would imply the demise of parliamentary strategies as a method for social change (Lundquist 1975, 15). In other words, if forty-four years of uninterrupted incumbency do not suffice to implement reformist policies successfully, then the reformist model must be called into serious question.

The interpretation of results poses a further problem. What degree of congruence between intentions and results is required for a reform to be judged a success or a failure? Let us begin with the two extremes: a perfectly successful reform that fully matches intentions, and one that falls short altogether. It would seem neither is particularly likely to occur. Such concepts as "policy success" and "policy failure" should therefore be considered relative.

Furthermore, a special problem arises in evaluating policy results. As indicated earlier, a social reform that fails to achieve its policy objectives may yet be judged a success by its instigators, if it serves an important purpose in fields other than the policy area in question. I therefore supplement my quantitative evaluations of the results of the two reforms with some assessments offered by the Social Democrats themselves as the party's forty-four years in government drew to a close.

Including such a subjective element in the evaluation of a political process amounts to making use of political self-assessments. The reason for using it in this analysis is based on the assumption that a political agent such as the Swedish Social Democrats cannot claim credit for policy results falling far short of original intentions, for doing so would conflict with the party's need to maintain political legitimacy (cf. Mayntz 1975).

Such a method is certainly questionable, inasmuch as intentions and the measurement of their fulfillment are both derived from the same source—a political agent with evident vested interests, no less. If used alone this method is clearly unacceptable, but I believe it may contribute to our understanding by supplementing objective measures and the evaluations of more independent analysts. Thus, if the evaluative research is contradicted by the political self-assessment, conclusions about the degree of goal fulfillment should be drawn with caution.

Similarly, if the independent evaluation and the political self-assessment concur with each other, we may reasonably consider the former result to be strengthened by the latter. Political parties are prone to vaunt their successful reforms and disinclined to admit failure, so the difference in self-assessment between cases of success and failure is liable to be one of degree. A particularly successful policy will probably figure prominently in the party's own account of history, while unsuccessful efforts will likely be played down or ignored altogether.

### Results of School Policy

The impact of the school reform on inequality has usually been measured in terms of social recruitment to postsecondary education. Social bias of this type can be traced back to primary school (Gesser 1985, 124). By this yardstick, the degree to which the school reform has achieved its objective is clearly very small. The main finding of all studies in this field is shown in table 2, which measures the recruitment to traditional university education in 1962 (the official first year of the comprehensive school) and 1977 (the year after the SAP lost power for the first time in forty-four years).

Strikingly enough, social recruitment to higher education was less unequal in 1962, when the new school system was officially introduced, than in 1977, when it had been in operation for fifteen years.[6] Recruitment of students of working-class background dropped from 27 to 20 percent during that period. In absolute numbers, it fell from 2,818 in 1962 to 2,278 in 1977. The conclusion must be that, more than three decades after the comprehensive school reform was introduced, there are no signs of an increased recruitment of students with working-class backgrounds to higher education in Sweden.

Another measure of goal fulfillment centers on the provision of a nine-year basic education for all Swedish pupils. Official studies indicate that the proportion of pupils not completing their basic education rose in the 1970s from 3.5 percent in 1973 to 5.5 percent in 1975 and 8 percent in 1980 (and the last figure is probably on the low side) (Wingborg 1982). Those pupils so excluded from basic education have come predominantly from the working class; the lowest and highest levels of the educational system therefore exhibit the same social skew. Referring to this as the "surreptitious" school reform, Donald Broady argues that "if one pupil in ten leaves basic education prematurely then the system is not compulsory and if it breaks down into socially segregated school systems then it is not a basic education" (Broady 1982, 8–9). Thus, even in the matter of ensuring

TABLE 2. Recruitment to Traditional Tertiary Education in Relation to Social
Background

| Year | 1962 (N=10,438) | 1977 (N=11, 201) | 1990 (N=50,989) |
|---|---|---|---|
| Professional background | 22% | 25% | 31% |
| Middle-class background | 50 | 51 | 50 |
| Working-class background | 27 | 20 | 19 |
| Unknown | 1 | 4 | not incl. |

Note: Calculated from Kim 1983, 66–69 and from SCB Statistika Meddelanden 1992 U 20
SM 9292 "Högskolan 1985/86–1990/91", table 2 "Statlig högskoleutbildning." For similar results see Gesser 1985, 171–203; Gesser and Fasth 1973; Härnquist and Svensson 1980; SCB
Utbildningsstatisk Årsbok 1983, 1984. Social background is determined by the parent with
the highest formal education. Professional refers to persons with some university training.
Middle class corresponds to the Swedish term "Tjänsteman"—which refers to white-collar
employees without academic education. The working class includes persons in blue-collar
occupations, both skilled and unskilled. The operationalization of these categories is that
used by the Swedish National Bureau of Statistics. The figures from 1990 are not quite
comparable to those from 1962 and 1977, on account of the changed meaning of a university education. The reform of higher education launched in 1977 brought many formerly
nonuniversity branches into the university system (such as the training of nursery school
and preschool teachers). If only "traditional" university branches are included, the 1990
figures for the proportion of students of professional background are even higher and the
proportion of students of working-class background even lower.

students a nine-year basic education, the reform was to a considerable extent a failure.

Given the criteria of evaluation chosen in this study, it is obvious
that these findings present a clear picture of the school reform as a
failure. This is particularly evident as regards the primary objective
in the general equality model. The findings of Göran Arnman and
Ingrid Jönsson are particularly relevant, showing indisputably that
the school system's social dualism, which the reform was intended to
abolish, lived on in the new comprehensive school. Similar arguments have been put forward by prominent researchers in education; Ulf Lundgren, for instance, asserts that "practice in schools remained much the same throughout the attempts at reform and the
curricular revisions" (in Palme and Östling 1981, 50; cf. SOU 1988,
no. 20, 9–10).

These evaluations are reflected, as one might expect, in Social
Democratic rhetoric in the mid-1970s. Addressing the 1975 party
congress, the executive's representative and later minister of educa-

tion, Lena Hjelm-Wallén, struck a much less optimistic tone than had been taken at earlier party congresses: "we are forced to note that today's school is very largely characterized by a time-honored transference of knowledge, handed down from school system to school system and founded on values from a social system very different from ours" (SAP-protokoll 1975, 309). Replying to criticism of the current school system, she remarked that "we have extended the school system in organizational terms but this debate has indeed shown that it is not exactly any fine tuning of the system that is left but that very fundamental and far-reaching changes are still needed" (SAP-protokoll 1975, 339). She ventured an even more critical assessment of the results of her party's school policy at the 1978 party congress, when she criticized the gap between goal and reality as "unacceptably wide," and called for a "strong battle with the traditional forces of education" (SAP-protokoll 1978, 895–96).

Another example of Social Democratic disappointment with the results of the school reform is the exceedingly sharp criticism of compulsory basic education expressed by the LO in the 1970s. A report to the 1976 LO congress noted "the persistently skewed and class-based recruitment to higher education" and argued that the system contributed "to a bias in the environment of young people that leads to an unfortunate stratification of society" (LO 1976, 61–62). Compulsory education is said in the report to preserve the class society (84). The report contained the following observations as well:

The objectives of equality and democratization have been laid down in a number of policy decisions as well as in the ensuing instructions in school law, school statutes and curricula. But today's school has not managed to achieve these objectives to more than a very limited extent. . . . Compulsory education has failed to give a large group of young people even the most fundamental and essential knowledge and skills. The system has also failed to stimulate and motivate young people for education, which means that an even larger group refrains from going on to post-compulsory education. (81)

### Results of Labor Market Policy

The success of the active labor market policy in Sweden has been hailed in so many studies, not least by American scholars, that it has nearly become a truth beyond questioning.[7] Yet I think it necessary

TABLE 3. Unemployment as a Percentage of the Labor
Force: Five Year Averages.

|  | 1965–69 | 1970–74 | 1975–79 | 1980–84 |
|---|---|---|---|---|
| OECD | 2.4 | 2.8 | 5.2 | 7.8 |
| Swedem | 1.6 | 1.8 | 1.9 | 2.9 |

Sources: Lane et al. 1991, table 3:11. OECD countries: All save
Iceland, Luxemburg (whose economies are too small and unusual),
and Greece (no data available for the first period).

TABLE 4. Inflation: OECD Countries and Sweden. Average
Rates.

|  | 1960–68 | 1968–73 | 1973–79 | 1979–80 |
|---|---|---|---|---|
| OECD | 5.5 | 7.6 | 11.9 | 10.5 |
| Sweden | 4.2 | 5.9 | 10.6 | 9.0 |

Source: Lane et al. 1991, table 4.7. Inflation is calculated on the basis
of the implicit GDP price index, which provides a comprehensive
measure of the aggregate price movements of goods and services
making up the GDP. Countries are the same as in table 3.

to explain in greater detail what this success has consisted in, for the
policy is here analyzed in terms of its role in the Rehn-Meidner
model. Choosing an appropriate yardstick by which to measure results is less obvious for labor market policy than for school policy,
on account of the complexity of the model of which labor market
policy is a part. The model embraces a number of parallel objectives;
more than two measures are therefore needed.

In regard to the objective of combining low inflation with low
unemployment, an international comparison reveals considerable
success up to the end of the 1970s. As shown in tables 3 and 4, the
unemployment level in Sweden has been one of the lowest in the
OECD area, while inflation has been a shade below the average
(Hedborg and Meidner 1984, 138–42). Sweden was unique among industrialized countries, according to Therborn, in successfully coping
with unemployment crises in 1973–83 by means of an active labor
market policy (1986). It is also generally agreed that Sweden managed during that decade to maintain full employment without in-
curring high inflation (Hibbs 1977; Katzenstein 1985, 119). It should
be recalled here that the primary objective from a trade union
standpoint is low unemployment, for this minimizes competition
between workers.

TABLE 5. Trade-Union Membership Among Blue-Collar Workers in Select Countries 1940–75.

| | 1940 | 1950 | 1960 | 1970 | 1975 |
|---|---|---|---|---|---|
| Sweden | 66 | 76 | 78 | 80 | 89 |
| Denmark | 56 | 65 | 69 | 71 | 80 |
| Norway | 59 | 70 | 72 | 74 | 59* |
| Austria | | 74 | 77 | 73 | 58* |
| Belgium | | 56 | 74 | 74 | 66* |
| United Kingdom | 34 | 48 | 50 | 54 | 58 |
| Federal Republic of Germany | 31 | 36 | 35 | 33 | 39 |
| Netherlands* | 31 | 40 | 39 | 37 | 38 |
| France | 30 | 39 | 22 | 23 | 25 |
| United States of America | 22 | 32 | 29 | 28 | 29 |

Source: Kjellberg 1983, 37.
*Indicates that the figures represent degree of unionization among the total number of wage earners.

Wage solidarity was another objective of the Rehn-Meidner model. In a comparison of ten OECD countries around 1970, Sweden had the second most even income distribution before tax A study of industrial wages in fourteen OECD countries likewise put Sweden in second place in 1970 and 1975 (Hedborg and Meidner 1984, 143–44). Wage differentials between blue-collar workers in Sweden decreased until the early 1980s. In 1959, the average wage differential between workers in different contract areas of the LO-SAF sector was 29.6 percent. By 1980, this difference had fallen to about 10 percent (Elvander 1988, 36).

As regards rates of union membership, finally, an international comparison shows that, at the end of the period measured, Sweden stood at the top (table 5).

Judged in terms of the political intentions attributed to it here, then, the Rehn-Meidner model must be considered a political success story. This does not mean all the model's instruments functioned as intended (cf. Tilton 1990, 204–09). The main shortcoming has been the state's inability to maintain a sufficiently restrictive fiscal policy (Rehn, interview). Still, there is good reason to agree with Hedborg and Meidner that:

The international comparison has shown that Swedish employment and labor market policy has yielded very good results. The selective labor market policy has . . . made an appreciable contribution to this. . . . the Rehn model has been most successful in contributing to the achievement of the fundamental objectives: full employment and equality. (1984, 149, 156; cf. Therborn 1986)

As expected, the Social Democrats' self-assessment in regard to the results of labor market policy has been very positive. The party has been portrayed itself as the guardian of full employment, citing the successful labor market policy as evidence of this. A case in point was the opening address by the party chairman (Olof Palme) to the 1975 party congress; in this speech, the National Labor Market Board (AMS) figured as the good fairy:

Sten-Yngve Smed, a lathe operator, was told by the doctor that his hips and back were worn out. He was fifty-four. A broken leg as a child, polio at the age of fourteen and hard work had all left their mark. He drew sickness pay, and there was talk of a disability pension. But he protested: he was still strong enough to go on working for a long time. Now he is back at his old job. The adjustment group where he worked found a solution. His lathe could be modified to eliminate an number of awkward operations. The AMS contributed 20,000 crowns and the company 50,000 crowns. A car with special fittings was arranged by the AMS so that he could drive to work. A physically disabled worker is now able thereby to continue a meaningful job. (SAP-protokoll 1975, 18)

Addressing the same congress, the LO chairman (Gunnar Nilsson) described the labor market policy as one of the main bonds between the party and the LO (SAP-protokoll 1975, 959–60; cf. the speech by his predecessor, Arne Geijer, to the 1972 party congress, SAP-protokoll 1975, 42–44). Many such positive Social Democratic self-assessments may be found in regard to labor market policy (e.g., Palme 1977, 177).

As in the case of education policy, a report on the active labor market policy was presented to the 1976 LO congress. It contained a very positive assessment of the results, and called for even more selective labor market measures (*Fackföreningsrörelsen och arbetsmarknadspolitiken* 1976).

## Intentions and Results: Conclusion

To understand the limits of reformism, it is important to investigate cases in which these limits have had differential effects on the outcome. If we concentrate only on successful *or* on failed reformist policies, we cannot solve the puzzle. Seeking to ascertain policy success and failure is of course to enter choppy waters. Policies may be evaluated from many different standpoints, and there are as many assessments as there are approaches.

This study focuses on the ability of the elected (Social Democratic) government to implement its ideas for social change in two areas. Its success in the two areas has varied dramatically. Judged against intentions, the labor-market policy has been an undoubted success and the education policy an equally evident failure. I should stress that the concepts of success and failure are to be understood as relative; I do not claim that either of these policies has succeeded completely or failed altogether. But the evidence presented, both "objective" and "subjective," shows clearly that the goals of the active labor market policy have been achieved to a much greater extent than have the goals of the comprehensive school policy. In the chapters that follow, I seek to demonstrate that an appreciable part of the explanation for this can be found in the institutional differences between the agencies responsible for implementing the two policies.

# 5. Organization and Policy as Historical Structures

## Introduction

When the Swedish Social Democrats announced their policy intentions for education and the labor market in the second half of the 1940s, they did not act in an institutional vacuum. In both sectors, an administrative apparatus was already in place and had been operating for decades. Institutionally, then, the reforms would not begin from scratch. As mentioned earlier, this study attaches considerable theoretical importance to the institutional history of government administration (cf. Weir 1992).

This chapter clarifies the main events in the genesis of the two administrations and their characteristics at the time the policies were implemented. To begin with, however, it is necessary to explain a few general facts about the organization of government in Sweden. First, since the mid-nineteenth century, the Weberian ideal has left a powerful imprint on the Swedish state. No patronage or spoils systems have existed in modern times, and corruption has been negligible (Heckscher 1958, 18). On the contrary, a strong legalistic tradition of loyalty to the government and of service to the public interest has dominated the Swedish civil service (Mellbourn 1979).

Secondly, the responsibility for carrying out public policies has not been in the hands of the ministries, which have in fact been rather small organizations dealing mainly with policy formulation. Policy implementation has instead been the responsibility of a large number of semi-independent national boards and agencies (Sw. centrala ämbetsverk), such as the National School Board. These agencies and boards are usually led by a director-general appointed by the government, and they are supposed to act under their own legal responsibility according to general rules and regulations issued by the Riksdag or Cabinet.

This unique system, with roots reaching back to the seventeenth century (and which exists only in Sweden and Finland), means that the central agencies and boards do not take direct orders from the minister in their policy sector, but only from the cabinet *as a whole*. Furthermore, instructions from the cabinet to the boards must be stated as formal decisions, and ministers are forbidden, according to the constitution, to give orders about how particular cases should be dealt with. This expresses the idea that administration is mainly a legal affair, in which cabinet members should not interfere (as they should not intervene, say, with court decisions). Informal contacts between boards and ministries are of course frequent, but in the end it is the director-general of the board, or his subordinates, who bears the responsibility of ensuring that the board's actions accord with the laws and regulations (SOU 1985, no. 40). This system is usually thought, seen in comparative perspective, to grant the administrative branch of the Swedish state a strong position vis-à-vis the cabinet.

### Origins of the Labor Market Administration

The administrative structure that in 1948 was transformed into the National Labor Market Board (Sw. Arbetsmarknadsstyrelsen, or AMS), and which was assigned the responsibility of implementing the active labor market policy, had its origins in four previous public agencies established to influence the Swedish labor market. These were (1) the public labor system established 1903–1907, (2) the Unemployment Commission (Sw. Arbetslöshetskommissionen, or AK), which operated from 1914 to 1940, (3) two government commissions of inquiry in the late 1930s, and (4) the Labor Market Commission (Sw. Arbetsmarknadskommissionen, or AMK), a wartime crisis agency set up during World War II.

## The Public Employment Service

Public employment agencies in Sweden began not as central government initiatives but as local enterprises with municipal ties. Beginning in 1902, the system spread fairly quickly and, from 1907, the government provided financial support. The manner in which these local labor exchanges were organized affected their subsequent development greatly. The first agencies established in 1902 institutionalized the organizational principle for the relationship between government, capital, and labor that subsequently prevailed in the central government's labor market administration. The statutes prescribed that the boards of these local exchanges were to consist of equal numbers of representatives for organized capital and organized labor, respectively, together with an impartial chairman, usually a senior municipal official. Here can be discerned the embryo of the corporative public administration in which organized class interests are directly represented. This organizational recipe from 1902 was to become one of the principal features of what in the postwar era came to be known as "the Swedish model" (Rothstein 1982; Schiller 1967, chap. 1).

The local regulations also stated that the operations of the labor exchanges were to be neutral in relation to organized class interests. These public employment offices were not tied to specific occupations and industries, but were designed to provide information about all types of work. All trades would be served, and services would be free of charge. This is remarkable on several counts. For one thing, the employment agencies in Sweden emerged at a time of numerous sharp disputes between organized class interests, culminating in the general strike of 1909 (Schiller 1967).

The arrangement also differed from the general pattern in other countries, where the interested parties had striven for a monopoly in this field. The trade unions saw labor exchanges as a way of controlling the labor supply, which would strengthen their hand during industrial conflicts. Similarly, control of job referral could be used by capital to filter out union organizers and strikers as well as to recruit unorganized labor. Such a system, established in parts of Germany, was described in 1904 by the director of the Swedish Employers' Federation (SAF) as being "of eminent importance," in part because strikers and their leaders could be weeded out in the process of recruiting workers. Indeed, the control of job referral was a major object of contention between organized class interests in Germany and in other European countries (Falkenström 1904; cf. Schiller 1967, 8–33).

In Sweden, however, neither labor nor capital had initiated the local public labor exchanges. These were promoted instead by politically and socially active members of the emerging liberal bourgeoisie and, more importantly, by the central state apparatus. The SAF and the labor movement both housed differences of opinion over the organization of the employment agencies. The Social Democratic newspapers in Stockholm feared that employers would use the system to break strikes by recruiting unorganized labor, whereas their colleagues in Malmö favored the idea.

When the issue was debated in the Riksdag in 1903, the leader of the Social Democrats, Hjalmar Branting, was not enthusiastic, arguing that the principle of neutrality could not be maintained as long as the municipal franchise was limited to the affluent class. On the other hand, a corporate organization of public labor exchanges had found favor with the trade unions in Stockholm as early as in 1895 (King and Rothstein 1993; Rothstein 1991). The debate focused on how the exchanges should function in connection with labor disputes. The principle of neutrality was usually taken to mean that, if a dispute were in progress at a workplace, job referrals to that workplace would not be discontinued; an effort would be made, however, to inform applicants of the dispute. This procedure was adopted in 1902 (Skogh 1963).

There were those in the SAF who strongly favored the German system of employment exchanges controlled by the capitalists' organizations. In Malmö, however, a member of the SAF executive strongly promoted the neutral public system. When the first labor exchange in Stockholm was set up in 1904, the Central Employers' Confederation, a rival of the SAF, sanctioned the arrangement by agreeing to representation on the board (Schiller 1967, 33).

The SAF did not adopt a position on the labor exchanges until 1907, by which time the militant Gustaf Falkenström had been replaced as the leading figure by Hjalmar Von Sydow, a lawyer and by inclination a public servant. Speaking in 1907, von Sydow noted that a job referral system controlled by the SAF would be highly advantageous in struggles with the trade unions, but he still thought such a system should not be adopted in Sweden. His reasons are worth quoting:

The great power which this system places in the hands of the labor bureau raises misgivings, nor can it be denied that there is something repugnant in the way in which the workers are at the disposal of the system, to be moved about like pieces on a chessboard. Moreover, the introduction of such a labor exchange would no doubt encounter determined resistance from the labor organizations, and probably could not be undertaken except at the end of a general labor dispute in which the workers have been completely defeated. (von Sydow 1907, 14)

This assessment of the potential organized resistance was one reason why, after 1907, the employers accepted the public system of labor exchanges for the time being. Differences of opinion had prevented the SAF from reaching a decision earlier, and in this way the initiative had been lost. By 1907, ten corporatively organized labor exchanges, handling more than 36,000 vacancies, had already been established (for the most part in the major cities and towns) (Rothstein 1982, 27).

The principles that came to govern the operations of the public labor exchanges—corporative structure, neutrality, and cost-free service—were adopted on the national level by a series of *Employment Office Conferences*. It was the civil servants in the National Board of Trade—the government agency responsible for commercial and industrial issues—who organized these meetings beginning in 1906. Leading representatives from the SAF and LO were among the conference participants, together with representatives from the local employment exchanges. The following year, the Liberal government enacted legislation providing financial support to the municipal labor exchanges, on the condition that the above principles be observed (Skogh 1963, 177). This government subsidy was not large, but it institutionalized the system by requiring neutrality and equal representation for employers and employees. Furthermore, the fact that the bill was unanimously adopted, and was not debated in either chamber of the Riksdag, indicates the widespread acceptance of these principles (ibid.).

The system expanded rapidly, and by 1914 there were about a

hundred labor exchanges handling more than 100,000 vacancies (cf. Öhman 1970, 101). By 1920, a national network had been established with more than 130 offices handling around 200,000 vacancies (Rothstein 1982, 27). A public labor exchange could be found in every sizable town and industrial center. The introduction of public unemployment insurance in 1934 led to renewed expansion, and by the time the system was nationalized in 1939, there were 166 offices handling almost half a million vacancies. As regards the central administration, finally, it should be mentioned that the provision of government support had given rise to a central inspectorate in 1911 (Rothstein 1991).

The institutional principles that had been adopted for job referral in 1902 remained unchanged. There was virtually no political disagreement on this count, even when fierce disputes were being fought out on the labor market, or debates raged over employment policy. In a 1916 report, the National Board found that the public labor exchanges had managed to gain the confidence of both organized capital and the unions, "which in our country have fortunately abstained from utilizing the referral of jobs as a weapon in the social struggle, . . . in Germany [this] has partially distorted the whole employment office issue." The board also observed that:

Despite the sharp social and political conflicts that have emerged in other areas of public life between members of the employers' and workers' camps, on the boards of the employment offices the same persons have, in the experience of the National Social Welfare Board, continued to cooperate faithfully in the interest of objectivity. (Quoted in Rothstein 1991, 165)

Another distinctive feature of the Swedish public labor exchanges in the interwar years was their connection with public unemployment insurance. Most comparable countries had introduced such insurance much earlier and had assigned the public employment agencies the task of ensuring that those applying for benefits were prepared to work (cf. Marklund 1982b). The working class in these countries therefore perceived the public labor exchanges— particularly during the severe unemployment of the 1930s—as a repressive supervisory body rather than a neutral agency. This gave the employment service a bad image in many countries. In Great Britain, for instance, the public labor exchanges' lack of legitimacy has impeded efforts to implement an active labor market policy, for labor exchanges cannot operate successfully unless the jobless are convinced of their effectiveness and impartiality (Blankenburg 1978, 281; King and Rothstein 1993; L. Levine 1969; Mukherje 1976; Showler 1976, 19–37; cf. Hill 1981, 91–93).

However, public unemployment insurance was not introduced in Sweden until 1934, giving the labor exchanges plenty of time to establish a reputation as a neutral agency rather than a supervisory body. The insurance system did require the jobless to register with the public labor exchanges as job seekers, and if an applicant rejected a suitable work assignment, the staff were required to report the fact. In the Swedish unemployment insurance system, however, it was not a public authority but the unemployment associations— established and regulated by the trade unions—that decided whether refusal to accept a work assignment constituted grounds for depriving a person of unemployment benefits. This relieved the public labor exchanges of the need to act repressively (King & Rothstein 1993; Rothstein 1991).

The introduction of unemployment insurance was hotly debated by the Left and Right in the Riksdag (AK 1934, no. 40, 3–71; FK 1934, no. 37, 7–56). A manual issued by the National Social Welfare Board in 1936 emphasized that the new unemployment insurance legislation was *not* designed to turn the labor exchanges into a control system; they were to continue, rather, to act as service agencies. This was also underscored in a circular to the labor exchanges, which stated that "the chairman of an unemployment committee should not simultaneously be the labor exchange's representative." The supervision of unemployment assistance was to be kept separate from job referral. Nor was the distinction to a mere "formal arrangement." Employment officers were not to serve on the local unemployment committees, and their activities would be housed in separate premises (*Handbok för den offentliga arbetsförmedlning* 1936; cf. SNA, Socialstyrelsens arkiv, no. 7:e byrån, diarenr. M 550/36, (AK arkiv), Thomson's documents).

## The Labor Market Administration Before 1940

Public unemployment assistance was accordingly supervised not by the labor exchanges but by local unemployment committees under the direction of a central body, the National Unemployment Commission (AK), which had been set up by the government in 1914 as an emergency advisory body. During the severe unemployment of the early 1920s, the AK became an executive body, and became as well, in sharp contrast to the labor exchanges, an extremely divisive political issue (cf. Nordström 1944, 38). Two Social Democratic minority cabinets resigned (in 1923 and 1926) when they failed to gain control over the AK, which was supported by the nonsocialist majority in the Riksdag. The underlying causes of this dispute were as follows.

The political power of the Swedish labor movement—founded as it was on the organizational strength of the trade unions—was threatened by three policies enforced by the AK: (1) the AK's wage policy in regard to relief work, (2) the scale of the AK's public assistance, and (3) the AK's approach to labor disputes. The AK developed unemployment assistance fairly independently of central direction, and attained such an unrivaled position in state administration as to earn it the epithet of "a state within the state" (Nordström 1944, 40). The AK's unemployment policy took the form of massive relief-work projects rather than cash benefits. The unemployed could receive (means-tested) cash benefits, but only in exceptional cases—if such workers could not be sent to the work camps.

It is important to note that these cash benefits *were not* unemployment insurance; that is, the unemployed had no insurance-based right to assistance. Instead, the decision was at the complete discretion of the local unemployment committees working under the AK (Unga 1976, 70–71). In this respect, too, Sweden deviated from the prevailing international pattern, and indeed this approach came to be known as "the Swedish system."[1]

In the AK's view, relief-work wages should be no higher than about 70 percent of the lowest market rate for unskilled labor. This, it was thought, would give the jobless an incentive to find regular employment as soon as possible. It also reflected the prevailing economic doctrine that the crisis could be resolved only by cutting wage costs (Unga 1976). This wage policy encouraged many municipalities and some state agencies to arrange their regular projects as AK relief work; that way, the central government covered an appreciable share of the costs (cf. Thomson 1944, 70). As a result, a municipality's laborers were liable to be dismissed, only to find themselves doing the same work—now officially on a relief project—for considerably less pay. This development clearly threatened one of the foundations of trade union organization: the negotiation of a minimum wage level.

The second problem was that the AK deliberately rationed relief work and means-tested cash benefits in such a way that barely half of the applicants could obtain any assistance (N.B.: no public unemployment insurance had yet been introduced). This undercut wage demands, for the unions could not maintain a control over labor supply under such conditions. Moreover, the local unemployment committees were free to determine whether individual applicants really needed assistance; the result was a close scrutiny of applicants' personal circumstances (Nordström 1944, 47; Unga 1976, 70–71). Criticizing the AK's practice of restricting assistance to a certain quota of applicants, the leading Social Democratic spokesman on this issue (Gustav Möller) declared sarcastically in a speech in the Riksdag:

I have to admit that as a flower in the garden of bureaucracy this quota is a truly magnificent achievement. . . . To regulate unemployment assistance with the aid of a slide rule without heeding individual circumstances is undoubtedly a brilliant bureaucratic invention. (FK 1927, no. 39, 8)

The third and main source of political disagreement concerned the right of the AK to require, during certain types of industrial dispute, that the jobless accept work at private as well as public workplaces where strikes were in progress, on pain of losing benefits or being excluded from relief work. This amounted in practice to the state forcing the unemployed to act as strikebreakers. The AK thereby prevented the unions from making effective use of strikes and blockades, their principal weapons. The essential basis of union power was directly threatened: they could no longer maintain their control over labor supply. The Social Democrats severely criticized the fact that the AK was able to operate in this way. The resignation of minority Social Democratic governments in 1923 and 1926 occurred when their efforts to alter the AK's line in this vital area came up against the nonsocialist majority in the Riksdag (Rothstein 1982, 19; Unga 1976, chap. 10).

It has been demonstrated that the Social Democrats' adoption of a new unemployment policy around 1930 was driven by these institutional concerns about the AK's policy vis-à-vis the unions, rather than by any inspiration drawn from new (primarily Keynesian) economic theories (Unga 1976, chap. 10). In order to maintain their own strength, the SAP and LO were compelled to alter national labor market policy. Another factor was the power the AK exerted over municipal unemployment assistance—a municipality's failure to comply with the commission's directives could lead to the loss of government support. Indeed, since the late 1920s a number of municipalities under Social Democratic rule had pursued unemployment policies at variance with those of the AK, and hence without government support. In practice, then, the AK system was beginning to fall apart even before 1930 (Unga 1976, chaps. 7 and 9). This account of Social Democratic unemployment policy in the 1930s—as motivated by a solicitude for the conditions of the reproduction of trade union organization—may be regarded as directly parallel to the previous chapter's interpretation of the Rehn-Meidner model in terms of organizational efficiency.

It should be added that the relief work provided by the AK was very demanding. The projects consisted mainly of road construction in remote parts of the country. A minimum of machinery was used in order to provide work for as many as possible. The location of the projects also meant that the workers lost touch with their accustomed labor market. Conditions in the work camps were known to be very harsh. The Social Democratic platform for the 1930 election included as a major point the abolition of the AK and its system for handling unemployment. The demeaning circumstances under which unemployment assistance was provided meant that Social Democratic voters and the working class in general detested the AK system (Nordström 1944, 47). This confrontation between the AK and the labor movement was the fruit of an ambition among leading right-wing administrators to match the operations of the AK as closely as possible with the principles of the SAF and the political Right (Andersson 1967, 188–90).

The retention of the AK in 1933 was part of the price the Social Democrats had to pay for their famous coalition agreement with the Agrarian party. Yet a number of significant changes were made. Wage rates for public works were raised, though not to market level. The AK was no longer permitted to assign the jobless to workplaces affected by strikes, and assistance was expanded to cover more than 70 percent of applicants, instead of the earlier 50 percent. More important, however, was the creation of altogether new relief-work projects paying market wages.

Politically and administratively, the agreement is of interest not for the establishment of any Keynesian budget policy (none such was ever implemented) but for the arrangement whereby the AK no longer obtained the major share of appropriations for unemployment assistance. These funds were instead put at the direct disposal of the new minister of social affairs, Gustav Möller. Writing in the LO periodical, he described the essence of the agreement as follows:

The funds assigned by the Riksdag for combating unemployment must first be divided into *two* approximately equal items: 80 million crowns to be administered by the AK and 100 million to be administered by the government. (*Fackföreningsrörelsen* 1933, 597)

Two parallel administrative systems were thereby responsible for national unemployment policy: a modified AK system and a purely Social Democratic system. Moreover, besides eliminating the threat to trade-union organization from the AK's policy, the new arrangement did away with the AK's power over the municipalities—those deviating from the AK system could now obtain financial support directly from the Social Democratic government.

During the late 1930s, the predominantly Social Democratic governments gradually eroded the power of the AK by cutting its funds. Accordingly, in the last year of its existence (1939), the AK received only 10.3 million crowns, while the government appropriated 64 million crowns for its own unemployment policy. When the 1936 party congress criticized the Social Democratic leadership for not fulfilling its election promise to abolish the AK, Gustav Möller concluded his defence with the words that "it is after all an indirect rather than a direct method that I recommended as appropriate in the struggle against the AK" (SAP-protokoll 1936, 150).

## The National Labor Market Administration 1940–47

The Social Democratic struggle against the AK system was crowned with success in 1940, when the organization was formally disbanded and replaced by a new administration, the National Labor Market Commission (AMK). The transition from the AK to the AMK has been described in earlier research as a continuation or transformation of the existing organization (Furåker 1976, 132; Sjöström 1985, 23; cf. Öhman 1970, 94, 122). As shown below, this interpretation misses the whole point.

The AMK was established in September 1939 as an emergency advisory body to follow developments in the labor market in conjunction with the war in Europe. The board consisted of representatives of the principal organizations in the labor market and was chaired by Arthur Thomson, a former Social Democratic member of the Riksdag. The primary task for the new commission was to regulate the labor market; that is, to function as a national labor exchange and to procure labor for vital parts of the wartime economy.

In December that year, the Riksdag approved a national service act which would be administered by a national labor board (Prop. 1939, no. 92). This board would have exceptional powers to commandeer labor in the national interest. The AMK soon became an executive body, however, in the autumn of 1939 (Prop. 1940, no. 216, 2), yet it had nothing to do with the AK until April 1940, when the government proposed that the latter be made subordinate to the AMK (ibid.).

Three primary tasks were proposed for the reorganized commission: (1) to coordinate and direct the public labor exchanges, (2) to regulate the utilization of labor during the crisis, and (3) to constitute a national labor board—that is, to implement the new national service law (Prop. 1940, no. 216, 4). These were very extensive commitments. The labor exchanges were nationalized and their management transferred to the AMK, along with the right, previously reserved to the ministry of social affairs, to initiate relief work (Öhman 1970, 121). This indicates the ministry regarded the new AMK as reliable.

According to the bill itself, the proposal was based on a memorandum from the ministry "concerning a reorganization of the AMK." In contrast to that memorandum, however, the bill proposed as well that the coordination of assistance to the unemployed (i.e., the tasks performed by the AK) be assigned to the new organization (SNA, AMK archives, kanslisek. adm det 1940; cf. Prop. 1940, no. 216, 9). The bill also included the following statement by the Minister Gustav Möller:

However, I consider the time has come for a reorganization that was only mentioned in the memorandum as a further step on the intended road; I refer to the issue of the central management of unemployment assistance. For reasons I elaborate in the context of appropriations for this activity, the current situation appears to require that the various public measures to do with the labor market are coordinated, making it suitable to organize them under a single authority. (Prop. 1940, no. 216, 9)

This statement is, to say the least, a free interpretation of the memorandum, which actually suggests that the AK and the new body would work in parallel. Nor does the bill offer any reasons for the coordination proposed by the minister. In practice, the remains of the AK were simply incorporated into the AMK. That the AK was demoted is also evident from the fact that it contributed only two of the eight senior staff in the new organization (Rothstein 1982, 23).

When the AMK's field organization was set up, moreover, the AK's structure of county assistance committees and local unemployment committees were passed over in favor of a new arrangement based on the employment offices run be the local governments (which were independent of the AK). The striking manner in which the AK was converted into the AMK has several conceivable explanations. One has to do with the exceptional powers invested in the body responsible for implementing the national service act. Commenting on the draft, the LO had expressed strong reservations about such a law, which in principle would entitle the state to dictate the utilization of labor (Prop. 1939, no. 92, 33–34). The LO would hardly have approved the new law at all, had it been administered by the AK or one of its subordinate bodies.

Another explanation may lie in the political controversy that had surrounded the AK for two decades. The fight over the AK had become highly charged, so it was uncertain a majority in the Riksdag would have supported an open abolition of the AK even in 1939. The way in which the organization was wound down in 1940 enabled the Social Democrats to present the move as a reasonable and uncontroversial step in the organization of the wartime economy.

There is, however, a third and more convincing explanation. Contrary to what the bill indicates or previous research has shown, advanced plans were in the works by 1940 to organize a new national institution for the labor market. Two committees of inquiry, appointed by the government in 1936 and 1937, respectively, had submitted detailed proposals for a reorganization of the labor market arrangements established by the central government in 1940. The ministry of social affairs had drawn up the terms of reference for both inquiries, of which the more important in this context was the 1937 Committee of Unemployment Experts, chaired by Gustav Möller himself. The vice chairman was Arthur Thomson, the former Social Democratic member of the Riksdag who became the head of the new AMK. The third member of the executive body was Tage Erlander, who in this way joined the inner circle of the Social Democratic party (and later served as party chairman and prime minister from 1946 to 1969).

This committee disbanded in 1943 without publishing a final report, which is probably why its work has escaped the attention of researchers (RD 1943 års riksdagsberättelse, 63; cf. SOU 1938, no. 21 and 1939, no. 24). A final report had been drafted in the summer of 1939, however, and a final meeting of the committee was convened for September but was canceled in the last minute because of the outbreak of the war (SNA 1937 års arbetslöshetssakunnigas arkiv, vol. 2). The committee archives, which may be found in the National Archives in Stockholm (fifty volumes including the abovementioned draft for a final report), make plain that a new public body for the labor market, which would be entrusted with the tasks then performed by the AMK, had been under preparation since 1937 by the committee. One memorandum in particular (which largely mirrors the draft report) proposes a new, more active labor market policy, and a new government agency to implement it as well (SNA 1937 års arbetslöshetssakunnigas arkiv, vol. 2).

This agency was to tackle the problem of residual unemployment caused by rationalizations in the production process—pockets of workers in certain occupations and districts who found themselves jobless even when the rest of the economy was booming. The minutes show these proposals were drawn up in close collaboration with the other committee, the 1936 Industrial Efficiency Inquiry, whose report (published in June 1939) proposed a new government body, which it termed a labor market institute (SOU 1939, no. 13). The terms of reference for that committee had called for "measures for preventing and ameliorating harmful social effects of industrial rationalization and closures" (ibid., 7)—the major harmful effect being residual unemployment.

The report was adopted unanimously by the committee, whose members included the vice chairman of the LO and the chairman of the SAF. According to the terms of the compromise between the LO and the SAF, the union movement would take a positive stand toward the rationalization of industry. The labor movement would not try to interfere, by means of state planning or other measures, with the ongoing rationalization process. The employers in return would support assistance to workers hit by unemployment caused by this process in order to ease their way back into production. It should be added that new research has called attention to this agreement about how to handle the consequences of industrial rationalization as *the* major ingredient in the famous class compromise between labor and capital in Sweden during the late 1930s (Johansson 1989; cf. Pontusson 1992, 45).[2]

These proposals in many respects presaged the LO plan for an active labor market policy a decade later (though without the theoretical foundation provided by Gösta Rehn and Rudolf Meidner). The practical construction is virtually identical, the main principle being that government efforts for the labor market should be coordinated by a *single* body which would follow developments in the labor market continuously and would attempt to prevent bouts of unemployment. Extensive information collected from firms would enable the new body to stave off unemployment by planning and adjusting government efforts to cyclical fluctuations in the economy (SNA 1937 års arbetslöshetssakunnigas arkiv, vol. 2; cf. SOU 1939, no. 13, 75). The Social Democratic government and the union movement would refrain from trying to prevent companies from rationalizing the production process (and thereby creating unemployment). The government would take steps to ease the unemployment produced by industrial rationalization, "so that the jobless would be restored to production as soon as possible." Economic efficiency would also be promoted, for trade union opposition to structural change would be softened or eliminated (SOU 1939, no. 13, 75).

The means proposed by the two committees included government support for the establishment of new enterprises, an improved and nationalized employment service, the promotion of labor mobility by means of occupational training, job referral between localities, and travel and moving allowances. Dwellings would be purchased to enable redundant workers to move elsewhere, and there would be assistance for disabled labor, early retirement, and so on (SNA 1937 års arbetslöshetssakunnigas arkiv, vols. 1 and 2; SOU 1939, no. 13). These proposals from the late 1930s make up the core of the policy arsenal applied to the labor market after the war. The Rehn model, as Öhman rightly points out, was primarily an enlargement of existing instruments of labor market policy (Öhman 1974, 23). What Gösta Rehn contributed was the realization that these instruments, together with the policy of wage solidarity and a tight fiscal approach, could be of strategic importance for the LO in the inflationary postwar economy (Öhman 1974).

Addressing the first chamber of the Riksdag in 1941 on the subject of labor market policy, Gustav Möller described the new orientation as *active* (FK 1941, no. 17, 9; italics in original). It was indeed active during the war, when the staff grew from about one hundred to around five hundred, and the number of employment offices was doubled.

The regional organization established in 1940 consisted of a corporative labor board in each county, directly under the national body. The traditional arrangement would have been to incorporate this tier into the administration presided over by the county governor. An unsigned AMK document states that this special arrangement was adopted on account of the bureaucratic nature of the county governors' offices, which were competent at "executing decisions where certain formal conditions are shown to exist"; such a manner of operation was considered unsuitable for the active, interventionist role envisaged for the new county labor market administrations (SNA, AMK's arkiv, PM ang. organisation för krisarbetslagens genomförande, Kanslisek, adm. det. 1940). This distinctive regional organization of Social Democratic policy—independent of the county governors' offices—became generally characteristic of the administration of the welfare state after the war (Rothstein 1985).

The key appointment as head of the new county labor board was generally filled by the head of the county's main employment office, i.e., not by a civil servant but by a municipal official whose earlier recruitment had been subject to trade union influence (Prop. 1940, no. 216, 23–27). As early as 1941, the central management of the AMK took charge of recruitment throughout the organization; previously this had been arranged locally (Prop. 1942, no. 344, 80).

The central agent in the construction of the predominantly Social Democratic labor market organization during the war years seems to have been Arthur Thomson (cf. Thomson 1944). As office manager of the AK from 1934 on, he had participated in the demise of that organization, while at the same time preparing for the birth of the AMK as vice-chairman of the 1937 unemployment committee. As the wartime director of the AMK, with full control over recruitment to the rapidly expanding organization, he was in a good position to determine its course. The need to plan employment for wartime conditions provided opportunities for practical experiments with the new administrative apparatus (Engvall 1980; Engvall and B. Olsson, interviews; cf. Hjern 1982, 75).

In addition, Thomson chaired the two committees which proposed after the war's end that the government's provisional labor market administration (which had lasted for thirty-four years) be terminated—by transforming the AMK into the National Labor Market Board (AMS). This was done in 1948. The practical effect was largely to give the activities and administration of the AMK a permanent form. As a civil servant, Thomson regarded himself as an instrument for Social Democratic labor market policy, as is evident from the draft of a reply (the only document of any political significance which he left in his personal archive at the Lund University Library) written in 1951 to Tage Erlander, who was then prime minister:

What you write about my contributions as a "practical politician" gives me great pleasure—contrary to what you write—though I am aware that the assessment is correct in only *one* respect: as regards labor market policy. No one apart from you and, to some extent, Bertil Olsson knows what I consider that I know about this. It is clear to me that I implemented the party's unemployment policy *in practice*. (Arthur Thomson's documents, Lund University Library)[3]

Thomson's dual position as politician and civil servant renders problematic the classical distinction between explanatory models focusing on the state and on society (cf. Skocpol 1985).

One significant difference between the AK and the AMK lay in the latter's wider mandate and more extensive means. The AMK also had a flexible, dynamic administration fired by a common ideology (SOU 1947, no. 24; Engvall and B. Olsson, interviews; cf. Gustav Möller in FK 1941, no. 17, 9–10). The AK was geared to providing unemployment assistance as stipulated by the government and Riksdag, while the AMK exhibited considerably greater flexibility in regulating labor supply and demand as the situation required. The AMK also frequently applied a preventive approach, which the AK did but little.

Comparing the then-current situation with unemployment policy during the crisis of 1932–34, Gustav Möller told the Riksdag in 1941: "What is now required of the AMK is a much smoother adjustment to *different* needs in society than was needed during the previous crisis. . . . I hope this will form the starting point for a very active unemployment policy, where activity must not obstruct adaptability" (FK 1941, no. 17, 9, 13). In sum, the transition from the AK to the AMK may be said to mark the advent of large scale sociopolitical interventionism in Swedish government administration.

## Origins of Public Educational Administration

For the hundred years following 1850 or so, public education in Sweden was the source of much hostility between social groups, for different types of schools served different social classes—grammar schools (*läroverken*) for the upper and middle classes, elementary and vocational schools (*folkskola* and *yrkesskola*) for workers and farmers (Herrström 1966, 5–46; Isling 1980; Wennås 1966). This larger social antagonism was mirrored in the conflict, founded in social and financial differences, between academically trained teachers at grammar schools and their nonacademic colleagues at elementary schools. When professional and group interests were affected by educational reform, furthermore, this opposition was accentuated.[4] These social and group conflicts were mirrored in the structure and development of the public administration of education.

### The Administration of "Higher Education"

In this context, schooling preparatory to academic study is referred to as "higher education," as opposed to the basic education provided in elementary schools (which had been introduced in Sweden in 1842). The term refers accordingly to the type of education provided by the school, not to the age of its pupils. From its medieval origins up to 1904, the grammar school was, like all other public educational institutions, the concern primarily of the church. Indeed, during the nineteenth century, these schools still served mainly would-be clergymen, and their statutes were part of the ecclesiastical system (Richardson 1977, 11–32; Wennås 1966, 9).

The emergence of industrial and commercial capital then led to demands for a corresponding adjustment of higher education, and for a different educational ideal as well. The driving force behind this change was the rising bourgeois class. In response, a separate division of the Ministry of Ecclesiastical Affairs was established for school matters in 1858. It was divided in 1864 into one division for the "higher" school system and another for elementary education (Prop. 1904, no. 50, 178). As described in a later bill, this administrative dichotomy "established a dualism in the direction of the two main branches of the school system for a long time to come" (Prop. 1913, no. 204, 8).

In 1904, the Riksdag transferred the management of grammar schools from the church to a new administrative body, the National

Board of Public Grammar Schools. The critical task of appointing teachers was thus transferred from church to state (Marklund 1979, 26). The grammar schools became a purely national institution, formally independent of the church and the municipalities. The separation from the church and the provision of a specific central administration increased the distance from the elementary school system in the public administration. It was symptomatic of this distance that, when local boards for grammar schools were set up in 1928, they were kept separate from the municipal direction of elementary and occupational schools (SOU 1955, no. 31, 36).

This administrative dualism in the school system was underscored in 1913 when the Riksdag, following widespread representations from elementary school teachers, approved the establishment of a National Board of Elementary Schools (Marklund 1979, 28). The Liberal government had proposed a joint national board for elementary schools and higher education (Prop. 1913, no. 204, 138; cf. Isling 1980, 145–52), but this was opposed by the existing grammar school board (Prop. 1913, no. 204, 136) and by grammar school teachers and the universities as well. The creation of a joint board was regarded as a move to abandon the two-tiered system, with its class distinctions, in favor of a comprehensive system of primary schools, followed by secondary education (Isling 1980, 145–52). A majority of the standing committee in the Riksdag opposed such a move (RD Statsutskottet 1913, no. 130), and in the ensuing debate the government agreed to the proposal for two separate boards. The class-based dualism in the school system was reflected thereby in the existence of two central boards. This situation lasted only five years, however.

The first step toward a comprehensive central administration was taken in 1918, when a third central board (for vocational education) was proposed (Marklund 1979, 33–34; cf. Isling 1980). The standing committee opposed any further division of the central administration, however, and recommended that matters having to do with vocational education be assigned to the National Board of Elementary Schools (RD Statsutskottet 1918, no. 105), which was then renamed the National Board of Education (SÖ, Sw. Skolöverstyrelsen).

The next step came the following year, when the Social Democratic minister of education proposed that the SÖ and the National Board of Grammar Schools be merged (Prop. 1919, no. 52). He argued that cooperation between the two boards had been "excessively superficial and formal" (Prop. 1919, no. 52, 27), and that, according to expert opinion, a joint national board would facilitate cooperation in the central administration. Another reason against continuing a divided administration was that:

It is also to be feared that the separatist opinions—founded not infrequently on mutual distrust—that unfortunately have not been unknown to date among the two corps of teachers representing the different spheres of education, would find cause for accentuation rather than the reverse if such an arrangement . . . were to be made. (Prop. 1919, no. 52, 25)

The proposed merger met with some opposition. The head of the National Board of Grammar Schools entered a reservation in favor of a continued division of the central administration (Prop. 1919, no. 52, 19–21), and the board concurred (ibid., 22). The SÖ favored a merger, however (ibid., no. 24, 25) as did the Riksdag. A joint SÖ for the different types of schools was therefore instituted in 1920, with three departments—for elementary, grammar school, and occupational education, respectively (Marklund 1979, 35). The extent to which the merger actually promoted unification is considered in the next section. After this there was little change in the administration of higher education until the 1950s. One notable feature of the grammar-school system was the close links between the central administration and the individual schools. This was administratively feasible because the number of grammar schools and students was comparatively small.

## Administration of Elementary Education

The main difference between the public administration of elementary education and that of higher education lay in the strong municipal influence and continuing power of the clergy in the former system. The first statute for elementary schools (passed in 1842) had assigned responsibility to the clergy. Local school boards were chaired by the vicar *ex officio* (Tegborg 1969, 17). The ecclesiastical nature of elementary education was evident from the fact that, when ecclesiastical and civil municipalities were separated from each other in 1863, the elementary schools remained in the clerical sphere. "The social development that resulted in the local government legislation of 1862 had not altered the status of elementary education as the church's school but rather strengthened it in that the laws made it clear that matters to do with elementary education differed in kind from civil matters" (ibid., 18). As for the *ex officio* right of the clergy to chair local school boards, it was debated in the Riksdag almost annually between 1867 and 1877. In the second chamber, which was dominated by farmers, a majority regularly opposed this clerical privilege; the conservative and aristocratic first chamber managed, however, to maintain the status quo (ibid., 21, 32).

The social status of elementary school teachers, and of their training colleges, was generally low. A bill in 1913 noted that these colleges' low status rendered the recruitment of qualified staff difficult, as did the limited prospects for promotion at such institutions; furthermore, "elementary teacher training still stands for a meagre, superficial education" (Prop. 1913, no. 205, 6, 7; cf. Isling 1980, 139–40). In addition, the regional administration of elementary education was divided during this period. The regional branches of the established church held the primary responsibility, a role not abolished until the late 1950s. Certain matters, however—the control and disbursement of government grants especially—were supervised by the county governor's offices.

When the new joint SÖ was established in 1920, its executive structure matched the division into different types of schools. The strong local influence over elementary education had the consequence that the central administration's impact on elementary schools was less than on grammar schools. Moreover, the elementary school system was many times larger than the grammar school system throughout this period, whereas the SÖ's department for elementary education was but slightly larger than its department for grammar schools.

When the National Board of Elementary Education was set up in 1913, the pitfalls in central administration were indicated by the minister of education in terms worth noting. He expressed the hope that widespread external contacts and visits to schools would enable the board "to counteract the tendencies to formalism and bureaucracy that otherwise arise all too easily in the confines of an office" (Prop. 1913, no. 204, 35). He formulated one of the reasons for instituting the new board was as follows:

It is namely not enough that the major issues have been investigated and proposals submitted; neither does it suffice that the Riksdag and the government agree on their execution. It is also a matter of initiating and supervising the implementation. (Prop. 1913, no. 204, 48)

As for whether the 1919 merger into a joint central administration for the entire school system achieved the desired reconciliation, the answer must be no. The major issues in the period between 1920 and 1948 split the SÖ into one faction for elementary education and another for grammar schools. This conflict was particularly acute during the 1920s over the proposal for a basic education; the resulting compromise was rather meager for the Social Democrats and meant the retention of the parallel system (Isling 1980, 163–67; cf. Richardson 1977, 47). The SÖ's response to the 1918 commission's proposal for a universal six-year elementary education indicated how class and professional antagonisms over education pervaded even the highest echelons of the administration. The manner of the proposal's submission also indicates that the board's members perceived themselves as divided into two different groups; instead of being presented by individual members, the reservation was entitled: "Reservation to the National Board's submission . . . presented by the members participating in the matter from the grammar school department of the Board" (SOU 1984, no. 24, 171). The submission and the reservation are almost the same length and are more in the nature of two alternative submissions.

The appointment of Otto Holmdahl as director-general of the SÖ by a conservative government in 1929 did little to heal the divisions. Holmdahl, who held this post until 1947, was a conservative member of the second chamber of the Riksdag, and continued in that capacity until 1944. He had actively opposed a universal basic education, and had been his party's spokesman in the decisive Riksdag debate of 1927.[5] This educational issue still divided the SÖ when, in 1945, the time had come to consider a comprehensive school, following an important inquiry begun in 1940. It again proved necessary to present two submissions, just as eighteen years earlier, and sides were again taken on a departmental basis (Richardson 1978, 213–14). These differences also affected personal relations (ibid., 347, n. 8). Nils-Gustav Rosén, who served for seventeen years after his appointment as director-general by the Social Democratic government in 1947, describes the situation as follows:

On my arrival in 1947 I was dismayed to find that the SÖ consisted of one department for grammar schools and another for elementary education and they worked separately. People stuck to their own matters and views.

There was no discussion at board meetings; the grammar school department had their say and so did the elementary side, after which the matter was put to the vote and reservations were compiled. The antagonism was also evident in minor matters. At lunch the grammar school and the elementary sides never sat together and I had to alternate between them. An anecdote, of course, but it says everything about the atmosphere at the SÖ. It was a divided agency. One explanation lay in its origins. It had had a terribly poor start. The different groups had brought their attitudes to the new set-up and this inevitably led to the two sides. Things were still like that in 1947. (Rosén, interview)

When a review of the SÖ was begun in 1936, the minister of education (Arthur Engberg) stated in the terms of reference that the educational direction of the school system—the agency's primary task—had been crowded out by purely administrative routines. The fears for bureaucracy, voiced among others by the National Board of Grammar Schools at the time of the merger in 1919, had "to no small extent been confirmed." He also observed that,

Mounting administrative and office work has left little time in which to acquire the desirable insight into personal and local conditions at different educational establishments, thereby obstructing the maintenance of connections with work in the schools and the procurement of the unifying and comprehensive experience that must be regarded as indispensable prerequisites for proper direction by the Board in the educational sphere. (SOU 1938, no. 14, iv)

It is worth noting that the SÖ still functioned as a collegiate body, which meant that, when matters were presented to the board, each member had to voice an opinion. Since the middle of the nineteenth century, this time-consuming and cumbersome process had been replaced in other administrations by a system in which decisions were taken by the chairman alone. The 1936 review met with demands to detach the department for vocational education and organize it as a separate administration, but the experts concluded that the organization of the SÖ should remain unchanged, aside from some expansion of the administrative staff. Nor was any change proposed in the collegiate system (ibid., 21). Since the merger in 1920, the three departments had each developed "a more independent status than appears to be indicated by the current instructions for the Board" (SOU 1948, no. 14, 16). The ensuing proposals did not reach the *Riksdag* (SOU 1951, no. 29, 271). As a member of the inquiry, the director-general of the SÖ submitted a lengthy reservation against many of the suggestions (SOU 1938, no. 14, 283–90).

An analysis of voting in the Riksdag between 1931 and 1936 reveals that the Social Democratic party was particularly divided on educational issues. Strikingly, these differences covaried with the educational background of the members (gymnasium graduates vs. others). With Arthur Engberg heading the ministry of education, the ideal of a classical education predominated (Isling 1980, 211–19).

School issues generally did not feature prominently in Social Democratic policy in Engberg's day. The proposal for a universal basic education, around which heated debates had earlier raged, was shelved (ibid., 204–36). Engberg adopted an elitist position and to some extent opposed the move toward a comprehensive school system, as well as other far-reaching reforms in this field (ibid., 211–17). The section on school policy during the 1930s in Tage Erlander's autobiography is headed "Unforthcoming Reforms," and includes the somewhat laconic assessment that "Arthur Engberg was a brilliant minister from 1932 to 1939, but the school system did not capture his interest" (Erlander 1973, 234).

A surprisingly severe obituary of Engberg, published in the party's theoretical journal by a prominent Social Democrat, compared his political contribution and style unfavorably with Gustav Möller's. The first sentence states that "Arthur Engberg was a politician who never commanded any decisive influence," and his performance in education policy elicited the following assessment: "he never really grasped the issue. He held brilliant speeches about the future of our educational system, displayed great enthusiasm for new paths but never set out along them. Whereas Gustav Möller achieved a breakthrough with a new social policy, in Arthur Engberg's sphere there was no decisive movement" (Lindström 1946, 341).

When the wartime coalition government took over in 1939, the education portfolio went to Gösta Bagge, the leader of the Conservative party. His major initiative in school policy was to appoint a commission of inquiry in 1940. This had the effect of suspending any real reforms. The wartime coalition was dissolved in 1945, and Erlander appointed a new school commission in 1946 (Isling 1980, 237–67; cf. Richardsson 1978). It was this commission that launched the plans for the comprehensive school reform in 1948 (cf. chap. 4).

## The Administration of Vocational Education

Vocational education was supervised to some extent by the state from the middle of the nineteenth century. In 1919, a separate department for vocational schools was established at the National Board of Elementary Schools (SOU 1938, no. 54, 7–10). This reform established local boards for vocational schools, organized separately from those serving the other schools. There was no regional direction of vocational education at the time (SOU 1955, no. 31, 33). Widespread unemployment during the 1930s, not least among youth, elicited a proposal to expand and reorganize vocational education as a means of combating unemployment. Significantly, it was not Arthur Engberg but Gustav Möller, the minister of social affairs, who promoted this innovation in the school system (Thomson 1944; cf. Isling 1980, 217). An inquiry into apprentice training, set up in 1937 and chaired by Thomson, resulted in the establishment of national apprenticeship schools, and thus a major expansion of vocational education. The report also proposed that vocational education be removed from the SÖ's responsibilities and assigned to a separate national board (SOU 1938, no. 54).

The manner in which the SÖ handled vocational education was sharply criticized in the report. The director-general was accused of devoting insufficient interest to such matters. A separate organization was desired, mainly to make the administration more flexible in dealing with fluctuations in employment. The SÖ was deemed incapable of handling vocational education in a dynamic fashion (SOU 1938, no. 54, 28–29, 39–44, 96, 142–43). The LO and employers' organizations had marshaled similar arguments for divesting the SÖ of vocational education (ibid., 37). The report envisaged that the proposed board would consist, in addition to the director-general, of equal numbers of representatives from trade union and employers' organizations. The new board would also be transferred from the education to the commerce department, where the minister at the time was Gustav Möller (ibid., 97–100).

It was not until 1944 that these plans could be put into practice. The proposals of the inquiry were adopted almost in full. The reasons for the five-year delay are a matter for speculation. The fact that the education portfolio was held by the Conservative leader Gösta Bagge probably contributed. It is clear from the bill that he would have preferred an *internal* SÖ link between vocational education and the labor market organizations, but deferred to a concerted opinion elsewhere: the SAF and the LO, for instance, were united in demanding an independent board (Prop. 1943, no. 232, 13, 17–18). As the initiative came from the ministry of social affairs, there is reason to suppose that the delay had political grounds. As usual, the submission from the SÖ failed to reach agreement on the composition of the board. The majority preferred the direct representation of the labor market organizations, while the director-general strongly opposed this in a separate submission, recommending instead a board made up of government officials (Prop. 1943, 232:35–36; AK 1943, no. 25, 16–18).

## Conclusion: Building a Social Democratic State?

During the war years, the labor market authority was converted into a unified and coordinated administration, whereas the administrative and policy divisions in the governance of education persisted. These divisions ran vertically as well as horizontally. Besides mirroring the different types of schools and their class affiliations, they were evident as well in the administrative leadership of the various regions and localities. Another crucial difference was that the AMK constituted an entirely national administration, as against the substantial municipal and ecclesiastical influence in the field of education.

These differences reflect the discrepancies between these two fields as regards the Social Democrats' political initiatives and actions in the 1930s. The controversies over unemployment policy elicited plans for a completely new approach that in some respects came to be implemented already during that decade. In administrative terms, this involved disbanding the old organization (the AK) and building up a new one, the AMK.

It can be said that the harsh conflicts over labor market policy in the 1920s were resolved by the Social Democrats in the 1930s, and in a way that benefitted the party. The political situation occasioned by the outbreak of war in Europe, moreover, was turned to good account—the new administrative arrangement planned by Möller, Thomson, and Erlander was introduced with virtually no opposition. The demise of the AK may be seen as a peculiarly Swedish and Social Democratic version of a "successful" attack by organized labor on the bourgeois nature of the bureaucratic capitalist state. The prime political mover in the process (Gustav Möller) had thoroughly prepared an antibureaucratic strategy for this.

In education, on the other hand, the 1930s were a passive, divided decade for social democracy, both as regards the substance of policy and the administrative apparatus. The minor successes the party scored in this field during the 1920s were not followed up with new policy initiatives or plans. The efforts to bring the SÖ more into line with future policy objectives proved largely fruitless. The one area (vocational education) where changes were accomplished (primarily by Möller) was of secondary importance in the subsequent work of reform.

Moreover, the organized working class continued to enjoy little influence over the administration of elementary and grammar school education. In labor market policy, on the other hand, the LO had regional as well as central representation. The direction of labor market policy, at both ministry and board levels, was in Social Democratic hands for most of the 1940s, whereas the corresponding posts in education were held by Conservatives. The SÖ, moreover, retained its bureaucratic organization and procedures (such as the collegiate principle), whereas the provisional nature of the AMK permitted more modern and flexible forms of organization under the conditions created by the wartime emergency.

The state which Swedish social democracy had at its disposal for postwar policy offensives was thus a heterogeneous organization. The administrative capacity, organizational character, and ideological orientation of its various agencies ranged considerably, as illustrated by the cases analyzed above (cf. Skocpol and Finegold 1982). If in fact the institutional capacity of the state is of central importance for the implementation of policy, these differences must be analyzed in greater detail.

# 6. Organizational Connection One: The AMS

## Introduction

I have tried in the preceding chapters to make the following points. First, that in order to understand the limits of political reformism, it is necessary to take the state as an organizational factor into account. No matter how wisely a reformist policy is designed, if the administrative arrangements are faulty, it will fail at the stage of implementation. Second, that the active labor market policy launched by the Swedish Social Democrats has, contrary to what has taken place in many other countries, been a success. Policy intentions were to a considerable extent realized in practice. Third, that there are different ways to organize state apparatuses, and that we should not take for granted that all branches of a capitalist state operate under the same organizational syndrome. In Marxian parlance, the class character of the state may vary between different state apparatuses.

Furthermore, I have for analytical reasons distinguished between two ideal types of organization, the Weberian bureaucracy and the cadre organization, and I have put forward an argument about how the differences between these two are politically generated and politically important. More precisely, I have argued that the strength of the cadre organization is its ability to operate flexibly according to a common ideology. The strength of the bureaucracy is the mirror image of that of the cadre organization—its nonideological, neutral orientation and its rule-based predictability. For implementing policies of the sort examined here, however, the weaknesses of a bureaucratic organization are decisive.

I have showed lastly that, when the Social Democrats in Sweden after World War II launched the two reforms at hand, they also had to deal with two very different state apparatuses. Both the active labor market policy and the comprehensive school reform must be considered "socially invasive" policies requiring flexible implementation. Both policies also contain strong ideological commitments. In the following two chapters, I will compare these ideas with my empirical findings from the Social Democratic state.

This chapter and the next contain empirical analysis of the two agencies that are the focus of this study. I will try in the process to determine which of the two ideal types fit which organization. In this chapter, I will analyze the character of the National Labor Market Board. The question is whether one finds, behind the success of the Swedish active labor market policy, not just a carefully designed and theoretically advanced policy (i.e., the Rehn-Meidner model), but a specific organizational connection as well. Did the agents who constructed the active labor market policy take into account the problematic relation between working-class policies and the bureaucratic capitalist state identified by both Marx and Weber? And if so, what measures did they take to solve the problem?

The existing empirical material about the organization and operation of the government agencies under consideration here is of course overwhelming. Most of the data is taken from open sources such as public records and government archives. In addition, interviews with thirty-one key persons were done. The larger part of this material is not used in the text, however, either because the information was given under guarantees that it would not be used in the text, or because similar evidence could be gathered from open sources.

Following standard practice in organization theory, I here consider organizations to consist of (1) program content, (2) personnel, and (3) funding (Rose 1984, 7; cf. Therborn 1980, 34). Each of these will be treated separately in what follows. In keeping with the comparative approach, finally, the conclusions drawn from this and the next chapter are presented separately in chapter 8.

## Program Content

The plans drafted by the 1937 Committee of Unemployment Experts and the 1936 Efficiency Inquiry aimed to create a central government agency that would handle all public policy aimed at counteracting unemployment. The agency would also be responsible for labor market regulation in general, primarily via the employment service. The findings were never published, for reasons mentioned earlier, but the proposals were followed in detail when it came to creating the National Labor Market Commission (AMK) in 1940. The extensive tasks proposed for the new agency, coupled with the exceptional circumstances of the war years, led the government to give the AMK very "wide powers" (SOU 1947, no. 24, 70).

Both the inquiries and the bill leading to the creation of the National Labor Market Board (AMS) in 1948 underscored the importance of making the new agency independent of central direction. The inquiry observed that the "varying conditions in the labor market will no doubt make the tasks extremely changeable. To a large extent, they will concern activities that are incompletely regulated in the statutes, thereby demanding a great deal of initiative and independent action on the part of the agency" (ibid., 128). This *change-oriented* line was echoed in the bill, in which the minister stated that, in the event of any substantial unemployment, it would be necessary to "assign the Labor Market Board extensive powers and thus an independence of the government that the central agencies generally do not have" (*Prop.* 1947, 239:79).

This independence was perceived, in the inquiry and the bill, as leaving the new agency untrammeled by any precise rules or other specific instructions from the central government. The minister declared:

It is inevitable in my opinion that the central labor market body, even though it be organized as a central agency, must be able to have the same status in emergencies as the emergency authorities have had to date in this field. The Labor Market Board should accordingly have extensive freedom to act independently and consequently not be tied down by detailed instructions. (ibid., 36–37)

The primary reason for avoiding precise regulations lay, according to the inquiry, in the nature of the tasks—that is, "the often rapidly changing circumstances that characterize the labor market" (ibid., 37). The inquiry found that the new labor market agency had the task of "activating labor market policy." The earlier policy for combating unemployment was said to have been largely passive; instead of aiming to influence developments, it had served "only to ameliorate unemployment when it happened, usually even some time after it had become a fact." The inquiry proposed that the new agency depart from the earlier passive line and continue the development of labor market policy initiated by the AMK in the war years. The task was described as "not being satisfied to wait upon events but trying to anticipate and—insofar as is feasible—influence them" (SOU 1947, no. 24, 59–60).

The arrangements for control should be constructed to permit "rapid and not excessively formalized action" (ibid., 65). The report goes on to note that it "does not appear possible to draw up any general instructions in the matter in advance; the allocation of powers will no doubt have to be determined from case to case" (ibid., 73). This *nonroutine* operational logic was indicated by experience from the wartime organization, which had been characterized by close but "scarcely formalized" cooperation between the AMK and the government (ibid., 70). The importance of being able to initiate sizable work projects without delay was underscored in particular. Another argument was that precise rules would detract from the initiative and flexibility that were essential were the organization to succeed in its tasks (ibid., 36–37). In sum, the Social Democratic government clearly wanted the new agency to operate according to a *substantive* rather than formal rationality.

The fact that the board would be dominated by the major labor market organizations served as a guarantee that the agency would operate as intended by the government. It is thus not entirely correct to describe this organizational principle as "corporative" (cf. Pontusson 1992). It should be noted that the employees' organizations had more seats on the board than did the SAF. The Social Democratic government overcame some resistance in arranging that the civil servants who were division heads would not be voting members of the board (ibid., 46). This form of management, unusual at the time, was justified in terms of legitimizing the policy. In a report presented to the 1952 Social Democratic party congress, the reasons for the composition of the board were specified as follows:

Participation by the representatives of the organizations in decisions would serve to create confidence among the general public and thus strengthen the authority of the Board. This would be particularly important in that many decisions by the Board are likely to be sensitive and impinge on large groups of the population." (*Demokrati inom statsförvaltningen* 1952, 26; cf. *Prop.* 1947, 23:39)

The government also got its way as regards a delegation that would settle matters having to do with unemployment insurance: representatives of the trade union unemployment associations were to enjoy a majority in this body. The employers' representative in the inquiry took exception to this proposal, which was also opposed by the nonsocialist members of the Riksdag (Prop. 1947, no. 239, 44–50; RD Statsutskottet 1947, no. 227, 80). The gist of the proposal was to give the unemployment associations—the trade unions, in practice—a majority in the final ruling over such sensitive matters as unemployment insurance entitlements. Accordingly, responsibility for these exceedingly intricate matters was, as a practical matter, handed over to the trade union movement.

In 1960, after the bourgeois opposition had criticized the independent position of the organization, a major inquiry was set up to look into the principles behind the AMS and labor market policy. The committee included the opposition leader as well as a representative of the SAF; even so it managed to reach agreement on all important issues. The report emphasized in particular that the AMS should be allowed considerable, and in certain respects even increased, independence (SOU 1965, no. 9, 485–89). The ensuing bill pointed out the relationship between the tasks of the agency and the appropriate form for government control. The government spokesman stated in the bill:

The development of labor market policy since the war, in particular during the past decade, has placed heavy demands on the administration. In this context it has been of the utmost importance that society has possessed a modern, versatile labor market administration that is full of initiative and the ability to act, capable of quickly and smoothly adapting the practical implementation of labor market policy in the field to continuously shifting requirements, and with access to staff who have been well equipped to perform the demanding tasks. In this context I should like to express my appreciation of the skillful and efficient way in which the Labor Market Board has carried out the difficult tasks entrusted to it by the government and the Riksdag." (Prop. 1966, no. 52, 179)

The last two sentences seem to suggest that the agency managed to combine its independent status with an ability to earn the confidence of the Social Democratic government. The *negligible* degree of formal control has been documented in a major international comparison from 1965, which found the AMS to be a notably strong and independent public organization (Shonfield 1965, 201; cf. Hjern 1982). This is also underscored by Nils Elvander in his study of interest organizations in Swedish politics:

The AMS has a very strong position today. Its independence, subject to the directives issued by the government and the Riksdag, would seem to be greater than that of other agencies. The instructions are drafted and implemented without any informal contacts with the government office. The AMS appears to be a real power in its field. (Elvander 1972, 229; cf. Rehn 1982, 12)

Instead of using precise rules, activities were supervised via informal contacts between the responsible ministers and leading representatives of the LO. The decision to begin implementing in full the Rehn model for labor market policy, for instance, was taken, according to the prime minister of the day, at an informal conference in 1955 between the government and the LO leadership (Erlander 1976, 37–42). An important factor here is said to have been the change to a new director-general of the AMS in 1957—Bertil Olsson (Rehn 1977).

As mentioned above, criticism from the nonsocialist opposition to the effect that the Riksdag had been excluded from the formulation of labor market policy led to a major inquiry in 1960. In all important respects, this led to Riksdag's confirmation of the objectives established earlier. The bourgeois resistance to this policy probably ceased when the matter came to be perceived as part of a wider class compromise between the LO and the SAF. Commenting on the findings, the LO interpreted the report primarily as an expression of confidence in the objectives for labor market policy to date, now summarized for the first time in an official document (Prop. 1966, no. 52, 18).

The influence of the top management of the AMS over the lower levels of the organization is difficult to document from public records. Those I interviewed about whether the organization was united or divided on policy issues emphasized the *strong internal cohesion* in the agency. Similarly, policy implementation was said to be characterized by flexibility as opposed to formalism. It was frequently mentioned, however, that the management, particularly after the change of director-general in 1957, had a very strong say in activities at the central as well as local level (interviews 1, 4, 8, 11–13, 19, 21–24, 29–30; Rehn 1982; SOU 1968, no. 61, 67). Conflicts between management and field staff over policy matters seem to have been rare and the internal cohesion of the organization *strong*. This situation is exemplified in an interview with a former head of a county employment board (Martin Engvall):

*Bo Rothstein:* Can you describe your relationship with the agency management? Were there policy disagreements?
*Martin Engvall:* Our relationship was very good and informal. I do not recollect any controversy over policy.
*B. R.:* Was the good relationship you describe an exception or do you think it was the same for the other county directors?
*M. E.:* It was probably the same for most. Conflicts were rare. I suppose we all had the same outlook and those who did not, acquired it when they found this expedient. There was no opposition.

Informal mechanisms seem to have been very important in the management of the organization. Labor market training, for instance, could be initiated by a county labor board even though the regulations required a central decision. As long as they followed central policy, local initiatives were encouraged and did not incur any reprimand from superiors (Hart 1978, 89, 93; cf. Hanf et al. 1978).

As regards the commencement of relief work, when the county labor boards submitted their official proposals to the AMS, they had already been told informally what the formal decisions would be. The necessary regional planning would not have been feasible without this informal procedure (Hart 1978, 96). The system benefitted from the fact that virtually all those appointed county employment directors from the mid-1960s onward had previously held posts in the central organization of the AMS, and from the fact that the ideology of the organization was *explicit* (Engvall, Jönsson, and B. Olsson, interviews). The informal style also permeated the links between employment officers and their superiors in the area of regular referral work (Hart 1978, 114–15, 152).

Informal contacts were also the rule when it came to relations between the management and the representatives of interested parties on the agency board. The management made great efforts to ensure the support of the organizations represented on the board (Rehn 1982). There were no differences over matters of principle. On the contrary, the SAF took pains to support the AMS, and expressed irritation internally when the nonsocialist political parties attacked its activities in the 1960s (Elvander 1972, 227–29; Jerneck 1986; SOU 1965, no. 9). The relationship was described by Director-General Bertil Olsson in a 1967 speech to a conference of representatives of the central union organizations in Stockholm:

When the organizations are agreed on labor market policy there is really no one who can dissent—there is no point in expressing a different opinion—and the decision is approved. As civil servants we have naturally used that a lot and tried as far as possible to secure unanimity on labor market policy among people from the organizations. (Olsson 1967, 9–10)

An inquiry into management forms in the AMS, including interviews with division heads, was commissioned by the government in 1968. It was carried out by the Agency for Administrative Development (SOU 1968, no. 61). One of the conclusions was that the management exercised little explicit, formal control over the division heads; rather, the objectives had "evolved over time," were "generally recognized internationally," or "established via informal contacts within the organization" (ibid., 67). This suggests that the key personnel had so internalized the objectives of labor market policy that there was no need for specific managerial control. In the words of the inquiry, "either the important element of control is arranged via centralized decisions above the level in question or the management considers that the existing perception of objectives among the division heads is so suitable that a further specification would be superfluous." Instead of universal rules, then, internal direction was achieved through making the *ideology* of the organization explicit.

The AMS gradually acquired a considerable arsenal of instruments with which to influence the labor market. Aside from the employment service, there was the greatly expanded range of measures for influencing labor supply and demand (Ettarp 1980; Furåker 1976;

SOU 1978, no. 60, 89–103). Policy publications from the agency often emphasized the importance of having access to a great many *different* instruments (*AMS-handboken* 1975; *Förändring och trygghet* 1967, 20–23). Most of the means were of the usual financial or legal kind. Various types of grants and subsidies could be used to influence the number of jobs as well as the number of applicants, while the employment service monopoly enhanced this influence (Ettarp 1980; *Förändring och trygghet* 1967).

My focus here, however, is on an instrument of a different kind, unlike the sort usually associated with public bureaucratic organizations. The direction exercised by the AMS was notable for its extensive use of *ideological instruments and persuasion*—that is, public propaganda by means of which the active labor market policy was marketed. The chief economist at the SAF, K-O Faxén, indicted in 1960 what this was all about:

The task has been to find jobs for the unemployed, and as job opportunities have existed in certain parts of the country or in certain occupations, the natural thing in the first place has been to try to move the unemployed. Here in Sweden we regard such migration as quite self-evident. Not least after energetic public relations activities by Mr. Chairman (Bertil Olsson), it is generally considered that one should move. It is, I almost said, virtually criminal not to be mobile. This has become so self-evident that we do not give a thought to how remarkable it actually is. I do not believe that other countries have the same general attitude at all. There you would find a good deal of romantic talk about the local community, tradition and the importance of soldiering on, of maintaining the culture of a particular area, so that one does not say—in the ruthless way we are doing here in Sweden and that we consider to be morally right—that when an area ceases to have a good economic potential, we should institute a labor market policy for stimulating mobility to make it easier for people to move away. (AMS archives, Arbetsmarknadsinformation series L 1/1960)

Writing retrospectively about the contribution of the LO economists to the construction of the new labor market policy, Gösta Rehn noted that a central feature of the policy implementation was the ideological support for and marketing of the reform by the AMS management (1977, 222). Vigorous efforts were made to influence social ideology, using many different channels. A constant stream of newspaper and magazine articles was published to promote the basic ideas underlying the active labor market policy. Films and filmstrips were produced for presentations at public exhibitions and the like (AMS archives, Arbetsmarknadsinformation series R 1967, 2; Furåker 1976, 110–11).

The *persuasive* approach toward clients shows clearly in how the agency's outreaching weekly magazine fired off bursts of propaganda from time to time.[1] The AMS was also assisted by the LO and its various federations in marketing the active labor market policy among the membership (Elander 1978, 77–86). In 1976, for instance, the LO study material on labor market policy issues strongly emphasized the logic behind the principles of the active labor market policy and the specific measures the AMS was taking to implement them:

The task book and the ensuing discussions will teach you a little more about what labor market policy stands for, what the various policy instruments consist of and why the trade union movement, together with social democracy, is so heavily engaged in promoting an active and comprehensive labor market policy. . . . The breakthrough for the new approach to labor market policy did not come, remarkably enough, until the recession of 1957–58. The AMS had a new chief, Bertil Olsson, who understood the importance of the new ideas put forward by the trade union movement. (Aktiv arbetsmarknadspolitik 1976, 2)

As the head of the agency, Bertil Olsson was often invited to various union study groups and seminars on labor market policy, primarily arranged by the LO (AMS archives; Bertil Olsson's documents; cf. B. Olsson 1967). This form of propaganda, which was particularly extensive from the late 1950s onward, was nothing new. When the AMK was set up in 1940 it commissioned Torsten Gårdlund, editor of the leading theoretical publication of the SAP (*Tiden*), to tour the regional trade union organizations and explain the background to and secure support for the new approach to labor market policy (SNA, AMK archives, Artur Thomson's documents).

One explanation for this massive deployment of ideological influence may lie in the nature of the task. As compared to the implementation of more traditional policies, carrying out an active labor market policy requires, as pointed out by Blankenburg, a greater measure of mediation, persuasion, and negotiation on the part of the labor market authorities, and less of such traditional bureaucratic instruments as specific legislative rules codified by parliament (1978). Citing examples from West German labor market administration, Krautkrämer argues that, due to the need for flexibility and a dynamic approach, an active labor market policy is not congruent with traditional bureaucratic lines of thought; bureaucrats wish to give the impression that they simply take prescribed measures to implement decisions that have already been formulated on the foundation of legally defined forms of activity. (1978, 12; cf. 5, 65, 137; cf. Morel and Dupuy 1978, 35, 44, 62–63)

When headed by Gösta Rehn, the OECD commission for labor market issues identified the task of changing the public image of the labor market administration as one of the primary instruments in the implementation of an active labor market policy. People should not perceive public bodies in this field as a bureaucracy for the regulation and possible disbursement of unemployment support. Instead, one should create the image of a public service. Rehn argued that encounters between employment officers and their clients should be arranged under the same external conditions and with the same atmosphere of service as between a bank and its customers. This called for, among other things, an extensive ideological marketing of the new policy.[2]

## Personnel

The two inquiries preceding the final nationalization in 1948 of the labor exchanges and the transformation of the AMK into a regular agency, the AMS, proposed that recruitment to the new organization not be bound by any specific formal qualifications (SOU 1946, no. 51, 44–45). Job referral work was said to be "of such a nature that formal qualifications as such cannot be said to determine how successful an employment officer will be" (ibid.). The employment officers generally worked independently, and it was emphasized that they would have a key position in the organization. It was also stressed that their intermediate position between employer and job seeker called for a high standard of purely personal characteristics and a general suitability for the task (ibid., 43–44).

The inquiry was aware that the absence of such customary qualifications as education, years of service, and so on, might lead to arbitrary and subjective appointments. Both the Swedish constitution and current practice prescribed that recruitment to the central administration be on strict grounds of formal merit. Yet the inquiry sought a freer form of recruitment so as not to "limit the recruitment of employment officers to a relatively narrow circle" (ibid., 44).

In order to counteract the negative consequences of such a system, it was stressed that "the very greatest care would be devoted" to recruitment. To this end, traineeships would be set up at the agency, and recruitment decisions would be exercised centrally by management (ibid., 45). This system had been in operation since 1941.

The freedom in recruitment proposed by the inquiry was accentuated in the bill. The committee of experts had pointed to the value of a theoretical education and proposed that the trainees have qualifications equivalent to a degree from a school of social work (at that time a semiacademic institution) (*Prop.* 1947, 239:45). However, the government (i.e., Gustav Möller) took the view that:

The work of job referral is of such a nature that for recruitment, suitable personal characteristics as well as practical knowledge about working life and contacts with the labor market organizations should regularly carry more weight than formal qualifications. (ibid., 236)

Both the LO and the SAF, as well as the AMK and the National Union of Employment Service Officers, expressed themselves in favor of recruitment without formal qualifications (ibid., 231–34). There were some critical comments from various government organizations, however, to the effect that the problem was a matter of principle for the government administration, and that the danger of arbitrary selection should be confronted (ibid.).

The Riksdag had debated the issue of recruitment to the employment service on an earlier occasion, in 1943. Sven Andersson, a Social Democrat and later a minister, raised the matter in connection with the appropriation for the AMK; he considered that recruitment to the nationalized employment exchanges paid too much heed to theoretical and formal qualifications at the expense of practical experience of working life and its organizations. He had nothing against the concentration of power inherent in the centralization of recruitment to the AMK; under the heading "Bureaucratization Must be Avoided," however, he called for a change in recruitment on account of the civic importance of the employment service (AK 1943, no. 26, 155–57). As mentioned in the previous chapter, a large proportion of the staff at the labor exchanges had habitually been recruited from organizations in the labor movement.

In the same year another Social Democrat, J. J. Lundberg, referring to the labor exchanges, argued that civil service appointments should disregard "paper qualifications and degrees" and concentrate instead on practical suitability for the task (AK 1943, no. 31, 8–9). Gustav Möller, minister of social affairs, replied:

I likewise consider that, in general, practical familiarity with labor market problems and the psychology of job applicants gives a person a better chance of performing his tasks than theoretical merits. Strict recruitment principles, comprising formal qualifications, should therefore not be applied to the employment service. The personal suitability of the applicant should be assessed from case to case, paying primary consideration to proven practical ability. The existence of theoretical training should obviously not be regarded as a drawback. (AK 1943, no. 35, 30–31)

This principle for AMS recruitment was upheld in all the relevant inquiries and bills during the period investigated. Further examples may be mentioned. Replying to a question in 1962, the minister of social affairs (Torsten Nilsson) laid down that "No one should be excluded (from AMS training courses) solely by lack of educational qualifications" (AK 1962, no. 13, 3). The inquiry preceding the important labor market bill of 1966 (SOU 1965, no. 9) proposed that the AMS staff handling matters of occupational rehabilitation should have university qualifications in psychology and social legislation. In their comments, the LO and the AMS disagreed, and were supported in the bill by the responsible minister (Rune B. Johansson), who "underscored" that no formal qualifications were to be required for AMS recruitment (Prop. 1966, no. 52, 25–31, 196).

A couple of years later, the Agency for Administrative Development proposed that, while freedom in recruitment should be retained, the use of various tests in the selection procedure should be increased. In its comment, the LO again asserted the particular importance of a broad base for recruitment, with no demands for formal qualifications. Nor did the LO favor selection instruments that might benefit individuals with formal qualifications and more advanced education. The LO assumed that such applicants would find it easier to perform well on such tests. Again, the minister took this line explicitly in the bill (Prop. 1970, no. 1, 13:58, 82; SOU 1968, no. 60, 177).

This account of the formal principles for AMS recruitment raises two questions: (1) What were the immediate effects of these principles, that is, what categories were recruited? and (2) Why was this arrangement, which represented a departure from the constitution and from prevailing practice, introduced? As regards the first question, a large proportion of former trade union representatives was recruited throughout the period studied here. They came mainly and initially from the LO, but later from the Swedish Federation of Salaried Employees (TCO) as well, and to some small extent from the Confederation of Professional Associations (SACO) (interviews 1, 4, 11–13, 17, 19, 21–24, 29–30; see also Rehn 1982, 12).

The inquiries and bills mentioned above tended, moreover, to emphasize how important it was for AMS staff to have experience from the labor market organizations.[3] The union journal also promoted this form of recruitment (e.g., *Arbetsförmedlingen* 1944, no. 5, 88–89). SAF representatives on the board claim that employers were well aware that trade union personnel were being recruited to the AMS (Bergom-Larsson and Lindström, interviews). The policy was formally to welcome people from the employer side as well, but this came to virtually nothing in practice, since the salaries paid to AMS trainees could not compete with those offered by employer organizations (Lindström and B. Olsson, interviews).

The available statistics do not reveal the exact scale of recruitment from trade unions. Recruitment was never from this source exclusively, except possibly during one or two years. From the interviews and other material, I estimate the unions contributed from about 15 to around 50 percent of the annual totals. In fact, the management of the agency sometimes turned directly to the union representatives on the board and asked for suitable candidates (Molin, Nilsson, Olsson, and Östergren, interviews).

Senior appointments were almost invariably made internally. Concerning directors-general, it may be noted that the first person of significance in this post, Gustav Vahlberg (who held the position from 1947 to 1957), was taken directly from the trade union movement, where he had been vice-chairman of the LO. The third and most important director-general during the period studied was Bertil Olsson (1957–72), who was likewise a Social Democrat who had worked his way up through the agency, which he had joined in 1940. After rapid promotion, including a stint in the personnel department, he was transferred to the Ministry of Social Affairs, where he was made responsible for labor market issues. He also served as the chief secretary of the 1946 Committee of Inquiry on the nationalization of the public employment service (SOU 1946, no. 51), which laid down the recruitment principles and organization of the agency. Early on, his writing had earned him a name as an energetic advocate of an extended, active, and selective labor market policy (B. Olsson 1951, 1953, 1954; cf. Rehn 1977).

The justification provided for the unusual recruitment policy centered on the need to secure legitimacy among target groups and the necessity for being flexible. As regards legitimacy, it was stated openly that the delicate nature of the agency's tasks made it extremely important that the staff gain the confidence of the labor market organizations as well as of clients. Persons with experience of labor market organizations were assumed to be in a better position to win that confidence than those with formal degrees (*Demokrati i statsförvaltningen* 1952, 27–28; cf. *Arbetsförmedlingen* 1944, no. 4, 88–89; Prop. 1966, no. 52, 25–26; SOU 1946, no. 51, 43–45). This argument was stressed by Gösta Rehn in an interview:

It was a deliberate policy on the part of me and Nils Kellgren. I was, as you know, on the Thomson inquiry that laid the foundation of the AMS, and Kellgren can be said to have had inside experience from his employment during the war. It was essential to recruit people with practical knowledge of working life, in whom the workers could have confidence. We argued for that in the inquiry. It would not have worked with academically trained professionals.

Besides formulating the theoretical foundation of "the Swedish model," then, Rehn contributed to shaping the special organization of the AMS. According to Bertil Olsson, the recruitment policy had already been drawn up when Arthur Thomson was head of the AMK; this is also suggested by the inquiry chaired by Thomson on the nationalization of labor exchanges (SOU 1946, no. 51, 45). The focus on flexibility and on *substantive* rather than formal rationality is evident from an interview with Bertil Olsson:

*Bo Rothstein:* What was the origin of the idea that recruitment should not be governed by the formal qualifications of applicants?
*Bertil Olsson:* It was Thomson, among others, who pushed that. In his opinion, if there was to be a labor market policy, it would be necessary to have a supple, flexible organization, not one that was bureaucratic and formal as in the case of schools, for instance.
*B. R.:* Did he make that particular comparison, that is, with schools?
*B. O.:* Yes, frequently. He taught us to work in a completely nonbureaucratic way. His earlier experience as a division head at the National Board of Education had introduced him to organizational bureaucracy and rigidity. . . . He had developed this line when he was in charge of youth unemployment assistance at the old AK.

The director-general frequently took a personal interest in the particular business of recruitment, at least from the late 1950s onward (AMS archives, kanslibyrån, Jur-adm sekt, vol. E III, 6). Private letters from Bertil Olsson to some ministers (for instance Gunnar Sträng, then minister of finance, with a copy to Torsten Nilsson, then minister of social affairs), show that the government was kept informed about the recruitment of trade union personnel. There is no date, but the filing indicates this letter is from 1962:

The Ministry of Finance has inquired informally as to how large-scale recruitment to the employment service could be undertaken, and how the related personnel training is to be organized. I therefore want to give you my view on this matter. . . . Moreover, I have been in touch with trade unions, from which we have previously obtained our very best employment officers. If the initial wage is raised as we requested, there will be better prospects for recruiting capable trade unionists, which is what the employment service needs. Their prior knowledge of the labor market is invaluable to us. I have also made soundings among the trade associations, where people also have training and experience suitable for the employment service; but as a rule it is difficult to compete with their salaries (AMS archives; Bertil Olsson's documents, Ica. vol. 8)

Information about recruitment policy also seems to have traveled in the opposite direction, from leading Social Democrats to the director-general of the AMS. In two letters to Bertil Olsson (04–21–71 and 04–22–72), LO chairman Arne Geijer recommended individuals with sound union records as potential employment officers (AMS archives, kanslibyrån, personalsekt, GD's korrespondens i personalfrågor). In a letter from an under secretary of state (Tage G. Peterson, 10–08–71), an individual was recommended for an AMS post on the basis of the writer's personal knowledge of the individual in question from the Social Democratic youth section, and on account of "his political base, resourcefulness and independent way of working." In sum, the recruitment policy was based on ensuring the field personnel's *ideological commitment* to the goals of the active labor market policy.

In addition to recruitment, promotion and internal training were two important elements in ensuring the ideological commitment of the personnel. The attitudes of staff unions will also be considered here. The inquiry and the bill resulting in the AMS laid down that promotion in the agency would not be formally regulated, as was the practice in most other parts of the Swedish civil service. This was a departure from the system that dominated the state administration at the time, which placed a premium on years of service. It was also stressed that exclusive staff categories were to be avoided as far as possible at the AMS (Prop. 1947, no. 239, 237; SOU 1946, no. 51, 445). This proposal was supported by most of the interested parties, but some criticism was also heard, for instance from the administrative board of Malmöhus county:

The experts have resolved the matter in a radical way, but apparently at the expense of values that cannot be disregarded. As the experts themselves point out, the matter of personal suitability must be judged more or less subjectively, and the guarantees against arbitrary appointments are not likely to be better *a priori* in the employment service than in other branches of public activity. A free, unregulated recruitment and promotion policy can thus lead to appreciable inconvenience also for those concerned, in that they evidently would not be able to count on the security and assurance provided by tolerably normal and foreseeable promotion. (Prop. 1947, no. 239, 231)

Promotion policy was based to a large extent on the same principles as recruitment policy: many of those who rose to senior posts had served in the LO (Rehn 1982, 18). Two decades after the agency had been set up in 1948, at least nine of the twenty-four county employment directors had a union background (T. Olsson, interview). The AMS was criticized in 1982 by Center party representatives with experience as political advisers in the Ministry of Industry. They claimed, for instance, that without exception the twenty-four county employment directors were members of the Social Democratic party (Sjöström 1982; 1985). This caused something of a stir, and it was not denied.[4] The county employment directors were key figures in the organization, and the management took great pains to find people suitable for these posts (Engvall, Jönsson, B. Olsson, and Rehnberg, interviews). The following is an extract from an interview with Bertil Olsson, the director-general.

*Bo Rothstein:* Promotion policy in the AMS was also completely unregulated. How were the county employment directors, for instance, appointed?

*Bertil Olsson:* They were picked individually. The posts did not have to be advertised; the appointments were made by the government on the recommendation of the director-general, not the board! They were key posts and it was important to find the right people. I put a lot of effort into training them. A couple of years before a post became vacant we were already looking for suitable candidates and relocating them to Stockholm. The labor market demands quick decisions also at the regional level, and the responsibility is great. Consequently the head of the agency must have absolute confidence in his county employment directors.

B. R.: How did you know whom to choose?

B. O.: You could see who was showing his paces. There were many courses and conferences at which you could see what people were worth. I had also acquired a considerable knowledge of people at the agency ever since my time in the personnel division.

The significance of employment officers' background for the character of implementation is illustrated in an interesting study by James O'Toole. The objectives of labor market policy have been similar in Sweden and West Germany, but the outcome has been considerably better in Sweden. O'Toole assumes that the discrepancy has to do with the very different implementation of the policy in the two countries (1983, 130). To study this, he compared a successful employment service region with a less successful one in each country. The two successful regions were distinguished above all in having key officials with trade union backgrounds. This strongly influenced their priorities in the implementation of employment programs (ibid., 143).

With no specific, uniform regulations governing staff qualifications, the agency management placed great emphasis on internal training. This had been initiated during the war by the National Union of Employment Service Officers (ATR), and was supported financially by the AMK from 1944 onward (*Arbetsförmedlingen* 1943, 5; 1945, 10; 1946, 10). When the system was nationalized in 1948, trainee courses were instituted at the agency, lasting a total of twelve weeks to begin with, and considerably longer later. Besides dealing with administrative technicalities, the program included a good deal of ideological education in the social role of labor market policy (AMS archives, personalsektionen). The activation of labor market policy in 1957–58 led to the inclusion of basic instruction in the Rehn-Meidner model (Jönsson, interview; cf. *Förändring och trygghet* 1967).

It is noteworthy that Bertil Olsson was one of the lecturers at *every* trainee course from 1948 until he left the agency in 1974 (AMS archives, personalsektionens handlingar ang aspirantkurser). He justified this unusual custom (for a director-general) on two grounds:

the importance of communicating and establishing the ideological foundation of the current labor market policy, and a desire to get to know as many of the new recruits as possible, partly with a view to future promotion (B. Olsson, interview).

Extensive further training was also arranged internally in the form of courses and conferences (AMS archives, personalsektionen). The county employment directors were usually assembled four times a year, mainly to discuss and settle policy issues. These meetings were considered very important, particularly after the activation of labor market policy in 1957–58 (Engvall, Jönsson, B. Olsson, and Wittrock, interviews; AMS archives, personalsektionen). From 1952 onward, the agency also arranged what were known as "promotion courses." Ove Jönsson, personnel manager from 1960 to 1965, was asked about their purpose:

*Bo Rothstein:* Was it necessary to attend them in order to gain promotion?

*Ove Jönsson:* Not necessary but, as someone put it, an avenue to advancement, and also to making a hash of things. By talking too much in such a course you could reveal that you were unsuitable for promotion. The lecturers included Bertil Olsson and Curtman. There were also people from the LO, the TCO, and the SAF. . . . Many of those who attended these courses became county employment directors later.

*B. R.:* Was their formal title "courses for inspectors?"

*O. J.:* No, "promotion courses." The post of inspector was the rung above a trainee employment officer. The courses also enabled the management and those concerned with promotion to get to know the staff and compare individuals.

*B. R.:* Were there other courses?

*O. J.:* Special courses for vocational counsellors and occupational rehabilitation officers. There were also "ideological summer courses."

*B. R.:* What were those?

*O. J.:* Each county labor board nominated a number of participants. The idea was that people would get to know each other. It was not a matter of training but of labor market policy in general; the Rehn-Meidner line. The leading speaker was Bertil Olsson. . . . The summer courses were not so much training as a sort of encouragement for the staff to get together. A way of creating a sense of unity. People got to know each other and used these contacts in their work.

Without doubt, the leadership of the AMS put great efforts into ensuring the ideological commitment of the personnel. In this respect, the relationship between the AMS and the National Federation of Employment Service Officials (ATR) was important. Formed in 1937, the ATR was an independent federation until 1949, when it merged with the Federation of Civil Servants. It supported the nationalization of labor exchanges right from the start (*Arbetsförmedlingen* 1939, 2).

The federation appears to have supported the agency and its tasks almost without reservation. It favored all the major proposals when the AMS was set up in the late 1940s, and its journal contains no criticism at all on matters of principle. On the contrary, it published a number of ideological justifications by leading figures in the AMS. Bertil Olsson, for instance, contributed six long pieces in favor of a further expansion of the selective labor market policy (ibid. 1951, 2–6). Perhaps the clearest indication that staff who were active in union matters also supported the agency's ideology is that four union chairmen and the first editor of the journal all rose to be county employment directors (Arvid Odlöw, Gunnar Strand, Göte Elmer, Carl Lerin, and Lars-Gösta Skogh).

The strategic function of the local employment service is a common theme in AMS documents (*Arbetsförmedlingen* 1952; *Förändring och trygghet* 1967). From the viewpoint of the street-level bureaucracy, it is the staff-client encounter that determines whether the intentions behind labor market policy are translated into practice. The aim of all preceding links in the chain is to mold the influence that employment officers endeavor to exercise over buyers and sellers of labor. In the Weberian model of the bureaucratic organization, it is the knowledge of the staff that is the primary consideration. Such knowledge is of two kinds: knowledge of a particular subject and knowledge of an existing rule system. The process of recruitment and socialization outlined above suggests that the organization of the AMS expressed a rationality different from that of the bureaucratic model.

The successful implementation of an active labor market policy presupposes that the labor market organizations, and individual enterprises and employees as well, have *confidence* in the authorities, that is, that they perceive them as *legitimate*. This reasoning was used primarily to justify the inclusion of representatives of the organized class interests in the policy-making body of the agency. In my view, the specific form of recruitment to the AMS also had the purpose of gaining the confidence of the working class. One of the principal elements in this process was the separation of job referral functions from responsibility for unemployment benefits. This was made quite clear in the 1952 training manual:

To be able to perform its tasks, the employment service—and the members of its staff—must have the confidence of the labor market organizations. Much remains to be done in this respect, and many habitual misconceptions need to be overcome. They are partly attributable to a general tendency not to burden labor market agreements with intervention by society and "bureaucracy". . . . One of the main reasons why people are skeptical about the employment service is its connection with the control of unemployment, and the forms for this during crises in the past. (*Arbetsförmedlingen* 1952 del. 4:1–8; cf. *Förändring och trygghet* 1967, 29)

The 1946 inquiry into the nationalization of labor exchanges contains a similar passage: "The great majority of assistants are required to undertake job referral on their own. The assistants have a key position in the organization of the service in that it is primarily they who are in continuous touch with its customers: employers and job seekers. The delicate nature of referral work accordingly places great demands on the tact and judgement of the referral officer" (SOU 1946, no. 51, 43). An argument for not basing recruitment on formal qualifications was that "The experts wish strongly to emphasize that the hallmark of a competent referral officer is just as much personal characteristics as knowledge. The intermediate position that employment officials to some extent occupy between parties in the labor market demands a great deal of their purely personal characteristics" (ibid., 44). Similarly, writing in the ATR journal in 1951, Bertil Olsson made the point that "the employment service cannot be one institution among other time-honored administrations directed by civil servants. Its functions require that the employment service be a part of the teeming daily round of working life. It exists to serve the parties in the labor market under their direct influence" (Olsson 1951, 47).

A bill from 1975, which recommended that the district boards of the AMS be comprised of representatives of the interested parties, stated that "a reason for increasing the participation of laymen in individual cases is said to be the great importance of these cases for the applicant and the appropriateness of decisions being made close to the individual by persons in whom he or she has confidence" (Prop. 1975–76, no. 84, 56; cf. Ds. A 1975, no. 9, 32). In a joint submission to the government (04–14–75), the LO and the TCO justified these composite district boards (dominated in practice by the trade union side) as follows:

The marked expansion of public administration in the past three decades, centrally, regionally and locally, has been accompanied by a radical change in the composition of the public services that are provided for citizens. This change is mirrored in organizational and procedural changes as regards the performance of administrative tasks. It is now virtually impossible to regulate in advance all the different situations encountered by an administrative authority. The authority accordingly has a very great discretion, subject to current guidelines, to make decisions about various matters in the light of politically determined general objectives. (Prop. 1975–76, no. 84, 51)

The extent to which the political intentions were in fact realized in the implementation phase is difficult to measure, but the support forthcoming from the organized class interests does suggest the outcome was that desired. A comparative study of the Swedish and the West German labor market administrations in the mid-1970s also highlights the efforts that Swedish employment officers, unlike their German colleagues, devoted to the creation of good relations with enterprises and local trade unions. This effort formed a principle part of a successfully implemented labor market policy (Hanf et al. 1978, 319, 337–38).

Another characteristic of the ideal typical bureaucracy is its adherence to a precise system of universal rules in its dealings with the public. In this respect, too, the AMS organization departed from the *rational form* of the bureaucratic model. In their contacts with the labor market, the AMS staff were not to have their hands tied by detailed regulations. The reasoning was instead that they should act in accordance with a *common but constantly changing line, established centrally and applied in the light of varying regional and local circumstances.* For this it was necessary, above all, that the priorities of the personnel be continuously congruent with the overarching strategic objectives for labor market policy (that is, the Rehn-Meidner model), as well as with the more detailed objectives stated by the board in respect to specific regions, economic activities, and occupational groups.

A couple of quotations will serve to illustrate this difference between a static, rule-governed method and a dynamic, strategic approach. An AMS training manual from the mid-1960s (*Förändring och trygghet* 1967) contains this passage: "Such is the nature of the work of the employment service that it cannot be molded via instructions alone. An employment officer must be aware of the content of circulars, but in addition must know about the objectives of labor market policy and the ensuing requirements concerning the direction of job referral work" (AMS archives, Arbetsmarknadsservice 1967, 1). Trainees were also required to study the labor market policy program of the LO but not, remarkably, any corresponding document from the SAF or any other labor market organization (ibid., 2). The preface to the main textbook, written by the director-general, Bertil Olsson, declares that:

> The employment service . . . is the principal instrument for achieving the objectives of labor market policy. It is therefore highly important that these objectives, as well as the instruments for attaining them, are familiar to and implanted in the staff of the service. The primary task of this book is to provide the basic knowledge that this requires about the contexts and intentions of labor market policy. The other main task is to provide a normative description of various aspects of employment service activities. This description, in other words, provides guidelines for how the work should be conducted in order to achieve the stated objectives. (*Förändring och trygghet* 1967, 7)

The following quotation is from an OECD report from a meeting about conceivable improvements in the organization of labor market administrations: "An excellent example of an important instrument for the development of staff training—a manual or textbook produced in Sweden—was discussed at some length. It was quite evident that the training material was designed not to provide mechanical or procedural instructions but to create an understanding and appreciation of policy and program objectives" (L. Levine 1969, 28). The two foremost aims of the training seem to have been to convey the *ideology* behind policy to the personnel, as well as the *link* between this ideology and the practice of active labor market policy. All the instructive examples in the book are designed to show how measures for varying situations in the labor market can be brought into line with overriding policy objectives (*Förändring och trygghet* 1967, del. IV). The director-general's preface states:

> Employment service activities are of a kind that neither can nor should be regulated with specific instructions for every aspect and every conceivable situation. The individual employment officer, besides knowing about and following the instructions that have been issued, must also be capable of deciding which measures are needed, and of acting independently in the light of general objectives and guidelines. (ibid. 8; cf. 64)

A similar though less explicit line is expressed in the first printed manual for internal training, from 1952. This stressed the importance of constantly adapting to the level of activity in the labor market. It also stated that the employment service "must ensure that it does not become a bureaucratic institution, regulated by documents and hard and fast instructions" (*Arbetsförmedlingen* 1952, del. 4:7).

The importance of staff being *dynamic and flexible* was also underscored. Being dynamic implied the opposite of a routinized and passive approach; staff were to be constantly on the offensive in pursuit of the policy objectives. The activities should be adjusted continuously to the changing situation in the labor market as a whole as well as in the various submarkets: "In view of the changes that constantly occur in the labor market and which are tending to become more widespread, the field organization needs to have a high degree of *readiness for adjustment*. The tasks change and it follows that the organization cannot be static; it must be capable of adjusting smoothly to the demands inherent in the changes in the labor market" (*Förändring och trygghet* 1967, 34; cf. *Arbetsförmedlingen* 1952, del. 4:7; B. Olsson 1954).

Flexibility implied that the nature of the measures applied by labor market policy was such as to rule out a universal application, with no distinction between the people or organizations applying to the employment service. Job referral work, for instance, deliberately differentiated between occupational groups. An internal circular provides the following example: "The aim in all referral work should not be a uniform procedure that is the same for every employment office. Instead the approach should be adapted as far as possible to the economic activities, occupations and individuals in question" (AMS archives, arbetsmarknadsinformation series A 1964, 11).

Field studies by Hart of some local employment offices in the mid-1970s indicate that relations with customers and clients were not governed to any major extent by the relevant instructions and rules, nor by direct supervision or control by superiors. The norm was instead set by established practice and by the outcome of regular internal meetings at which new guidelines and current tendencies were discussed. When the staff faced difficult cases and were uncertain about what to do, they first consulted their colleagues and superiors, rather than the rules in the manual (Hart 1978). It seems that rules and orders had given way to a comprehensive process of socialization in the agency.

The study also shows that staff input varied appreciably between different groups of applicants, and that employment offices facing different labor market problems worked very differently (ibid.). Similar regional differences are reported in the implementation of labor market training (Hanf et al. 1978). It should be added that the flexibility of the labor market administration was by no means an automatic consequence of the tasks involved.

Flexibility is rather something that had to be built into the institutional structure. An illustration of this is the rigid implementation that characterized the AK, the predecessor of the AMS (cf. chap. 4). Another example is the West German attempt at instituting active labor market policy. Labor market legislation inspired largely by the Swedish experience was introduced in that country in the late 1960s, as indeed it was in several other Western industrial countries as well (Blankenburg 1978; Lewis 1978, xii). This policy was implemented by an already existing bureaucratic authority, and in a manner governed by precise rules. Because the staff were neither dynamic nor flexible, the implementation was deficient.[5] As Bertil Olsson said in an interview, "There was no place for lawyers in the active labor market policy; they are trained to sit and judge in the static society."

## Funding

The right of deploying most of the funds for relief work was handed over to the AMK in 1940, having previously been in the hands of the Ministry of Social Affairs. In 1946, the financial regulation exercised by the government was further reduced, in that the AMK was given complete control of the appropriations for all work projects for combating unemployment. The importance of maintaining financial discretion for the organization was supported with arguments similar to those for avoiding a detailed network of regulations (SOU 1947, no. 24, 65–66, 71–73; Prop. 1947, no. 239, 36–37). In the Riksdag, a Social Democrat who had headed the AMK for a brief period in 1946–47 (K. J. Olsson) stressed the importance of financial flexibility and *an orientation to change:*

While the work of the ordinary government agencies runs along old and, you might say, habitual lines, the AMK has conducted and the future AMS will conduct operations that are extremely varied, covering a whole range of fields and dealing with numerous shifting problems, often of a very transient nature. It is thus not a matter of uniform, continuously ongoing activities; instead it is to a very large extent necessary to improvise, make quick decisions and act promptly. Operations of this kind call for an organization that is elastic. It must not become rigid. The new problems that constantly arise call for adaptability. . . . All this means that those who make decisions with economic consequences must act much more rapidly than is necessary for civil servants in general. (FK 1947, no. 31, 10)

The Riksdag fully approved this feature of the bill establishing the AMS. The 1966 bill on the principles of labor market policy further emphasized the importance of the agency remaining untrammeled by specific appropriations: "Labor market policy must be flexible in extent as well as content. Its institutions must therefore have considerable financial and administrative freedom. In recent years the AMS has acquired greater freedom in certain respects in that a number of large and small appropriations for different activities have been combined into groups of measures that can be used as alternatives. This applies not least to the large appropriations for public relief work etc." (Prop. 1966, no. 52, 137). Commenting on the result of the 1960 inquiry into labor market policy, Gösta Rehn wrote:

All the interested parties were convinced that an institution—a labor market administration directed by a strong labor market board—was needed that would be able to act very quickly, without too many parliamentary delays over the supply of funds and unhampered by specific rules concerning the tasks assigned to it. (1982, 12)

The virtual absence of (at least short-term) budgetary control by the Riksdag in this field is evident from the following passage in the bill: "The difficulty of foreseeing the financial requirement for relief work in particular is demonstrated by the fact that substantial supplementary funds have had to be requested for this purpose in recent years. With the current arrangement, the requested funds have as a rule been disposed of in practice by the time they are approved by the Riksdag" (Prop. 1966, no. 52, 137).

Two of the pillars of active labor market policy are the funds for relief work and for supporting enterprise location to areas hit by unemployment. Organizational control was achieved in this area by obliging the regional bodies to obtain the approval of the central management and board for the initiation of any sizable project, even if it conformed with the internal budget. In 1975, this included any project costing more than 500 thousand crowns, as well as all projects in such fields as agriculture, industrial facilities, recreation, tourism, and so on (Ds. K 1975, no. 5, 64–69; cf. *AMS-handboken* 1977, del. 2, pkt. 23.10.30; Hart 1978, 81–82). As a total of 1.3 billion crowns was appropriated for relief work in the fiscal year 1976–77, there must have been plenty of room for internal management via the allocation of these funds (Prop. 1967–67, no. 100, bil. 15, 92).

The funds for labor market training were controlled in a similar manner (Hart 1978, 89). The authorization stated that all appropriations for labor market measures were to go to the AMS for allocation by the governing board (Statsliggaren 1949, 76 regleringsbreven till arbetsmarknadsverket). Neither the central government nor the Riksdag, then, had any means of directing labor market funds to specific regions or districts. The composition of measures from region to region was largely determined in the course of deliberations and compromises within the board.[6]

The case-by-case implementation of labor market policy was characterized by a variety of *financial* instruments for influencing the supply and demand of labor power (Ettarp 1980). The individual job seeker was the target in many instances, as with direct unemployment support, business startup assistance, and various allowances for training, moving, and disposing of a dwelling. Other instruments were aimed at enterprises, such as localization support, grants for internal training, and wage subsidies for taking on disabled applicants. The AMS was also in a position to influence some of the investments by local authorities and other public or semi-public bodies, in that projects or other activities could be funded for their account as relief work. A notable feature of this exercise of financial influence was the large measure of discretion enjoyed by the executive staff of the AMS.

This freedom was part of the program for the leading administrators of the active labor market policy. This discretion, or rather the absence of precise legislative rules, was considered essential for the work in question. Those formulating the policy theory likewise emphasized the importance of giving the labor market administration a free hand in the choice of measures, in order to endow its operations with as much *substantive rationality* as possible. Rudolf Meidner regarded the program's feasibility as resting on:

Two essential conditions; *firstly,* the availability of a generous assortment of policy instruments, and *secondly,* the existence of an extensive network of regional and local administrations, with the task of deciding on the combination of instruments that they deem to be most effective. (Quoted in Hjern 1982, 77)

The drawback of this, of course, was that individuals and local authorities were not in a position to *demand* particular financial benefits specified in statutory regulations. There were small prospects of referring to such rules and thereby winning an argument against the AMS, along such lines as—*because* these particular circumstances apply in my case, *it follows* that I am *entitled* to certain financial benefits. The organization of the AMS accordingly deviated from the principles of consistency and universalism expressed in the ideal typical Weberian bureaucracy.

The statutes regulating the AMS contained numerous regulations about grants and benefits which the executive staff were able to disburse with a large measure of discretion. Discretionary assessments lay behind the decisions as to what benefits would be provided in which cases. Removal allowances, for instance, could be granted, according to the labor market ordinances, to those who "are or run the risk of becoming unemployed" (SFS 1966, no. 368), with the question of who "runs the risk of becoming unemployed" to be settled in each specific case. Internal manuals and instructions provided no specific juridical indications as to how the ordinances should be interpreted.

Efforts were instead made to enhance the individual staff person's ability to assess the distinctive requirements of each situation. Considerations not pertaining directly to the individual applicant might prove decisive, and the applicant had no legal grounds for questioning such decisions. Such considerations could, for example, concern the future outlook, as judged by the AMS, for a particular economic activity, occupation or region (cf. *Förändring och trygghet* 1967, 129–46; SOU 1965, no. 9, 117, 131–39).

That this *orientation to change* necessitated a discretionary element in case-by-case decision making at the local level was emphasized in particular in the context of individual allowances for labor market training. The AMS manuals and instructions did not provide any legal, rule-based explanation of the labor market ordinance; on the contrary, they stressed that no one had any legal right to labor market training (*Förändring och trygghet 1967*, 106; cf. Hanf et al. 1978, 309).

Decisions about labor market training should instead be founded, according to the manuals, on a balanced *assessment* of the applicant's background, motivation for training, and prospects for finding work afterward. An assessment of the applicant's ability to complete the training was also required: *"A strong desire to participate in a course is not, however, sufficient by itself. It is up to the employment officer to form an opinion as to whether the desire really does stem from a proper understanding of what will be required of the participants"* (*Förändring och trygghet* 1967, 106, 109–12).

Many of the decisions about individual allowances were handed down from the regional level to the districts, and from there to officials at the local offices. Formally, these officials' decisions were taken on behalf of the county labor boards. Admittedly, an appeal system existed for AMS decisions right up to the government level, but as a rule "the great majority" of complaints were rejected. A ministerial inquiry in 1975 into increased influence by the labor market organizations on the district level of the AMS expressed the opinion that "The latter [the district level] can be regarded as a theoretical construction of little practical importance." (Ds. A, 1975, no. 9, 12, 30, 35).

A comparison with conditions in West Germany (during the early 1970s) again shows that more precise rules were applied in that country, for instance with respect to the right to individual allowances, particularly for labor market training. Jobless individuals who could demonstrate that they met certain legally specified criteria were able to conduct legal proceedings and thereby to secure training allowances from the German labor market authorities. Instances have been reported of this system obstructing the application of the training instrument in accordance with the general objectives of the active labor market policy, especially the achievement of "flexibility in a rapidly changing task environment" (Blankenburg 1978, 292; cf. Krautkrämer 1978; Hanf et al. 1978).

## Organizational Connection One: A Last Comment

As mentioned above, the conclusions of this chapter and the one following will be presented in chapter 8. In the meantime, however, a quote from a study of the labor market agencies in West Germany can serve as an illustration of one of this chapter's main points:

In Germany, in addition to the legal prescriptions, guidelines are so numerous and detailed as to fill a bookcase in the office of a placement agent.

Standard letters suggesting a polite form of addressing clients, and even the amount of time to be spent on the counseling of each client are prescribed in detail. It is not astonishing that many of the placement agents become disoriented in the mass of prescriptions and their constant amendments, and finally tend to neglect many of them altogether. (Blankenburg 1978, 292).

# 7. Organizational Connection Two: The SÖ

## Introduction

As shown in chapter 4, the Swedish Social Democrats put great hope in comprehensive school reform during the 1940s and 1950s. They hoped not merely to change the school system as such—that is, to make it more egalitarian and accessible to children of working-class background; they also viewed the comprehensive school reform in a long-term strategic context. Their aim with the reform was no less than to change the character of their favorite instrument for social change, namely the state. By broadening the social recruitment to higher education and, thereby, to key positions in the state, the Social Democrats sought to assure that the implementation of future social reforms was not hindered by a predominantly conservative state bureaucratic corps.

As the figures presented in chapter 4 show, the reform has been a failure in this respect. More than three decades after the reform was begun, no improvement whatsoever has taken place in the social recruitment to higher education in Sweden. On the contrary, the percentage of students of working-class background was lower in 1990 than in the early 1960s (cf. table 4). How can a failure of this magnitude be explained?

Again, the reason may well be the construction of the policy itself. Although I will argue against such an interpretation, the question lies largely outside the scope of this study. As argued in chapter 2, one of the two major causes of policy failure is faulty implementation arising from the bureaucratic character of the capitalist state. The purpose of this chapter is therefore to describe, in light of the theoretical ideal types presented in chapter 3 (of bureaucratic and cadre organizations), the organizational landscape between policy formulation and policy implementation.

More precisely, I intend to show that the aims of the comprehensive school reform were never realized, *on account of the bureaucratic organization of the implementation process*. Irrespective of the nature of the planning behind the policy, in other words, the manner in which the changes were implemented would have hindered them from reaching classroom practice. Thus, I agree with John Chubb and Terry Moe that "all schools are shaped in pervasive and subtle ways by their institutional settings, and that the kind of organizations they become and how effectively they perform are largely reflections of the institutional contexts in which they operate" (1990, 29).

As shown in chapter 5, the structure of the central school bureaucracy had been left fairly intact by the Social Democrats during the interwar period. In contrast to the case with the labor market, the party made no effort to change the organizational structure of the state in the area of education. During the wartime coalition government, both the minister of education and the director-general of the National Board of Education were Conservatives; this of course minimized the Social Democrats' prospects of influencing the school administration. Summing up his findings about the causes of success and failure in government programs, Harold Wolman states that "programs placed in existing agencies are more likely to fail if they represent major deviations from programs previously administered or if they require the agency to change its perception of its mission" (1981, 436).

One important question therefore concerns how the Social Democratic government coped with the structural character of the state apparatus in question, namely the National Board of Education. If reformism faces the limits described in the previous chapter, they should become visible in the course of investigating this question. For reasons of comparability, finally, this chapter is organized in the same fashion as the previous one, and the conclusions from both are presented together in chapter 8.

## Program Content

The School Commission established in 1946 by Tage Erlander, in his capacity as the new minister of education and ecclesiastical affairs, served to torpedo the ongoing inquiry initiated in 1940 by Gösta Bagge, the Conservative leader. Erlander writes in his memoirs that he considered this necessary in order to avoid an unreasonable delay in the reform of the school system. The Bagge committee, which was comprised mainly of educationalists, slipped thereby into the political quagmire into which so many attempts at resolving school issues had sunk since the beginning of the century (Erlander 1973, 235–37; cf. Marklund 1980, 70–71; chap. 5). Unlike the Bagge committee, however, the 1946 School Commission had a majority of politicians (most of them Social Democrats). Its report, published in 1948, spelled out the political guidelines that served subsequently as the foundation for the reform of the school system (cf. chap. 5).

The theme of the report was a more democratic school system, to be achieved in part by a thorough reorganization, but above all by a change in the schools' internal procedures (Erlander 1973, 341–42).[1] The existing variety of schools would be replaced by a single comprehensive elementary school, with no differentiation of pupils in the first eight grades. This would be made feasible by the *individualization* of schoolwork, meaning that teaching would be adapted to the particular situation, circumstances, and ability of each pupil. A small number of progressive teachers in the elementary schools had used this method since the 1920s as a means of coping with heterogenous classes. It had then become increasingly popular among elementary school teachers (Fredrikson 1950, 402–09, 481–86; Marklund 1981, 63; SOU 1946, no. 31).[2]

The report described the prevailing system as authoritarian, formalistic, and insensitive to the varying needs and circumstances of individual pupils. It called for an emphasis on the individual and on cooperation, in order to encourage independence, teamwork, and a critical ability.[3] At the same time, the report declared much in the existing school system to be admirable and a fitting foundation for the work of reform; however, as the general tenor of the report was highly critical of the current forms for schoolwork, this gloss probably served to secure agreement and placate conservative educationalists (SOU 1948, no. 27, 2–6). The commission further held that a comprehensive school system, in which children were not assigned to different schools in a class-biased manner, would greatly enhance working-class children's prospects of advancing to higher education. If this "socially invasive" policy were to succeed, however, it was in the commission's view necessary to change not only the formal organization of the school system, but teaching methods as well, because children with very different abilities would be kept together in the same classes much longer than in the existing school system.

What role did the commission assign to the National Board of Education (SÖ, Sw. Skolöverstyrelsen) for achieving the goal of changing classroom practice in the Swedish schools? First, the commission recommended two approaches, which stood however in partial contradiction to each other. The commission argued, on the one hand, that major changes of method were essential, while on the other hand declared that there would be no departure from the principle of classroom autonomy for teachers (SOU 1948, no. 27, 15, 429, 431, 439). Secondly, the commission was reluctant to assign the central administration a significant role in the implementation of this aspect of the reform (ibid., 15, 431). It was outspokenly critical of the existing organization, as witnesses the following assessment:

only natural that school was marked by bureaucracy. The organizational strictures and rigidities that still characterize the school system were established in this period. . . . Democratic society has inherited bureaucratism from the days of the civil-servant state. In the educational sphere, as in other spheres of society, democracy must free itself from the fetters of bureaucracy. As far as school is concerned, this would seem to require greater lay influence and decentralization. (SOU 1948, no. 27, 2, 16)

The limited active contribution expected from the SÖ is evident from the exhortation that the school authorities "must feel obliged to encourage educational experiments regardless of whether they agree with the teacher about the best approach in a particular case." While the SÖ should "follow and inspire spontaneous experiments," it was not to take the initiative (SOU 1948, no. 27, 88–89). The report also argued that pilot projects with comprehensive schools required changes in the composition of the SÖ staff (ibid., 431). It was not even certain that the central body for supervising the reform should be incorporated into the SÖ (ibid., 101; cf. Prop. 1950, no. 70, 365). It is safe to say, I believe, that the commission drafting the reform plans distrusted the national school authority.

When the comprehensive school was initiated on a trial basis, moreover, this was done not by the central administrative agency but directly by the commission. As Marklund notes, this remarkable step can be explained by the direct link between the commission and the government, coupled with a desire among leading members of the commission to present the Riksdag and the SÖ with a fait accompli—the comprehensive school in action (Arvidson, interview). The anticipated resistance from the SÖ presumably influenced the government and the commission to bypass the agency with the initial trials. Marklund, who had been a department head at the SÖ, comments:

It is hardly surprising that the formally competent civil servants at the SÖ found this rather extraordinary. It may also help to explain the dissonance that the course of events gave rise to between the School Commission as the maker of policy and the SÖ as the supreme executive body. Ought the SÖ to give way to the Commission or not? . . . The head start that the trial stole as a result of this understanding between the government and the Commission left the SÖ nowhere. (Marklund 1981, 18, 20; cf. 28–29)

The SÖ publicly expressed displeasure at being thus ignored by the commission (ibid., 28–32). Considering that the SÖ must have perceived the commission as to some extent an extension of the government, the matter probably helped to sour relations between the agency and the government even before the reform began in earnest.

The bourgeois opposition, unlike the leading Social Democratic politicians in this field, favored putting the SÖ in charge of the trial comprehensive school. When the Riksdag debated the introduction of this system in 1950, a Liberal representative observed: "The reason why, with regard to these matters, one can look to the future with confidence is the fact that both the standing committee and the government have proposed that the results of the trial shall be assessed by the SÖ. Here we have an objective, competent body in which we have every reason to place the greatest confidence" (AK 1950, no. 23, 8). A Conservative representative voiced a similar opinion (ibid., 25).

In its comments on the report, the SÖ strongly criticized the commission's analysis of existing educational activities. In particular, the description of the common teaching methods was said to be unduly negative. The SÖ was also very skeptical of the individualized approach that the commission had recommended as an alternative to prevailing authoritarian practices (SOU 1949, no. 35, 11–44, 44, 105). Furthermore, the SÖ opposed the idea of undifferentiated teaching up to the ninth grade. In this debate, which subsequently became very heated, both the SÖ and a virtually unanimous opinion among grammar schools called for an earlier differentiation of pupils (SOU 1949, no. 35, 10, 29–30, 35, 40; cf. Marklund 1982).

The bill presented to the Riksdag in 1950 was drafted from the commission's report (Marklund 1980, 135). The government proposed that the comprehensive school be the subject of a ten-year trial period; further comprehensivization would then proceed "*to the extent*" the trial showed this was appropriate. A further complication was that the standing committee provided no clear definition of the Swedish term *enhetsskola* (which is generally translated as "comprehensive school," but which also denotes a "unified educational system") (Marklund 1980, 216–23; 1985, 37–40; Richardson 1967). The director-general of the SÖ from 1948 to 1964, Nils Gustav Rosén, asserts that these ambiguities posed a considerable problem for the agency in interpreting the government's intentions. Indeed, uncertainty as to whether or not a comprehensive school system would be introduced at all persisted until 1956 (Rosén, interview; Marklund 1980, 230–31; cf. Marklund 1985, 37–40).

The final decision to adopt the new school system was taken by the Riksdag in 1962. As a result of the pilot program, however, roughly every second pupil in the country was already attending some form of comprehensive school by 1960 (Marklund 1984, 43). The control of educational content that was adopted involved considerable ambiguities as well, not unlike those connected with the initiation of the trial. The political compromise of 1960 regulated in considerable detail the principles for differentiating pupils and for allocating teaching time between different compulsory and optional subjects; at the same time, however, it stressed the importance of leaving individual teachers free to arrange their work (Prop. 1962, no. 54, 42–43, 270). It is remarkable that, while the reform's prospects depended so heavily on changes in teaching methods, very little was done to achieve any such changes.

The government was, contrary to the School Commission's recommendations, very vague about the new school's general objectives. The instrument (the curriculum) by which teaching methods were to be changed was not specified in any detail.[4] The objectives were formulated in much the same terms as the compromise from 1950, allowing a variety of interpretations and serving to dampen conflicts (SOU 1988, no. 20, 9–10; cf. Marklund 1982, 60; Svingby 1981, 57). Commenting on the new system's first curriculum, Svingby adds: "the ideology expressed in the general sections does not permeate the specific instructions"; much the same could be said of the second curriculum, from 1969 (1981, 193).

The 1957 School Committee also adhered to the principle established by the 1946 commission, declaring that "the implementation of the curriculum in daily schoolwork is to be a matter for the individual teacher" (Marklund 1982, 79; cf. Hagelin 1968, 117). Obviously, the policy makers hoped to avoid souring the teachers on the reform proposals by guaranteeing them full discretion in classroom practice. This stands, on the other hand, in stark contrast to the weight the commission originally put on the need to change teaching methods.

At the same time, the *rules* of the school organization were laid down by the government in considerable detail. Virtually everything not having to do with the reform's main objectives or with teaching as such was precisely specified. These detailed rules concerned the regional and local organization, as well as the SÖ (SOU 1988, no. 20, 9–10). The explanation for this may be that the 1957 committee, in accordance with the terms of reference issued by the minister of education, concentrated on the external organization of the new school system, rather than on its objectives and methods (Marklund 1982, 20–22, 75). According to Lundgren, "Swedish education policy in the postwar period focused on the issue of differentiation and on organizational issues, while the essential questions concerning the organization and function of the curriculum were left to experts and administrators" (1979, 110).

The 1962 Education Act and, above all, the school statute from the same year were full of detailed regulations. The 1970 Education Act ran to sixteen printed pages, and the statute for compulsory education to more than 130 pages (*Skollag och skolstadga* 1971). The code of statutes published annually by the SÖ from 1962 onward, which Boucher described as a "bible" for the administration of the school system, came to almost 1,500 pages in the 1969–70 edition (Boucher 1982, 46). The bill presented in 1976 on internal schoolwork noted that "its organization is regulated in even greater detail than is the content of teaching" (Prop. 1975–76, no. 39, 9; cf. 221). In sum, while policy markets found no way to induce changes in teaching methods (Hadenius 1990, 170), they regulated almost everything else in the school system in a traditional bureaucratic manner.

As shown in chapter 5, the SÖ was a very divided organization. In order to overcome the SÖ's divisions in the late 1940s, when the reforms began, the new director-general (Nils Gustav Rosén) requested an organizational inquiry from the government. It was clear to him that the school reform could not be accomplished as long as the SÖ was ideologically as well as organizationally divided, with one side favoring elementary schools and the other favoring grammar schools (Rosén, interview).

As a result of this inquiry, the SÖ was organized instead by function, with separate departments for educational issues at all school levels, for trial activities, for organizational matters, and for administrative questions. The agency's governing board continued, however, to consist of civil servants, albeit now augmented by two lay representatives (SOU 1951, no. 29; Prop. 1952, no. 129). Yet in spite of this new arrangement, educational and organizational issues were still subdivided according to school type, though now at a lower administrative level (Marklund 1979, 48).

It is thus doubtful that the agency's reorganization resulted in the desired unity. In the 1960s at least, there were still leading officials who actively resisted the school reform (interviews 0, 10, 12, 16, and 25). The SÖ did present a united front in regard to the design for a comprehensive school proposed by the 1957 School Committee, but this may have had to do with the proposal's compromise character and great political significance—these made it difficult for anyone in the SÖ to oppose it. In addition, Rosén went to unusual lengths to unite the agency:

When it came to major matters of principle, I saw to it that we had frequent meetings and said that we would continue until we were in agreement. I went so far as to call for evening and night sessions if necessary. I did this so as to reach agreement just in order to break down that antipathy between the elementary school people and the grammar school side. (Rosén, interview)

Such centrally placed persons as Ragnar Edenman, Hans Löwbeer, and Sixten Marklund have all testified to Rosén's skill in this respect. The latter said also that Edenman, as minister of education and ecclesiastical affairs, was greatly surprised when he managed to persuade the SÖ to support the compromise over the structure of the comprehensive school. The deputy director-general actually resigned in protest over the school reform, according to Marklund.

Even after the formal establishment of the comprehensive school in 1962, there were still major conflicts between the SÖ's departments in regard to policy issues (Isling and Ulvhammar, interviews; Svingby 1981). Documentary evidence of these differences is unfortunately hard to come by, however, since the records do not contain any minutes or notes from the weekly meetings by means of which the agency was largely managed (after its governing board had been transformed in 1964 to represent interested parties, [SOU 1974, no. 36, 227]).

The SÖ was reorganized once more in 1964. It came now to incorporate the National Board of Vocational Education (KÖY, Sw. Kungliga Överstyrelsen för Yrkesutbildning), and the composition of its governing board was changed and would now consist of representatives of the parties on the labor market and other interest groups. In that the comprehensive school and the subsequent reform of secondary education meant that theoretical and practical education would be now undertaken in a common organization, it was deemed appropriate to dispense with the organizational division into two central agencies dating from 1943. The inquiry had been conducted by Hans Löwbeer, who served first as under secretary of state at the Ministry of Education and Ecclesiastical Affairs, and then as director-general of the new agency from 1964 to 1969. An interview with him included the following exchange:

*Bo Rothstein:* As regards the reorganization for which you were responsible in 1964, when you merged the SÖ and the KÖY, were there any other reasons for this apart from putting regular education and vocational education on the same footing?

*Hans Löwbeer:* We wanted an efficient agency in order to achieve the school reform. Moreover, the former tasks of the KÖY would no longer exist in that compulsory education was extended to nine years. The KÖY was, as you know, strongly against both the merger and the new school. We saw the merger as a means of gaining control over the KÖY.

*B. R.:* In fact, it was not just a simple merger but an entirely new agency. A look at the official yearbook suggests that a number of senior officials really disappeared down the hierarchy.

*H. L.:* Yes, they did, many lost their headships. It was very troublesome and not exactly easy to do.

*B. R.:* What were your criteria for senior positions?

*H. L.:* Only competence, we wanted an agency that was unified and efficient. An efficient civil servant is also a loyal civil servant.

*B. R.:* How successful was the merger?

*H. L.:* It was a meeting of two different agency cultures. The KÖY was sluggish, highly conservative. The director-general was good but there were troublesome people under him.

*B. R.:* What is agency culture?

*H. L.:* A particular spirit, a working style, a way of communicating internally.

*B. R.:* Was the merger successful?

*H. L.:* It took time. We had trouble with some small pockets of KÖY people. We did not achieve unity there until the end of my time as director-general.

There is no reason to suppose that the 1965 merger made the agency more united or strengthened its ideological cohesion. The SÖ/KÖY dichotomy still existed inside the agency in 1971, according to a report issued by the Agency for Administrative Development (Statskontoret 1985, 47).[5]

A specific instance of the policy division within the SÖ is provided by the rise and fall of the MUT project ("Goal determination and evaluation"). Initiated as a major project in the early 1970s, it grew into the dominant project at the agency. The aim was to specify both the general and the specific curriculum objectives down to the level of the individual lesson, as a way of integrating them in the teaching situation. Education would be controlled via the specification of objectives rather than by detailed organizational rules (Svingby 1981, 150). The project leaders saw the project as a way of promoting the implementation of the reform objectives laid down by the Riksdag and the government. The primary concern was to integrate the general curriculum objectives—the basic ideology behind the school reform, in other words—with the specific subject matter.

This was the first time the SÖ tried on a large scale to change teaching methods in the Swedish school system in the direction proposed by the School Commission in 1948 (Isling 1975; cf. Svingby 1981). In March 1975, however, the project was unexpectedly dropped, whereupon its leader, Åke Isling, the person next to the director-general in the hierarchy, protested by resigning from the SÖ. Considering the scope of the project and the importance attached to it only recently by the SÖ, this turnaround was remarkable (cf. SOU 1974, no. 36, 78–79).

What happened briefly, was the following: The reversal began, according to Isling, when the leaders of the project presented a catalogue of problems at a press conference in 1973. They stated that the new school had encountered difficulty so far in attaining the curriculum objectives, particularly those concerning teaching methods and classroom practice (which had been so important for the reform's planners). The project leaders dwelt especially on the difficulty of infusing practical work in the classroom with the overarching educational ideal of individualization (Isling 1975).

In November 1974, however, a newspaper campaign began which accused the project of seeking to regulate teaching in detail. The matter was raised in the Riksdag by members of the nonsocialist parties. When the standing committee broached the issue in February 1975, Director-General Jonas Orring and Åke Isling were interrogated, and both declared that the project would proceed according to plan (RD utbildningsutskottet 1975, no. 11). Less than a month later, however, Minister of Education Lena Hjelm-Wallén, replying to a question in the Riksdag, announced that the project would be greatly curtailed (RD 1975, no. 29, 20–23). This meant in practice that it would be closed down.

The minister's reply had been drafted by Director-General Orring, in his capacity as an expert at the Ministry of Education. (The draft, bearing his name, is among his other papers.) In a personal covering letter to the minister, Orring mentioned that he had drafted the answer in person (this would have been done by an assistant in the usual case), and that it had caused him "much agony and a great deal of trouble." His decision to close down the project had been preceded by lengthy discussions at the regular weekly meeting of senior officials, and the "enclosed draft can also be said to represent the opinion of most of my closest colleagues." The reasons he gave for the closure included the following:

I also believe that, in view of the growth of this project—also within the agency—and the way in which it has come to be scrutinized by public opinion, it is likely to be necessary to undertake an operation of the kind I indicate here sooner or later. It is then no doubt better not to postpone the measure any longer than necessary. (SNA, SÖ archives, Jonas Orring's documents, letter 02–18–75)

In the ensuing debate, the minister also admitted that the SÖ was not unified over the value of the project (RD 1975, no. 29, 31). There is no space here for a detailed account of the complicated political events leading to the demise of the project. Nor is this necessary in order to draw the conclusion that, in 1975, the SÖ's management was profoundly divided over the crucial issue of how to control the content of teaching methods. It is clear that the termination of the project did away with the possibility of changing the organization's operational logic from one of formal to one of *substantive* rationality, from management by precise rules to direction by means of objectives (Svingby 1981, 150).

The conclusion to be drawn from the fate of this large-scale project is, I believe, the following: because of the lack of ideological unity within the SÖ concerning how to achieve the goals of the school reform, and on account of the lack of political support from the Social Democratic government, the SÖ had to drop its ambitions to influence classroom practice in the way recommended by the reform's planners.

The SÖ lacked, then, the peculiar strengths of the cadre organization, with its substantive rationality and direction according to ideological objectives. This may be seen in the relations between the central and regional levels of the school administration. For an agency responsible for implementing a "socially invasive" reform, the management's relations with the lower levels—those responsible for day-to-day operations—are of course of the greatest importance. It should be noted that, up to 1958, the school administration's regional body was the church diocese. The concept of a unified school administration was therefore not applicable before that. The question is whether organizational unity was established after the county boards of education had been set up. Former Director-General Nils Gustav Rosén had this to say on the matter:

*Bo Rothstein:* Were the county boards of education an SÖ initiative?
*Nils Gustav Rosén:* No, I think not.
*B. R.:* What sort of relation existed between the SÖ and the county boards of education?
*N.G.R.:* We had annual meetings, very valuable, with their predecessors, the elementary school inspectors. With the county boards of education they were less frequent, they were not so productive.

*B. R.:* Can one see the county boards of education as the long arm of the SÖ in the field?

*N.G.R.:* No.

*B. R.:* Did the SÖ control them directly in any way?

*N.G.R.:* No, not in the sense that we instructed the county boards of education to do this or that. They were fairly independent of the SÖ. They set store by their independence too.

That these relations with the county education boards were less than adequate was one of the criticisms made by the National Audit Bureau in a 1971 report on the SÖ. The report averred that the SÖ did not support regional planning, that it played a limited role as the supreme authority, and that some county boards had a rather secondary existence in the school system (RRV 1971). Commenting on the report, the SÖ admitted to not performing as the supreme authority but contested the other criticisms, claiming to have close, daily contacts with the boards and arguing that they played a very important role in the school system (SNA, SÖ archives, dnr 6403/71 A). The fact remains, however, that in a private letter to the agency's head of information in 1977, the director-general wrote:

At the latest managerial meeting someone also raised the question of relations between the SÖ and the county education boards, the gist being that they were not particularly good. It was said at the meeting that the SÖ came in for a fair amount of criticism from the boards around the country.

He also mentioned the differences of opinion over the position of the boards in relation to the SÖ and asked whether "the boards are to be as at present *or* more decidedly regional units of the SÖ? The long arm of the SÖ in the field?" (SNA, SÖ archives, Jonas Orring's documents, letter 04–11–77, italics in original). Some dissatisfaction over the links with the county education boards was also evident in the SÖ's comments on a report from the 1973 inquiry about these boards (SOU 1973, no. 48). The agency emphasized that it wanted to have the county school inspectorate as its regional body and thought "one way of further emphasizing this relationship would be to amplify the standing instructions for the SÖ with a clause to the effect that the county education inspectorate is subordinate to the SÖ (*cf. the labor market board and the county labor boards*)" (SNA, SÖ archives, Dnr. A 73, 11710; italics mine). The SÖ management was evidently somewhat envious of the regional facilities at the disposal of the Labor Market Board. In sum, even if the

SÖ had had an explicit ideology concerning how to implement the school reform, the organization would have failed to convey it to the regional level.

Some comments are in order, finally, on the part played by local school managements in the formal chain of command. It is in this context remarkable that the statutes regulating the responsibilities of school principals in the 1970s exhibited a historical continuity back to 1694! As one scholar argues, periods of liberalism or radicalism in Swedish history have left little trace in these standing instructions (Axelsson 1974, 264). Nor was the introduction of the comprehensive school accompanied by any marked change in school statutes or curricula as regards the government view of the role of local school managements (Stålhammar 1984, 30).

The principals of Swedish comprehensive schools face, according to Stålhammar, the conflicts inherent in the choice between acting primarily as an interpreter of rules in a bureaucratic organization *or* as an educational leader in accordance with the content objectives expressed in the curriculum. According to Stålhammar, school principals have been largely accustomed to functioning in a bureaucratic way—that is, they have seen themselves as primarily responsible for implementing statutory regulations. Formal rationality has been their operative criterion (ibid., 64–65; cf. Stålhammar and Wennås 1975). They have had no influence over who worked in their schools and very little over resource allocation.

Stålhammar's empirical studies support the hypothesis that a majority of school principals in the Swedish school system have seen themselves mainly as administrators of a bureaucratic system of rules, not as educational leaders and innovators (Stålhammar 1984, 100–101, 133–37, 145–47, 255–56). He also found that the curriculum, particularly the general section containing the ideas of individualization and urging changes in classroom practices—the *explicit ideology* of the school reform, that is—had not been significant as an instrument for influencing school principals in their daily work: "The values that a principal decides to promote seem to have more to do with the individual's value system than with a deliberate interpretation of the curriculum" (ibid., 181).

The lack of *ideological commitment* on the part of the SÖ to the goals of the school reform is also evident in the publications by means of which the SÖ "marketed" the reform. In this material, there is absolutely no mention of the general theme of social change as a goal of the reform. The emphasis was instead on the organizational consequences for the individual pupil. It seems that the reform's ideological aspects, having already been diluted during the process of enactment by the *Riksdag,* were further attenuated when the SÖ presented the reform to the general public. Instead of being described as an active political break with the old system of parallel schools, the reform was presented as an evolutionary process arising out of the development of society in general (*Skolöverstyrelsens skriftserie* no. 15, 30, 59, 61).

One of the few people to have been a member of the governing board of both the SÖ and the AMS is Bertil Östergren, a former chairman of the Confederation of Professional Associations (SACO). According to him, the management and senior staff at the SÖ regarded themselves—unlike the leadership of the AMS—as primarily civil servants in the classical sense. As a result, the agency largely lacked a policy of its own. It was inclined rather to be "more faithful to the government than the government itself" (Östergren, interview). In another interview, moreover, Birgitta Ulvhammar, who had been deputy director-general under Director-General Jonas Orring, described the agency as very divided over policy; she said further that the management had difficulty establishing a common ideology concerning the school reform even among its own advisory officers.

It is difficult to measure precisely the extent to which the implementation process was affected by the SÖ's lack of ideological unity and outwardly directed *persuasive* activity à la AMS. Some research has indicated, however, that such activities are a very important ingredient of successful policy implementation in the area of educational reform. A comparative study of two federal agencies' implementation of equal educational opportunity policy in the American school system has identified two factors as crucial for achieving policy objectives: the degree to which the agency in question supports the policy objective and the extent of the agency's determination to direct policy content (Bullock 1981).[6]

## Personnel

In the system of parallel schools which the comprehensive school replaced, teachers' recruitment and training had been strictly segregated according to school type. In the late 1940s, when the reform was begun, grammar school teachers had a university training and were appointed as civil servants by the government, after having been nominated by the SÖ in accordance with a strict system based on *formal merit*. Elementary school teachers, on the other hand, attended separate training colleges and were appointed as municipal employees. The system involved a combination of merit and selection according to personal suitability, the municipal school board being entitled to choose between the three candidates with the highest formal qualifications (SOU 1955, no. 31, 397–401).

In the reformed school system, these disparate and partly hostile groups of teachers would work together in a comprehensive nine-year school. In its report from 1948, therefore, the commission urged the elimination of disparities between the teacher categories. In the new school system, there would be equivalent rules for recruitment and employment and joint training for all teachers. A new type of teacher training college was proposed for this purpose (SOU 1948, no. 27, 377–78, 403). As for appointments, the commission expressed "strong sympathy" for the idea that all teaching posts in comprehensive schools should be municipal appointments, along the same lines as previously for elementary schools. The reason given was that, "without the right to appoint the staff of municipal schools, the right of a municipality to determine its own school system would be illusory" (ibid., 436–37).

In order to guarantee this right, the commission recommended that the local school authorities not be confined by applicants' qualifications; appointments could be based on personal characteristics instead. To quote the report, "It can . . . hardly be reasonable to force a school district to accept a teacher whose good degree, normal service record, and long service admittedly make him formally superior to other applicants but who is in reality, or is considered by the school board to be, an indifferent teacher" (ibid., 436–37). Participation in voluntary adult education, for instance, was one type of merit that should count in an applicant's favor (ibid., 12). Such a procedure had encountered "weighty objections" within the commission, however, on the grounds that it could be abused (ibid., 436).

The secondary teachers' association, for its part, underscored "with great acerbity" that they were not prepared to relinquish their position as civil servants appointed by the state. Furthermore, "the constitutional principle that merit and skill are the only grounds for promotion is seen by the secondary teachers as one of their foremost assets, which they are not inclined to dispose of" (ibid., 48). During the Riksdag debate, it was claimed that more than four thousand signatures had been sent in from teachers in protest at the proposed municipal system of appointments (AK 1950, no. 28, 48). In the face of this opposition from the teachers, the government and Riksdag decided to shelve the matter, pending an inquiry (RD riksdagsskrivelse 1950, no. 404).

The proposal to establish new joint teacher training colleges for comprehensive schools, on the other hand, provoked little opposition. The government argued in the bill that "a teacher training system of the present type, which sorts the future teachers into different pens right from the start, would be an anachronism in a school system that specifically aims to overcome the division of the old system into separate educational pathways" (Prop. 1950, no. 219, 99).

The terms of reference for an inquiry into teacher appointments begun in 1951 and reporting in 1955 pointed out that, "as a matter of principle, a uniform procedure for appointing all comprehensive school teachers must be said to be close at hand," and that in the absence of "very weighty reasons," municipalities should not be deprived of the right to appoint teachers. Furthermore, "for a calm and harmonious development of the school system, it is of the utmost importance that this issue is resolved in a manner that is satisfactory and earns the confidence of different parties," and that the concept of a unified school system is not taken to such lengths that different appointment procedures cannot be considered even when strong reasons speak in their favor (SOU 1955, no. 31, 20–21). These terms of reference can clearly be said to reflect a government facing a classic dilemma.

The highly sensitive nature of the issue, for the political system in general and the teachers' unions in particular, is evident from the following passage in the report submitted by the inquiry:

Since the report from the School Commission on matters of principle, including proposals concerning the appointment of comprehensive school teachers, this matter has attracted conflicting interests, and it has become increasingly clear that a satisfactory solution is most important for the future of the school system. In its deliberations, the inquiry has attached the utmost importance to this circumstance and has attempted, as its most urgent task, to raise the issue to a factual level and to prevent a solution in one or the other direction from becoming a matter of general political or professional prestige. (SOU 1955, no. 31, 439)

The inquiry ultimately opted for a system of municipal appointments for teaching posts in the new comprehensive school, mainly on the same grounds as the School Commission had done. The inquiry further thought that impartiality could be assured by the scrutiny of teacher appointments by new state-county school boards (ibid., 439–41, 450).

The inquiry urged that the municipal school boards be entitled, when assessing applicants, to go beyond "purely formal" qualifications. The report particularly objected to the current system for recruiting grammar school teachers, in which formal merits were more or less decisive (ibid., 418). Yet the school boards should not be allowed to select applicants without any motivation either, as in the earlier system for elementary schools. In order to avoid a system of "automatic points" based solely on diplomas, degrees, and years of service, the report proposed that the boards also be able to consider "the need of a particular teaching competence in the municipality as well as . . . factors that can contribute to a better overall picture of the teacher" (ibid., 409, 442, 448, 493).

Factors that should be allowed to contribute to the overall picture of an applicant included "contributions to voluntary adult education, public positions of trust, and positions in associations" (ibid., 443). Finally, according to the report, the SÖ was to have no influence over the recruitment of teachers to the new school. Appointments by the municipal school boards could be appealed to the county education boards and from there directly to the government (ibid., 450).

In the ensuing bill submitted to the Riksdag in 1957, however, the government argued "that the proposals from the inquiry have not managed to resolve the conflicts of interest that have materialized in discussions around the issue of appointments ever since this was brought up by the 1948 report from the School Commission. The positions are still largely unchanged" (Prop. 1957, no. 61, 35–36). The Association of Local Authorities and the grammar school teachers' association criticized the proposal as well (albeit for opposite reasons). The former wished to retain the recruitment principle that had applied to teachers in the elementary school (ibid., 37), while the contrary view was taken by the grammar school teachers in words that, by Swedish standards, were exceedingly sharp:

The Association can find absolutely no way of accepting the proposed grounds for promotion, and explains that, for the Association, it is a definite condition that what the inquiry has proposed concerning the possibility, when appointing teachers and school principals, of heeding merits other than those directly connected with teacher training, be dropped (Prop. 1957, no. 61, 42).

The elementary school teachers were, as one might expect, largely in favor of the proposal, while the government generally opposed it, particularly that part of it concerning the system for ranking merits. The SÖ's submission even contained a "complete alternative" to the proposals of the inquiry: teachers would be appointed by the new regional government bodies, while municipalities would be able to express opinions about applicants. The SÖ also did not want the holding of positions of public trust or participation in voluntary associations to count as merits (ibid., 36–51).

The government largely followed the SÖ's recommendations as regards qualifications and the power of appointment (ibid., 63–64). The holding of positions of public confidence and participation in associations and organizations were accordingly rejected as merits, while contributions to adult education and youth leadership were to be recognized. A departure from the system of formal qualifications would be permitted, but only "when an applicant whose ranking is not unduly inferior has other merits that are substantial or there is documentary evidence that the aptitude of the applicant is appreciably greater than indicated by a diploma obtained earlier." The grammar school teachers, for their part, would be largely immune from departures from the ranking system: such deviations would, the government believed, primarily concern the appointment of teachers in the lower grades of the comprehensive school (ibid., 58).

The debate in the Riksdag elicited some interesting comments. The Liberal spokesman claimed that the cabinet (a coalition of Social Democrats and Agrarians) had agreed on the bill only after a partial crisis; this was not denied (AK 1957, no. 16, 9). The principal secretary of the 1946 School Commission, Stellan Arvidson, a Social Democrat, criticized the bill strongly and submitted a reservation in the standing committee. He protested that the government had reversed the commission's intentions in regard to municipal influence over the school system, and argued that the proposal would lead to formalism and red tape. Arvidson argued that the system of selecting one of three candidates enabled the local school boards to obtain informal information about the practical educational competence of the applicants. School boards were usually reluctant to commit such information to paper. The proposed system was deficient, according to Arvidson, because teaching competence could not be assessed objectively from written documents alone. The Riksdag approved the bill, however, and in this way the earlier principles for recruiting grammar school teachers were adopted for the future comprehensive school.

As regards teacher training, the changes proposed by the commission for the comprehensive school did not give rise to any innovations until the late 1960s. As pointed out in the Riksdag debate, when the first teachers trained specifically for the new school began to teach, two decades had passed since the comprehensive principle had been approved by the Riksdag in 1950 (AK 1967, no. 20, 54). The commission's proposal in 1948, to begin reforming teacher training in the existing school system, accordingly came to nothing (SOU 1948, no. 29, 498–500). Teacher training colleges were indeed established before the end of the 1960s, but they trained teachers only for the lower grades and did not have "the long-term perspective of the entire school reform" (SOU 1965, no. 29, 18; cf. Skog-Östlin 1984, 48; Erasmie and Marklund 1977, 6). The new comprehensive school system was divided into three levels: junior (grades 1–3), intermediate (4–6), and senior (7–9). Each level was staffed by teachers with completely different types of training; in this way, the earlier system of parallel schools was in practice largely retained in the new organization.

A new inquiry into teacher training was begun in 1960, at first just to tackle short-term organizational problems (the introduction of the comprehensive school had led to occasional acute shortages of teachers). After two years, however, the terms of reference were extended to include the long-term objectives and principles for teacher training for the new school (SOU 1965, no. 29, 32). When the inquiry was set up, attention was drawn to the lack of cohesion in the comprehensive school arising from differences in training and traditions among teachers. An awareness that the components of the reform had fallen into disarray is evident from the following: "As a result of the reform . . . the earlier system of parallel schools has been replaced by a unified educational system. But the corresponding thorough transformation of teacher training, whereby teachers are no longer trained for elementary school or grammar school, no longer for theoretical or practical schools, and no longer exclusively for either theoretical subjects, practical subjects or occupational subjects, has not yet taken place" (ibid., 16–17).

The work of the inquiry was transformed by the extension of its terms of reference in 1962. The new instructions emphasized that information about the objectives and societal function of the new school should feature prominently in future teacher training; "strong reasons" called for inserting these aspects at the beginning of the courses. The gulf between subject studies and practical educational training should be bridged by integrating the school reform's organizational features and *ideological goals* as well as the relevant instruction.

The main report, presented by the inquiry in 1965, pointed out that the objectives of the School Commission in regard to the equalization of social classes and a new type of schoolwork necessitated changes in the activities and methods of teachers as well. It was necessary, for instance, to "transform school work so that it can provide good conditions for the new categories of pupil: their interest must be caught and the work made meaningful to them" (ibid., 86–87). The report found, however, that very little had happened—particularly when it came to the individualization of teaching—in the seventeen years since the commission had published its findings (ibid., 79). The new teacher training would take care of this, however; a close study of the history and objectives of the school reform was envisaged for the teacher trainees, among other things because:

Without an insight into the circumstances that led up to the present situation, as well as the motives and values underlying the changes, the teacher will not be able to comprehend the nature of the task. . . . The external and internal organization of the school system is being changed, the nature of school work—for pupils as well as teachers—is changing, school work has acquired a new objective and teaching methods must be adapted accordingly. The teacher is personally responsible for continuing the transformation. If he is not familiar with the basic ideas behind the school reform, he will not be in a position to understand what is going on around him and will be liable to become negative and querulous. (ibid., 92)

Briefly, then, the report found that "a very marked shift in objectives" would be necessary in order to train teachers in accordance with the requirements of the new comprehensive school (ibid., 101). Clearly, this was a call for a change in the ideological orientation of the "street-level bureaucrats" of the Swedish school system.

Even so, the proposals amounted in principle to keeping the separate forms for teacher training at each three-year level of the nine-year system.[7] A reservation against this organizational separation was entered by Stellan Arvidson, who argued that teacher training for the lower levels would not attain a scientific standard, and that a danger existed of consolidating "the gap between subject teachers and class teachers that has existed for a long time but is quite unnecessary in today's and tomorrow's school" (SOU 1965, no. 29, 653–54). Subject teachers were the new label for the former university-trained grammar school teachers who now worked on the senior level of the comprehensive school, and who taught largely the same subjects as they had done in the old grammar school system. Class teachers were the former instructors at the elementary schools, who now in principle taught a class in almost every subject and worked on the lower levels (grades 1–6) of the comprehensive system.

The ensuing bill, presented to the Riksdag in 1967, departed from these proposals in important respects. It provided for "largely the same *teacher categories* as in the mentioned types of school today" (Prop. 1967, no. 4, 137). It also rejected the proposal to close down the training colleges for elementary school teachers and assemble all practical educational training at teacher training colleges in the university towns. The nine colleges of the former type would be retained, and would continue to provide training just for junior- and intermediate-level teachers, albeit in the same formal guise as the newer colleges (ibid., 228–31).

The bill met with the Riksdag's approval. In the standing committee, Stellan Arvidson and two other members (of whom one was also a Social Democrat) entered a reservation against a system in which the different teacher categories would still be trained separately (RD Statsutskottet 1967, no. 51). He argued in the ensuing debate that, "In that these training colleges are only for class teachers, there is evidence of the old dualism between class teachers and subject teachers—the dualism that we have tried to get rid of with the new school organization." He pointed in particular to the differences in social and other experience that would arise between subject teachers with their academic training on the one hand, and class teachers on the other, and noted that "the division does not accord with the spirit of the school reform and will obstruct cooperation across the three levels." He noted "somewhat bitterly" that, despite general agreement on the objective of bringing the different teacher categories together, support had not been forthcoming for his above-mentioned reservation. He feared the proposed system would threaten "the future of the school reform" (AK 1967, no. 70, 67–71). The standing committee's majority proposal was adopted by the Riksdag, however. The second chamber passed it by 156 votes to 31, and the first chamber without a vote (as the reservation entered by Arvidson and his two colleagues found no support) (AK 1967, no. 20, 90; FK 1967, no. 20, 81).

The bill did arouse some opposition elsewhere. For example, Torsten Husén, one of Sweden's most prominent scholars in the field of education and at the time a member of the teacher training inquiry, wrote articles and a booklet attacking the bill as a threat to the entire school reform, because the "system of parallel schools will be perpetuated in teacher training." The resultant dualism would create "differences of prestige between teacher categories in the comprehensive school." He also agreed with Arvidson that the comments on the inquiry's findings had expressed support for a divided teacher system, even while paying lip service—"benevolent platitudes"—to the school reform's overriding objectives (Husén 1966, 4–5; cf. Skolledaren 1967, 2). He concluded:

Those who seriously wish to realize the intentions behind the school reform—to replace the dualistic school system, a remnant of the class society, with a unified educational system—will arrive at a single reasonable solution: class teachers and subject teachers must be trained within one and the same organization. (Husén 1966)

Similar forebodings had been expressed by other researchers (cf. Marklund 1968, 123). It should be added that the inquiry's original proposal had been supported by the grammar school (i.e., the subject) Teachers' Federation (which was not always so favorably disposed to the school reform) and the Headmasters Association as well. The latter organization in particular agreed with Husén and Arvidson that the proposed system for teacher training would likely perpetuate parallel schools (Skolvärlden 1965, 18; 1965, 31; Skolledaren 1967, 2; cf. Marklund 1985, 277).

Concerning teacher appointments, the 1957 reform instituted a very strict ranking by points, in practice based exclusively on educational qualifications and years of service. Writing about teaching aptitude, a school researcher has this to say:

The regulations for assessing merit are followed meticulously as a rule. The total number of points, calculated according to detailed rules for each of the three grounds for promotion, have become the sole blessed criteria of suitability. Departures from them are extremely exceptional. It can even be argued that the regulations are consistently misinterpreted; the general rule, after all, is that the computed score is to serve only as a *main guide* and that the appointing authority is also to take unscored merits into account. Whether from timidity or only from a desire for consistency and order, the appointing authorities refrain from "having an opinion" or a "valuation" except in given quantities. As a result, the outcome may depend on differences on the order of two or three decimal places, even when the calculated merit is in the region of 100 points. A little quiet reflection suggests that this is a far cry from the original intention—a *factual* assessment— and amounts instead to a slavish obedience to numbers. (ibid., 176–77)

Where, finally, did the teachers as "street-level bureaucrats" stand in this process? As mentioned earlier, the 1946 School Commission held great hopes that individual teachers and school boards would be able to transform school activities in accordance with the educational ideas it had presented (Arvidson, interview). The comments on the report showed, however, that these ideas had not found favor with the great majority of teachers and school board members (Marklund 1980, 114–16; Munknäs 1983). The SÖ argued, for instance, that the commission's perception of the teachers in the new school "resembled an ideal vision floating on high rather than a human being" (SOU 1949, no. 35, 105). The central proposal—not to differentiate pupils until after the eighth grade—was opposed by a great majority of teaching staffs, which considered an earlier differentiation essential. Submissions were received from 234 teaching bodies at public grammar schools and municipal or private "higher" schools; only three favored late differentiation, while 213 were flatly against it. The teachers' unions were also opposed to or doubtful about such a late differentiation (Marklund 1980, 121–22).

The pilot projects initiated by the commission and approved by the Riksdag in 1950 did not alter attitudes toward differentiation even among those senior-level teachers at the schools concerned. A study by the SÖ showed that about three teachers in four preferred a parallel system at the senior level (ASÖ 1956, 1:28). The predominantly negative attitude of the grammar school teachers during the experiments with a comprehensive school gave cause for concern. Jonas Orring, for instance, at the time a senior official at the SÖ and subsequently its director-general, noted in a memorandum dated 04–22–56 that grammar school teachers as a group were disinclined to involve themselves in the trial:

On the contrary, there are numerous signs that they actively resist the implementation of the trial. Even where this must be regarded as entirely natural. A good illustration is the ongoing discussion about the comprehensive school at Hisingen in Göteborg, where, at a meeting to provide information, the incorporation of the lower grammar school into the senior-level organization is described by the head of a lower grammar school as treachery towards parents. There are many other similar examples. (SNA, SÖ archives, Jonas Orring's documents, letter 1953, 58)

The same memorandum expresses concern that the editorial line of the journal of the grammar school teachers' association was decidedly hostile to the reform. As the reform continued, moreover, the elementary school teachers tended to become more favorably disposed to the commission's proposals, while the grammar school teachers persisted in their unfriendly attitude.[8] Nor were the protests of the latter confined to commenting on the proposals. When the Riksdag was due to vote in 1962, each member received a petition signed by more than eleven thousand teachers opposing the construction of the senior level proposed in the bill (Marklund 1982, 72–73; 1985, 290–91). There were about thirteen thousand grammar school teachers at the time.

As indicated earlier, the government took an interest in teacher training at a relatively late stage in the process of reform. The Riksdag approved the introduction of the comprehensive school in 1956, while it was not until 1962 that the terms of reference were presented for an inquiry into teacher training. This inquiry examined trainees' attitudes to the school reform on behalf of the 1957 School Committee.

A questionnaire was distributed to all teacher trainees who were about to graduate. Their replies showed two interesting things: (1) the trainees were poorly informed, and (2) a clear majority of those destined to teach at the senior level preferred a school system with some form of selection. Most of these future senior-level teachers opposed the school reform as well. Fewer than 25 of 229 favored the comprehensive school, and more than 200 preferred the ordinary grammar school; as to which type of school they most wanted to avoid, about 140 said the comprehensive school. A summary of the findings noted that "an appreciable proportion of the senior-level teacher trainees seem to have been entirely disinclined to accept the fact that the lower grammar school is to be replaced by the comprehensive school." This study was done in 1959, three years after the introduction of the comprehensive school had been approved by the Riksdag (Marklund 1960).

When the 1957 School Committee was presented with the results of this study, they found it "shocking reading," according to Jonas Orring (SNA, SÖ archives, Jonas Orring's handl. korr inom och för skolberedningen—letter to Sixten Marklund 07–18–59). Another noteworthy finding of the study was that, the more these future teachers knew about the comprehensive school, the more favorable were their attitudes toward it (Marklund 1960).

The SÖ had also proposed in 1954 that pilot comprehensive school programs be linked to teacher training. The ensuing inquiry proposed in 1955 that six such trial schools be set up, but the SÖ opted for only four. By the time the bill was presented in 1957, the minister had concluded that he could recommend only one. One such school therefore opened, in 1958. By 1960, however, this school still had no direct organizational link to teacher training (Marklund 1960, 15–16; cf. Prop. 1957, no. 106). Future comprehensive school teachers, especially those who were to work as subject teachers, accordingly had virtually no opportunity to acquire practical experience of the comprehensive school during their teacher training. Their internship, which was a large part of their training, was thus mostly done in grammar school classes.

The government acted in a similar fashion when it came to the provision of extra training for teachers in connection with the school reform. Plainly, the new school would be staffed in the main by teachers drawn from the existing system of parallel schools. The 1946 School Commission had therefore underscored the importance of providing teachers further training—as a step in implementing the school reform—and the Riksdag's standing committee seconded this judgment in 1950, when the matter came up for parliamentary consideration (SOU 1948, no. 27, 422; RD Särskilda utskottet 1950, no. 4, 53). Eleven years passed, however, before the Riksdag received any proposals in this matter.

The SÖ also arranged its own inquiry in 1956 to assess the need for further teacher training in connection with the school reform. The report found that such training as had been undertaken to date was clearly insufficient, unsystematic, and based on outdated methods (Marklund 1960, 17). In the following year, the SÖ requested increased appropriations for further teacher training to match the comprehensive school reform that had just been approved; the government denied this request, however (Prop. 1959, no. 1, bil. 10, ht. 8, 417).

Writing in 1958, Director-General Nils Gustav Rosén deplored the propensity of the government "to underestimate the significance of further training for teachers," and declared that the SÖ would request greatly increased appropriations for this purpose (1958, 136). A division head of the SÖ put forward the same argument a couple of years later (Brevner 1962).

Both Rosén and the under secretary of state at the Ministry of Education at the time (Hans Löwbeer) have stated that, despite the urging of the SÖ, the government was unduly restrained and tardy in funding further training, and this made it difficult to implement the school reform (Löwbeer and Rosén, interviews). It was not until the SÖ "with greater emphasis had declared the necessity of expanding and stepping up further training" that appropriations were increased markedly—in the 1961 budget. In putting his case, the minister of education (Ragnar Edenman) commented somewhat bitterly: "Experience shows that just the need for information on fundamental facts about the coming school reform is very great, even among those whose daily work is in the field of education." It was only in 1962, moreover, that funds for further training were provided on the scale that the SÖ had requested for 1958 (Prop. 1962, no. 1, bil. 10, 8 ht:653).

It may be asked whether the drive for further training strengthened teachers' ideological support for the school reform. Available studies suggest, however, that active teachers perceived the content of the further training as largely irrelevant to their work in school (Marklund and Eklund 1976). In 1974, the National Audit Bureau evaluated a program for further teacher training that had been designed by the SÖ. The program was intended to help teachers work more in accordance with the intentions of the curriculum regarding pupils' independent activities and cooperation. The bureau concluded that it doubted this objective had been attained (Gran 1977, 85).

The SÖ arranged further training for school principals as well, during the second half of the 1960s. By 1973, however, only 320 of more than two thousand principals of comprehensive schools had taken this training (SOU 1974, no. 53, 783). According to a report submitted to the SÖ's educational council, "No systematic attempts to direct school work with the aid of further training" were made until the mid-1970s; moreover, some county boards of education opposed further training for school principals (Sandkull 1981).

One may also inquire as to whether the new teacher training changed the opinions of subject teacher trainees as regards the school reform. According to a research survey, however, these trainees had been only weakly disposed toward the teaching profession when they entered university; it was their chosen academic subject itself, rather, that had interested them the most (Gran 1977, 22, 56). If this survey is any indication, then, there is little reason to suppose that the system of recruitment and training generated teacher support for the school reform's objectives.

Nor is there anything to suggest that the attitudes of future senior-level teachers were significantly influenced by the provision of a further year of training. According to a 1977 study, the attitudes of subject teacher trainees underwent an "undesirable" change (in relation to the school reform) over the course of their training (Erasmie and Marklund 1977; cf. SOU 1978, no. 86, 69). According to another report, "One of the major problems in subject teacher training is how to attain the overriding objectives. There has been an excessive concentration on subject matter, and the trainees have completed their university courses without coming into contact with the school curricula and their overriding objectives" (Christoffersson 1977, 10). It seems reasonable therefore to assume that socialization through training was rather weak in the school administration.

Some comments are in order, finally, on the subject of staff socialization through the career system. The 1946 School Commission proposed that the new school establish posts for senior teachers. These department heads would not be appointed on the basis of "formal qualifications," but primarily for their personal and educational qualities. Recruitment would be facilitated by the expansion of the central inspectorate. These senior teachers would be responsible for keeping abreast of educational research, and would serve as a link between the school management and the rest of the staff, "furnishing other teachers, particularly those who are younger and less experienced" with information and advice (SOU 1948, no. 27,

378–79). The importance the commission attached to this method of management is evident from the following passage:

In the opinion of the commission, a general implementation of the institution of the senior teacher—besides creating considerably greater opportunities for promotion for teachers and thereby stimulating recruitment to the profession—will be highly important for the development of the Swedish school. There is an inestimable value in providing each level of every school of any size with one or more teachers whose responsibilities specifically require them to keep up to date with educational development and to bring new ideas to fruition in everyday work in school. (ibid., 379)

The concrete result of the reform, however, was far from the proposed central control of promotion. Instead, senior teachers were nominated by the school principals and appointed by the municipal education boards (*Skolöverstyrelsens författningsbok* 1969–70, 567). School principals in turn were usually recruited internally, in that teachers were first invited to assist with administrative matters or appointed as deputies (Stålhammar 1984, 130–32; cf. SOU 1980, no. 19, 51–54). There seems to have been no national, regional, or even municipal policy in this area (Ekholm and Lagervall 1983, 8; cf. SOU 1980, no. 19, 49–50; 1974, 53:784; Munknäs 1981, 156).

As shown above, the reform's advocates had held high hopes about the possibility of changing the school system's internal workings and teaching methods. These hopes have not come to fruition, as is evident from the quote below. Minister of Education Hjelm-Wallén spoke these words three decades after the School Commission's establishment in 1946, in her opening address to the Riksdag in connection with the bill on the internal workings of the comprehensive school (RD 1975–76, no. 134, 28).

Bringing about change in teaching, the internal work, has been considerably more difficult than changing the external structure. We have learnt that such changes take time. It is often a matter of altering attitudes and values either inherited from older school systems or current because traditional ways of teaching have never been questioned. This is not a criticism of those whose valuable efforts are carrying our school forward. But together with many practical problems, it does explain the tension between highly ambitious policy decisions and reality in school.

This failure to achieve the policy objective of changing concrete practice in the classroom—which the commission had considered the central objective of the school reform—is confirmed by research. This is particularly true of the efforts to individualize teaching. Studies from the early 1970s show that teaching in the comprehensive schools took a predominantly traditional form, without adaptation to the individual student (Callewaert and Nilsson 1974, 1980; Torper 1982; SOU 1974, no. 53, 325). It has even been claimed that "school work contributes, analyses show, to the internalization of values other than those expressed in official documents" (Svingby 1977, 20; cf. SOU 1988, no. 20, 9–10). It has also been reported that, throughout the period of experiments and reforms, a majority of senior-level teachers and their associations had little sympathy for the commission's basic concept of individualized instruction within the framework of an undifferentiated school (Marklund 1985, 273; 1981, 293; 1982, 386; cf. Munknäs 1983, 33–43).

This is not to say the school reform would have been more successful had schoolwork been changed in accordance with the intentions of the 1946 School Commission and the general sections of the curriculum. This educational problem does not concern us here. The failure to achieve the desired change in this respect may have been the consequence of inadequate funding (cf. Lundgren 1979, 120). It is clear, however, that the educational instrument considered to be of greatest importance in achieving the reform never came into general use. The Social Democratic government appointed a major inquiry in 1971 to analyze the problems encountered in implementing the school reform. Its main report stated that:

Swedish schools today are well staffed, and the utilization of these resources is regulated in detail in statutes and instructions that are the same for all school facilities. Schools are above all directed not by objectives and the training of staff and principals, but by detailed rules that largely specify how the resources are to be used, irrespective of changes in the school environment and regardless of the social problems that are topical in a particular school. The answer to how a school should act is to be found in statutes, curricula and standing instructions. This probably weakens initiative and interest among school managers and staff in following up results. This is a system which scarcely makes use of the commitment and constructive capability of the schools themselves. (SOU 1974, no. 53, 93)

I want to stress that individual teachers may well have been extremely capable and committed to the objectives of the school reform as well. My point is simply that the organizational conditions under which they worked prevented them from achieving such objectives.

## Funding

In principle, the 1946 School Commission thought it appropriate that funds for the new school be provided mainly by the national government. If the municipalities were burdened with this expenditure, the commission feared, the reform would be "unpopular and opposed" in many localities. The government grants should be subject to a system of *universal rules,* so that the government would have no discretionary power to direct educational activities via the provision of funds (SOU 1948, no. 29, 429). The trials of the 1950s provided some room for discretion, however, as the state decided where the pilot comprehensive schools would be placed.

The system of government grants for compulsory education applied during the period studied here was established in 1957. This system, which was marked by detailed regulations and automatic cost reimbursement, served to distribute funds uniformly throughout the country. The system of grants for the new school, as a ministerial study pointed out in 1977, set no new trend in the central management of the school system. Rather, it was a product of tradition. Alternative ways of allocating funds were not discussed. The study noted that "the present system of government grants is not to any appreciable extent an instrument for directing the planning of education or its scale and national distribution" (Ds. U 1977, no. 8, 7–8; cf. SOU 1988, no. 20, 9). Another government inquiry from 1975 called attention to the discrepancy between the government's objectives for compulsory education and the detailed and automatic system of funding (SOU 1975, no. 9, 31).

With this grant system, no uniform financial planning linked the SÖ and the regional boards of education on the one hand, and the municipalities on the other. Only in very special instances was it possible, for example, to assign teachers to specific schools or municipalities—that is, to allocate funds as circumstances required (SOU 1974, no. 216, 194–216). The system was based on the notion that the circumstances surrounding the operation of schools were fully *predictable.* The grant system's automatic nature (i.e., its *formal rationality*) granted local school boards "very limited" powers to redistribute funds in favor of schools with special educational and social problems (SOU 1975, no. 9, 28–29, 31). The separate units of the school administration were in principle funded without any mutual coordination. We may reasonably conclude, then, that the government was in no position to promote the objectives of school policy by means of financial management.

These *universal rules* greatly restricted the ability of the leadership of the school administration to direct the lower levels by means of appropriations. Automatic provisions laid down by the government and/or Riksdag governed about 90 percent of the state's disbursements to the school system. There was virtually no way for the SÖ or the county education boards to direct the flow of funds to particular schools or activities deemed to be especially deserving or in particular need (SOU 1975, no. 9, 18–19). Little use was made of the provisions for obtaining supplementary funds outside the automatic system (see the ASÖ's special issue 1965, 75 "*Skolväsendet*" with a summary of the SÖ's budget requests). This left even less room for central and regional bodies to influence the financial resources of the individual schools. The difficulty of directing the comprehensive school system by means of appropriations is indicated by the following comments from the National Audit Bureau in 1976:

The government appropriations for the school system—the comprehensive school and the secondary school—are not derived from *budgeting based on the activity.* A link is lacking between municipal planning and budgeting (along with regional decisions in the state organization) on the one hand, and government budget work on the other. The central estimates, prepared by the SÖ and scrutinized by the Ministry of Education, start in the main from assessments and data of a general nature concerning the school system—that is, from a theoretical school organization with no real feedback from activities on the ground. . . . The only link to the expenditure of earlier years is the material based on survey data concerning municipal requests for government grants *before* scrutiny by the county education boards. The subsequent organizational decisions of the boards are not considered. (RRV 1976)

In a 1971 report, the National Audit Bureau had noted the SÖ's lack of control over the funds assigned by the government to the school system; the bureau claimed, moreover, that the agency monitored resource utilization poorly. The insufficient links between the SÖ and the county education boards were noted in particular (RRV 1971). The SÖ rebutted this criticism—especially the perception of the SÖ as a form of isolated central organization without links downward in the school system—in no uncertain terms. The SÖ stressed that its ability to influence appropriations to subordinate authorities was severely limited, by both the detailed nature of the appropriations system and the autonomy of local government (SNA, SÖ archives, dnr 6 403/71 A).

## Organizational Connection Two: A Last Comment

Before turning to the next chapter's concluding comparative analysis, I would like to stress two points. The first has to do with the nature of bureaucratic organization and its relation to schools. Why do bureaucracy and schooling make such a difficult pair? One answer, provided by John Chubb and Terry Moe in a recent analysis of the American school system, is that good schools need autonomy most of all. For without autonomy, it is difficult to create the dedication to a common goal among school staff that is the condition of good performance. Yet

> All public authorities, in seeking to impose higher-order values on schools—values that many in society, including many in the schools, may not embrace—face serious control problems that are endemic to the larger democratic "organization" in which they are forced to operate. They cannot solve these problems by granting the schools lots of discretion. Discretion is the very source of their problems. The best means of ensuring that their values get implemented is to engineer the schools' behavior through formal constraints—to bureaucratize. From a technical standpoint, of course, this is far from ideal. Given the "bottom-heavy technology" of education and the measurement problems inherent in trying to control it, bureaucracy is a clumsy and ineffective way of providing people with educational services. (Chubb and Moe 1990, 41)

The conclusion to be drawn is that school reformers face a difficult dilemma. They need to direct the school system, yet direction—at least of the traditional bureaucratic sort—creates more problems than it solves (cf. Ruther et al. 1979).

The second point I wish to make has to do with political legacies and "destined pathways." These concepts have been developed mainly for understanding the development of policies. Yet I believe the analysis above shows that, in addition to policy legacies, one must consider *organizational* legacies as well.

# 8. Summary and Conclusions

## State Apparatuses Compared

"As two different worlds." These words were uttered by the late Bertil Östergren, former president of the SACO (Swedish Confederation of Professional Associations); such was his characterization of the differences between the AMS and the SÖ. As one of the few individuals to have been a member of both boards, Östergren was particularly well equipped to compare them. He described the AMS as dominated ideologically by the Social Democrats and organizationally by the LO and to a lesser extent the TCO. The SÖ, by contrast, was "a traditional bureaucracy with an organizational culture very different from that of the AMS" (Östergren, interview). Another individual who served on both boards is Matts Bergom-Larsson, former director of the National Engineering Employers' Association. Asked to describe the differences between the two agencies, Mr. Bergom-Larsson said:

One must doubtless say that the SÖ was a much more bureaucratic organization than the AMS. The AMS was not so hooked on formal regulations—it could adapt to different situations. The SÖ, on the other hand, was much more bureaucratic, with a lot of rules and regulations, an old bureaucratic culture. It was also divided politically over the comprehensive school reform, while there was firm support in the AMS for the active labor market policy.

Another individual who has called attention to the differences between these organizations is the LO's former chairman, Gunnar Nilsson. In a 1978 interview for a journal published by one of the teachers' unions, he expressed his great disappointment over the labor movement's inability to influence the school system more profoundly. The school reform had, according to Nilsson, been mostly of a "technical nature," and not much had changed within the schools. Of special interest here is that Nilsson, without being prompted to compare the two agencies, nonetheless pointed out the differences between the AMS and the SÖ:

Gunnar Nilsson also mentions the role played by the SÖ and other school authorities in these matters. Most government agencies have nowadays adapted to the changes in society. This means that they are no longer agencies of the traditional kind. Instead they are working agencies. The labor exchanges, for example, go out to the companies and work actively—just as the authorities and the state want them to do.

But the SÖ does not work in this way. It has no possibilities whatsoever to follow up. What does the SÖ do, and what can be done to convert the political intentions into reality? . . .

I am also critical of many of the regional and local school boards. It is often the case that they just sit there and discuss petty details in the formal recruitment process. They should instead work out how to realize the goals. (*Facklääraren* 1978, no. 23/24, 20)

These statements nicely illustrate what the two previous chapters have shown—that the two agencies have indeed differed in their basic character. On every point examined (program content, personnel, and funding), the differences have been significant and systematic. In this section, I will summarize the major results of the empirical analysis.

In overseeing the SÖ, the government relied first and foremost on a complicated system of specific rules; yet it was vague and imprecise when it came to the general goals of the school policy. In the case of the AMS, the situation was precisely the opposite. Formal

FIGURE 1. Government Methods of Direction: The AMS and the SÖ.

MEANS

|  | Precise | Imprecise |
|---|---|---|
| **Precise** |  | AMS |
| **Imprecise** | SÖ |  |

GOALS

rules and regulations played a minor role, while the general goals—
linked as they were to the Rehn-Meidner model's overall objectives—were clearly specified. The AMS was granted great discretion
in the choice of methods for achieving its goals, especially when it
came to the allocation of economic resources—that is, when and the
agency could increase the demand for labor power. On this point
too, the contrast with the SÖ is striking: the School Commission and
the government stripped the SÖ of nearly every economic means of
influencing local schools. In the figure below, the major differences
between the government's methods of directing the two agencies are
summarized.

Inside the organization, moreover, the SÖ relied heavily on the
very same bureaucratic methods which the government used to direct it; the AMS, by contrast, was a goal-oriented organization based
on substantive rather than formal rationality. The government also
gave the AMS management greater powers over the regional and local levels than it granted the leadership of the SÖ. The AMS was also
a much more cohesive organization than the SÖ. The AMS had a
strong connection to the parties on the labor market, especially the
LO, which enhanced its chances of successfully implementing policies of a socially invasive nature. The SÖ's position in the educational arena, by contrast, was weak. The corporatist organization of the
AMS enabled it to use, together with the LO, ideological means to
persuade its target groups to accept the active labor market policy.

The SÖ, on the other hand, did not count the dissemination of information among its tasks, nor did the organization seek to mobilize ideological support outside the educational sector for the comprehensive school reform.

The manner in which the organization functioned at the very beginning of the implementation process is also important. While the leadership of the AMK and subsequently of the AMS played an active role in the formulation of the active labor market policy, the SÖ leadership was much more passive in regard to the school reform (at times verging on the negative) and was viewed by Social Democratic policy makers as to some extent a hindrance. The AMS disposed of a great range of specific means for implementing the active labor market policy; the SÖ employed a more general method for directing the school system, which it was unable to adapt to the varying circumstances of different geographical areas or schools. If flexibility and an orientation to change are important for implementing "socially invasive" reforms, then, the AMS was well equipped for the task, while the SÖ just was not.

Another important distinction between these two agencies becomes evident when we compare the pattern of recruitment, promotion, and training of personnel. As James Fesler has argued, we should not forget that "institutions of the State have organization cultures, themselves the products of history, which through recruitment and socialization of their members assure a continuity of outlook that channels individual behavior" (1990, 87; cf. Kaufman 1960, 6). The recruitment and promotion of personnel at the AMS can be characterized as, at all levels, a special Social Democratic *cadre-recruitment* system, in which the LO had an important say and, most importantly, provided both the model to be implemented and the personnel to do it.

It is important to underline, however, that this system is in no way similar to an American-style spoils system, in which government jobs are handed out as rewards for political support (cf. Shefter 1977; Weir 1992, 119–29). The AMS was not a patronage system, but was intended rather to recruit staff who (1) would be legitimate in the eyes of the target group, and (2) could be socialized to understand and support the objectives articulated by the leadership and to implement the policy accordingly.

The best U.S. equivalent of the AMS is therefore not the spoils system, but the Forest Service described by Herbert Kaufman in his

1960 classic, *The Forest Ranger*. He asks why the 792 district rangers he studied did not apply 792 different policies at the stage of implementation. The answers he finds are largely similar to those that emerge in the AMS case. Kaufman stresses the importance of the leadership's methods of directing the Forest Service for the creation of a common ideological orientation in the organization. These methods involve (1) recruiting persons strongly inclined to the type of work (those "by nature fitted for forestry"), (2) using extensive internal training to nurture "the will to conform" to the organization's goals, and (3) organizing the work in such a manner that the will to identify with the Forest Service is strengthened.

"Without realizing it," wrote Kaufman, "members of the Forest Service thus 'internalize' the perceptions, values, and premises of action that prevail in the bureau; unconsciously, very often, they tend to act in the agency-prescribed fashion because that has become natural to them" (Kaufman 1960, 162, 173, 176). Similarly, what was special about the staff at the AMS was, I would argue, less their political orientation than their "sense of mission" and loyalty to the goals of the organization.

In contrast to the pattern of recruitment, promotion, and training in the AMS (and the Forest Service), the SÖ relied almost exclusively on a traditional Weberian system of recruitment and promotion. It is noteworthy that the School Commission's proposals from 1946 for a less bureaucratic recruitment of teachers and a different teacher training system never took practical form, despite the fact that these issues were taken up in the Riksdag several times. The parallel system of teacher education from the prereform period was instead retained, despite the criticisms expressed that this would affect the implementation of the reform unfavorably. One could conclude that, given the "bottom-heavy" technology of teaching, this meant that the old parallel school system was left intact inside the comprehensive school.

The difference here is striking: in contrast to the training of the "street-level" personnel at the AMS, the SÖ neither took administrative control over the training of teachers, nor considered it necessary to give the ideological goals motivating the reform a prominent place in the training system. There was also an important difference between the two organizations in the timing of efforts to change the training system. While the AMS's cadre type of recruitment and training was instituted about a decade before the Rehn-Meidner model became an operative policy, the question of an alternative training program for teachers to match the comprehensive school arose more than a decade after the implementation of the school reform had started. In fact, it was not until the mid-1970s that teachers trained for comprehensive schools began working in the school system.

Lastly, the leadership of the AMS paid close attention to the recruitment of key midlevel personnel, and sought thereby to appoint persons who (1) strongly favored the Rehn-Meidner model, and (2) knew how to implement policy flexibly in a dynamic environment. By contrast, the leadership of the SÖ seems to have made no such efforts. For example, the SÖ lacked, or did not bother to obtain, control over the recruitment of school principals; the latter, for their part, lacked influence over the recruitment of teachers. Both formally and informally, then, the gap between the leadership and the field personnel was much wider at the SÖ than at the AMS.

Thus, on every point on which we have compared these two organizations, they have proved to be each other's opposite. It is therefore fair to conclude from the empirical analysis that one of these organizations (the SÖ) corresponds to the Weberian bureaucratic ideal type, and the other (the AMS) can be characterized as a Social Democratic cadre organization. The rest of this chapter is devoted to discussing the implications of these findings for our understanding of the political limits of reformism.

One of this study's major conclusions is that the problem of the limits of reformism is indeed multileveled—it must be analyzed on the micro-, meso-, and macrolevels. The theoretical challenge is to understand the success and failure of the two reforms considered here in terms of the "limits within limits" perspective laid out at the beginning of this book.

## The Implementation Perspective

The findings of my empirical analysis clearly support the major conclusions of the policy implementation literature about the possibility of implementing socially invasive reforms. The most significant findings concern the importance of precision in the articulation of policy goals, the degree of discretion granted the field personnel, and the staff's support of and commitment to the policies in question. The importance of training as a method of ideological direction is also reinforced by the findings of this study. This type of training can be used to bridge the gap between the demand for centralized control and the need for local flexibility in implementing interventionist policies. "In its most general form" writes Walter Williams, "an inquiry about implementation capability . . . seeks to determine whether an organization can bring together men and material in a cohesive organizational unit and motivate them in such a way as to carry out the organization's stated objectives" (1971, 144). There is every reason to believe that the SÖ failed on this count.

Moreover, strong "agency commitment" is one of the best predictors of successful implementation, as Charles Bullock has argued in his study of racial desegregation in the American school system (1981, 119). In the Swedish case, which concerned the less difficult task of class integration, agency commitment was clearly lacking. I believe Bullock is right on the money when he asserts that "any agency not committed to carrying out a programme can sabotage it even if other conditions are favorable" (ibid., 120).

While the AMS may be considered such a "committed" agency, it was at the same time a highly decentralized state apparatus with a high degree of independence from both ministerial supervision and parliamentary control. On the other hand, these discretionary powers were disciplined and checked by a careful recruitment and training policy. The unions held a dominant position on the agency's central and regional boards, and their influence over the implementation process was plain. This direct union control may have been critical for ensuring that the active labor market policy did not develop into a corrupt patronage system (cf. Shefter 1977). The corporatist principle of representation was also of great importance for this. This meant that not just union officials but employer representatives as well sat on the central and regional boards. This role was far from symbolic—these representatives were heavily involved in monitoring policy implementation through their participation in different subcommittees within the AMS (Arnestam 1983). If tendencies toward a corrupt patronage system based on the unions had emerged, the representatives of the Employers' Confederation would certainly have rung the bell. A critical reason that a patronage system did not develop, then, is that the successful implementation of an active labor market policy demands the collaboration not only of unions, but of employers as well, which was something the LO clearly understood (Blankenburg 1978; cf. Wilensky 1990).

It is precisely on the question of corruption that several writers have dwelt in seeking to explain the failure of efforts to institute an active labor market policy in the United States during the 1970s. According to Margaret Weir, accusations of abuse and corruption led to increased bureaucratic control, which left no room for local flexibility in the implementation process. Local control was exercised not by unions or employers associations, but by elected officials rather; the latter proceeded then to use the agency's resources to promote their own political interests—by rewarding supporters with relief jobs, for example. The mounting charges of corruption and waste made the policy an easy target for the Reagan administration's cutbacks (Weir 1992, 125–27; cf. Donahue 1989, 181; Mucciaroni 1992, chap. 7).

Local and regional flexibility could be permitted in the Swedish case because of the tight ideological control exercised by the agency management over recruitment, promotion, and training, and on account of the supervision exercised by representatives of the LO, the TCO, and the SAF. Thus, the AMS might appear to be a decentralized organization, by the standards of administrative studies stressing formal chains of command (cf. Hjern and Porter 1981; Hjern and Hull 1982); from a political and policy perspective, however, the AMS has been a strongly centralized state apparatus—a cadre organization. What was lost in formal control was gained through ideological cohesion, along with the advantage of local flexibility.

On the basis of the general knowledge existing today about the problems of implementing social reforms in a dynamic environment, we could have predicted that the comprehensive school reform would fail. Lack of support, understanding, and knowledge on the part of many field and midlevel personnel, a vague and divided organizational leadership, and inflexible bureaucratic modes of intervention were probably the most decisive factors. Perhaps the lack of political support should be mentioned as well. For while the Social Democrats and their union allies were firmly united behind the active labor market policy, in the matter of reforming the school system the party was more divided. Nor did it enjoy strong backing from the LO in this endeavor.

In his classical study, *Essence of Decision*, Graham Allison writes: "The fact that fixed programs . . . exhaust the range of buttons that leaders can push is not always perceived by these leaders. But in every case it is critical for an understanding of what is actually done"

(1971, 79). I have sought to demonstrate that, in order to overcome the limits of reformism, key figures in the Swedish labor movement instituted changes in the operational mode of the state apparatuses responsible for labor market policy. The limits of reformism were thereby overcome in the case of labor market policy.

Educational reform was another matter: the changes in the practical operations of local schools sought by Social Democratic reformers could not be implemented, because the responsible state agency did not have the capacity to engineer field-level changes in the school system. As Meyer Zald has written: "the more a policy depends upon depth penetration of bureaucratic procedures, the less likely it is to be easily implemented." If the technology is imprecise, if staff attitudes and values are important, and if the chain of command is weak, we would expect changes in policy "to be slow to be implemented and distorted when they are" (Zald 1981, 102).

It seems fair to conclude, in sum, that a good many weighty reasons account for the respective success and failure of these two reforms. Still, while the implementation perspective can tell us much about the causes of policies' success or failure, it cannot account for the existence of these causes as such. To understand why these factors occurred at all, it is therefore necessary to move on to the next (organizational) level of analysis.

## The Organization Perspective

To implement public policy is the task of government organizations and of the larger networks of which they are a part. Yet these institutions are not neutral executors of the policies assigned to them (March and Olsen 1989, 107). From an organizational perspective, the two state apparatuses under consideration were institutions of a fundamentally different character. Persuasive evidence may be found at all levels of comparison. The two agencies did not merely employ different systems of administration and implementation, they also embodied different organizational cultures, which influenced the ways in which their personnel defined their essential role and mission in society. Contrary to Mucciaroni's claim, the administrative capacity of the Swedish labor market authorities—which he rightly argues has been decisive for the success of the active labor market policy—has *not* been a general feature of the Swedish state. The AMS has rather been a unique institution, an exception within an, at least until the late 1960s, otherwise traditionally organized bureaucratic state (Mucciaroni 1992, 247–48; cf. Mellbourn 1979).

One of the central insights of modern organization research is here confirmed, namely that a strong common organizational ideology can replace traditional bureaucratic methods of direction, such as formal rules and regulations. The socialization process can be so effective that the organizational leadership is able to grant the lower levels considerable discretion in how exactly to implement policy and yet be assured things will be done in a manner consistent with overall policy goals. At the opposite end of the organizational spectrum, on the other hand, the socialization process is weak and policy goals are vaguely articulated and ill-understood by the lower-level staff; in such an organization, it is necessary to rely on formal rules and regulations. This severely circumscribes the capacity of the organization to adapt flexibly to different situations.

The institutional development of these two state agencies also confirms the notion of institutional stickiness (March and Olsen 1989, 106). When the AMS was established in the early 1940s, it was designed to implement a new type of interventionist government policy. Its creation represented a decisive break with the previous state apparatus in this policy field. On the local level, the employment exchanges had long been strongly influenced by the parties on the labor market and had traditionally recruited a significant proportion of their staff from the labor movement. Because these exchanges did not administer unemployment insurance, moreover, they remained legitimate in the eyes of their main target group, the blue-collar work force (King and Rothstein 1993; cf. Weir 1992, 81–82). This local organizational legacy was crucial to the establishment of the AMS as a Social Democratic cadre organization.

By contrast, the responsibility for implementing the comprehensive school reform was not assigned to a new state apparatus specifically established for the purpose. It was instead given to an already existing bureaucracy which had been partly responsible for the school system the reform was destined to replace. This agency was also badly divided over the merits of the new policy. The argument put forward by Charles Lindblom (1977), Renate Mayntz (1978), Wolfgang Heydebrand (1977), and many others that "old bureaucracies die hard," is thus confirmed in this study. Existing government institutions may indeed constrain new policy efforts; put differently, reforms can in fact run afoul of "institutional stickiness."

At the organizational level, then, we can identify a contradiction corresponding to that between the forces and relations of production identified by Marx. Much can be learned from organization theory, but its largely apolitical orientation is also a hindrance to a deeper understanding of the relation between modes of organization and political power. Organizations, especially government organizations, are not neutral, technical instruments which can simply be programmed to achieve the goals set out by politicians. Instead, they are institutionalized manifestations of the vested interests and power structures of the wider society. As there are modes of production, so are there modes of administration (Mouzelis 1984, 1990).

The question we are then left with is: how could one state contain two such different apparatuses? Clearly, the answer cannot be given by organization theory alone. In order to understand why these differences came to be, we must move on to the level of state theory.

## The State as an Arena for Class Conflict

From a historical and materialist perspective, it is clear that these administrative differences, with their consequences for the pursuit of reformist policies, did not arise in a social or political vacuum. Nor do they merely reflect two different organizational styles. Rather, they are firmly rooted in political struggles and class conflicts. The organizational differences between the two state agencies should be seen as an expression of these conflicts.

In the case of the school reform, the conflicts were built into the organization itself. The very idea that the academically oriented grammar schools and the popular elementary schools should be merged into a new comprehensive system caused severe intraorganizational conflict within the National School Board, and ideological confusion as well. Such conflicts were resolved differently in the case of the labor market policy, because the organization that took charge of this policy area was established as a Social Democratic cadre organization. The demise of the AK during the 1930s and the subsequent expansion of the AMK-AMS after 1940, completely changed the class character of the state apparatus responsible for labor market questions. The idea that the capitalist state's internal structure is important for determining which reformist policies are successfully implemented thus finds confirmation in this study. The limits of reformism are therefore an organizational problem, at least in part.

The importance of analyzing class interests for understanding the variation in government organizations is underlined by this study. As reported above, for example, many OECD countries have tried to institute programs similar to the Swedish active labor market policy. Between 1962 and 1974, Gösta Rehn himself headed the OECD Manpower and Social Affairs Commission; in this capacity, he strongly encouraged other countries to adopt an active labor market policy (cf. Blankenburg 1978; Rhen, interview). Yet few if any of these countries have succeeded in doing so (Wilensky and Turner 1987; Therborn 1986).

Sweden is still unmatched in the resources devoted to active labor market measures as a proportion of money spent on labor market policies in general. While many OECD nations spend as much as or more than Sweden on labor market policies, they concentrate their efforts on passive measures, primarily cash unemployment benefits (OECD 1989). One reason for the difficulty of exporting the successful Swedish policy may be the unique organizational context attending this policy's implementation in Sweden.

The context was set not only by the support of a uniquely strong labor movement, but also by the specific institutional structure described above. Two studies written recently by Margaret Weir and Gary Mucciaroni, who have each analyzed the failure of attempts to introduce an active labor market policy in the United States, confirm the importance of these variables (Weir 1992, chap. 3; Mucciaroni 1992). Other scholars have stressed the importance of differences in administrative setup and operational logic between the labor market authorities of different countries; in the process, they have highlighted the problems many countries have met with in applying excessively bureaucratic modes of intervention. Combining political legitimacy with flexibility and efficiency in implementing labor market policy seems to have been extremely difficult for countries other than Sweden.[1]

Another hypothesis finding support in this study concerns the problematic relation between the Weberian bureaucracy, on the one hand, and interventionist public policies, on the other. An organization guided principally by formal and precise rules and regulations will have difficulty adjusting to changing demands, and successful interventionism requires such flexibility. The Weberian bureaucracy is perfectly suited to administering a state agency—the foremost goal of which is predictability and calculability. It is not a good tool for implementing interventionist programs, however, precisely because it makes a virtue of not adjusting its actions to fit particular circumstances (Offe 1985). The need for such flexibility is the Achilles' heel of the bureaucratic organization.

However, establishing that these two state apparatuses have been organized differently does not suffice to answer the general theme of this study. The question of why these differences arose remains to be answered. The reader may recall that, in order to link the three levels of analysis (concerning implementation, institutions and the state) I posed the following three questions in chapter 2:

1. Have the National Labor Market Board and the National School Board been differently situated in the field of class conflicts in Sweden?

2. If so, have these differences influenced the organization of the two state apparatuses?

3. If so, have these organizational differences influenced the implementation of the two policies in question in such a way that their success or failure can be explained?

It is obvious that the Swedish Social Democrats' efforts to change the administrative character of the labor market authorities were not merely accidental. Nor were they not motivated by a narrow concern for administrative efficiency. Rather, the changes the Social Democrats made in these agencies were *politically* motivated; the labor movement needed, in order to ensure the reproduction of its organizational base, to achieve political control over the state apparatus responsible for labor market policy.

The lessons of the 1920s and 1930s, when two Social Democratic governments were forced to resign, were extremely important: they palpably demonstrated to the labor movement the practical consequences of not achieving control over the labor market authorities. It had become extremely important, then, for the Swedish labor movement to obtain control over the state apparatus intervening in the process of buying and selling labor power. At the same time, the Social Democrats understood that the need for local flexibility in the implementation process demanded more than tight ministerial control over the labor market authorities.

Their solution was to establish a completely new type of government agency, which would be sufficiently decentralized as to allow for local flexibility, yet would be centrally and effectively controlled on account of the personnel's ideological coherence and commitment to the policy goals enunciated by the leadership. Unlike the situation described in Philip Selznick's classical study of the Tennessee Valley Authority established by the New Deal administration, this was not a case where the state apparatus tried to incorporate the policy's target group in order to achieve acceptance in the implementation process (1949). Instead, the target groups incorporated the state apparatus.

All three questions above can therefore be answered with a "yes." The existing state apparatus for handling labor market questions was broken down and replaced by what I have here called a Social Democratic cadre organization—the AMS, which the Social Democrats have thoroughly dominated. The existing school bureaucracy, by contrast, was left intact. If the state is a terrain of class conflict, the AMS represents a part of that terrain which the labor movement has captured and administered as its own (Poulantzas 1978). We can also confirm that two state apparatuses of divergent class character can coexist within the same nation-state (Therborn 1980).

The discussion of the limits of reformism must therefore take the state—in its full complexity and variability—into more serious account. It is true, on the one hand, that the bureaucratically organized capitalist state sets limits upon reforms (at least of the type considered in this study). On the other hand, the class character of this capitalist state is not altogether resistant to change. The structure of the state, or of specific state apparatuses at least, can be changed so as to be more compatible with the policy objectives of a reformist government.

Explaining this variation in the class character of state agencies, however, is rather more complicated than explaining the variation in policies. Why did the Swedish labor movement lay such stress on changing the AMS as compared to changing the SÖ? One reason may lie in the organizational division within the labor movement between the party and the LO. Among the Social Democrats who formulated and championed the school reform, none had their political base in the LO. All were associated in one way or another with the established school system, as teachers, principals, or established school politicians.

The Rehn-Meidner reform program, by contrast, was a product of the LO; only after four or five years had passed was it accepted by the party leadership. Even before the model was accepted, moreover, the LO began to assert control over the AMS. The contrast with the school reform is telling: the LO did not even bother to issue a formal statement (Sw: *remiss*) on the School Commission's report in 1948, which is very uncommon in the Swedish political system. Clearly, what we see here is a division of labor between the party and the union movement. As an organization whose power was based on controlling the supply side of the labor market, the LO had a much stronger incentive to take active initiatives in this sector than in education. This study indicates that, as between political forces (the party) or organized class forces (the union movement), it is class that weighs more heavily.

In the area of school reform, one may fairly conclude that Weber's prediction came true (see p. 10): the Social Democratic *party* was captured by the bureaucratic state. Weber was correct that social democratic parties will over the long run be captured by the bureaucratic state rather than vice versa, and that accordingly they pose no threat to the capitalist order.

The case of labor market policy, on the other hand, leads one to conclude that the Swedish Social Democratic *union movement* proved Weber to be wrong. While one may object that the active labor market policy in itself posed no threat to the capitalist order, this policy *was* a critical part of a larger model aimed at strengthening labor as an organized social force. The strength of unions derives largely from their ability to control the supply of labor power. If the state keeps unemployment low, and if this is done in a manner facilitating the cohesion of the trade union movement, organized labor clearly gains in strength. The policy can therefore be said to have given the Swedish labor movement the necessary strength to confront the capitalist order (which it also did in the late 1970s) (Pontusson 1992). This would indicate that Marx's conclusion after the fall of the Paris Commune is more to the point. The Swedish Social Democratic *union movement* did not just take over the state machinery ready made and then attempt to turn it to its own purposes. Rather, it instituted far-reaching changes in the organization of that state agency—the actions of which impinged most directly on the reproduction of its organizational strength.

## Counterfactuals: Could Things Have Been Different?

The findings of this study may be of interest also for the debate over the relative importance of structure and agency. We have concluded that the state is indeed an institutional structure which sets limits on the prospects for a successful reformism. Contrary to the assumptions of the "state-centered" approach (Skocpol 1985), however, it is also true that a political agent—such as a working-class movement—can change the structure of the state in such a manner as to further its interests and enhance its future strength. Certainly, this cannot simply be done at will in any policy sector or at any time. Still, while "historical junctures" are important, whether or not they are exploited "depends partly on the support from key political groups and figures, in short on political leadership" (March and Olsen 1989, 106).

Some policy areas and state apparatuses are probably easier to change than others, and some historical junctures are more critical than others (in terms of the prospects they yield for instituting lasting changes). As Margaret Weir has argued, "in circumstances when established institutions or intellectual frameworks begin to break down, the scope for choice for political actors may widen" (1992, 23). However, instead of "historical junctures" (a phrase that seems to imply history without agents), I suggest we speak of *formative moments*. The advantage of this term is that it implies that both structural openings (or moments) and agents seizing that moment to form new institutions are necessary ingredients for understanding the limits and possibilities of politically imposed social change.

The hard part, in an empirical analysis, is identifying these *formative moments* and *critical actors*. In regard to labor market policy, one critical actor during the 1930s and 1940s was doubtless the Minister of Social Affairs, Gustav Möller. What Möller did in the area of labor market policy, as indeed in other social policy areas, was to "design political structures" (Rothstein 1985, 1992). Clearly, he could not have done this without the support of the trade union movement (although the LO did not play a crucial role in designing labor market institutions during the 1930s). The historical legacy of the Swedish system of employment exchanges founded at the beginning of the century also helps to explain the outcome. Finally, Gösta Rehn's unique combination of macrolevel economic theory and microlevel administrative insight must also be taken into account.

If these and other formative moments and critical actors can be identified as crucial for the success of the Swedish labor market policy, the question then arises of the role of counterfactual explanations in the social sciences. Was there a time at which the Swedish Social Democrats could have changed the SÖ and the school system, so as to make them more compatible with the party's reform ambitions in education? How "sticky" were the administrative institutions in this case? As in all counterfactual discussions, attempting an answer is a highly speculative (and quite entertaining) endeavor. Yet such a discussion has also the advantage of helping to concentrate our thoughts on the matter of what implications for reformist strategies may be drawn from this study.

This study has not been aimed at offering advice to policy makers, yet it contains some lessons to be learned. The most important is that institutions matter. In George Tsebelis's words: "Selecting institutions is the sophisticated equivalent of selecting policies" (1990, 118). A first lesson, then, is that policy makers should think much more carefully about institutional arrangements when designing policies. While institutions are indeed harder to change than policies, the payoffs of doing so may be much greater, since institutions form the structural limits of the politically possible (cf. Rothstein 1992). Secondly, institutions are not always a constraint; they can also be a resource (cf. Immergut 1992). They do indeed put limits on some political projects, but they open up political opportunities as well. Finally, if unsuitable institutional structures cannot be changed, it may be better to do nothing. Implementing a policy with faulty institutional means might leave everyone, including the policy makers, worse off.

I would at this point like to call the reader's attention to the existence of an extensive literature in the Marxist tradition claiming that fundamental changes in education are structurally impossible in a capitalist society. According to this line of reasoning, the educational system is severely constrained by the demands of the capitalist system; "the system reproduces the inequalities created by its system of reproduction" (Carnoy and Levin 1976, 7).[2]

The counterfactual question therefore is: was it at any point possible to establish a fundamentally different administrative structure for implementing the comprehensive school reform, given the prevailing political and social circumstances? Did a reasonable possibility exist at any time for the Social Democratic party to "act otherwise," so that the following sequence of events would have been different? Or was history in this case structurally bound, and the agents mere puppets of circumstances not of their own choosing? Could the Social Democrats have instituted educational changes comparable to their accomplishments in labor market policy?

One counterfactual history could have been the following: the comprehensive school reform would have been initiated already in the late 1930s, not by merging the two school systems but through gradually extending the elementary school, which already lasted seven years at this point (cf. the comparable transitional role of the employment exchanges). The lower level of the grammar school system would have been kept as a parallel system to the reformed higher level of elementary school system during the beginning of this transition, but would not have been allowed to expand.

Instead, the funds devoted to this part of the grammar school system would have been progressively reduced, thus diminishing the attractiveness of these schools as compared to the comprehensive schools. The grammar school system would have thereby shared the fate of the Unemployment Commission. In addition, the funds devoted to the expanded elementary/comprehensive school system would have been significantly increased; these schools would therefore have been able to attract more students and better qualified teachers (the AMK during World War II is the parallel here). Finally, the lower grades of the grammar school (which would now have overlapped with the higher grades of the comprehensive school) would have been closed down, on account of their lack of funding and low quality.

At the central level, a new educational agency would have been established to implement the reform, based largely on the School Commission of 1946 (which was not a large administration and which, most importantly, included the most prominent champions of the reform). This new organization would have been organized along largely the same lines as the AMS—it would have been given a considerable discretion over means, especially when it came to the recruitment of principals and teachers. This organization would have established a new teacher training system aimed at socializing a new corps of teachers committed to the comprehensive school reform. This new teacher training system would have built upon the already existing training colleges for elementary school teachers (among whom support for the comprehensive school reform was widespread).

Lastly, the major labor market organizations would have been represented on supervisory boards at different levels of the school system. The new school agency would have taken direct charge of the regional school boards and used its discretionary control of funds to press local schools to refashion their internal work to match the objectives of the comprehensive school reform.

It is of course extremely difficult to judge whether such an alternative development was ever possible. But if history is not totally bound by structural circumstances beyond the reach of political agents—if history, that is, consists of more than "destined pathways" (cf. Skocpol 1985)—then there must be room for this kind of admittedly rather speculative argumentation. If it was ever possible, in Giddens's (1979) words, to "act otherwise," we should try to discern what these alternative choices would have meant for political development. Or, as Jonas Pontusson has argued, "structuralist explanations must demonstrate how structural conditions impinge on the strategic choices of political or economic actors" (1992b, 306) It should be mentioned that, although an endeavor in speculation, the above-mentioned scenario is not very different from how educational reform proceeded in Denmark, where the comprehensive system was achieved not through merging the two types of school, but by expanding the elementary schools (*folkeskolen*) and building on their tradition of comprehensive popular education (Ussing 1982).

One may of course question whether such institutional changes would have had any impact on the performance of students from working-class backgrounds. This is mainly a question for educational research and thus outside the scope of this study. Nevertheless, there are studies showing that the factors stressed here—ideological commitment on the part of the central agency, the local school leaders, and the field-level personnel—have important implications for how students from socially disadvantaged backgrounds perform in school.

A large study done in Britain by Ruther et al. (1979) compares educational results in different socially disadvantaged neighborhoods. The study shows that the individual school made a great difference, and thus that educational results are not determined by the social or economic environment. Students' performance instead varied systematically accordingly to the character of the school. The most important factor, according to Rutters et al., was the school's "ethos." A variable such as "school ethos" is problematic, of course, but it appears to signify the local school's ideological commitment to specific educational goals.

A more recent study done in the United States by John Chubb and Terry Moe reports similar results. Chubb and Moe stress the commitment and ideological orientation of the school leadership and staff, and their autonomy from "external bureaucratic influence," as crucial factors for a school's success: "school organization does indeed have a significant impact" (1990, 23, 15; 1991).

In Sweden, Lennart Grosin has found similar results: the educational performance of socially disadvantaged students is not structurally determined by their situation *outside* school. It is the organization of the local school, the dedication of their teachers and principals, that makes the big difference (1991). Like any other organization, a public school needs to get one type of signal—when it does badly—and another when it does well. It will otherwise, on account of sheer disorientation, do more things wrong than right. In the case of the school reform, the schools were part of a signal-less system: they had no incentive to do more things right than wrong.

Comparing alternative historical developments requires that we seek to ascertain when the Social Democrats took critical decisions, or nondecisions, with respect to the two policy areas in question. In the case of the school reform, it seems the inaction during the 1930s of the Minister of Education and Ecclesiastical Affairs, Arthur Engberg, was crucial. Engberg's passivity is especially striking alongside the masterful assertiveness during the same period of the Minister of Social Affairs, Gustav Möller, who determinedly altered both labor market policy and the structure of the state agency requisite to its implementation. The time lost for school reform during the 1930s was probably critical, moreover, because parents' interest in having their children attend grammar schools increased markedly after the war. One reason for this increased demand for grammar school education was the lack of an alternative. This made breaking with the old system extremely difficult, since a large part of the demand for grammar schools actually came from Social Democratic voters.

Former Prime Minister Tage Erlander describes in his memoirs how, as the newly appointed minister of education and ecclesiastical affairs in 1945, he found that the demand for grammar school education was virtually exploding; he felt that this called for immediate political action. In addition, he had just come from the Ministry of Social Affairs, where he had served as Gustav Möller's second-in-command. He then describes how he found his new ministry a very different place:

At the Ministry of Social Affairs, we had a practical reform program ready to be implemented as soon as the financial situation of the state allowed. In the area of education policy, there was no equivalent. What existed was an enormous collection of data, compiled by Bagge's school inquiry, but no plans that could be implemented. And here was an unreformed school which was almost torn to pieces by the rush. (Erlander 1973, 235–36; cf. Erlander 1982, 272)

There was thus hardly any possibility to start "acting otherwise" in 1945–46. The Social Democrats were forced instead to begin their reform of the school system while largely relying on the existing organizational structure. Erlander himself explains this situation as having resulted from Arthur Engberg's lack of interest in educational questions, and from the fact that the party's main ambition during the 1930s was to solve the problem of unemployment. This, according to Erlander, was why the party's radical school policy from the 1920s was not followed up during the 1930s; he does not mention, however, that the party was in fact split between Arthur Engberg's elitist view of education and Oscar Olsson's popular program (cf. Isling 1980, 211–20, 228–34). It is in any case natural that, for a party built largely on the strength of a union movement, first things must come first. Or, in the words of James March and Johan Olsen: "The premise of organization is that not everything can be attended to at once" (1989, 16).

Still, the political events of the 1930s do not explain why the party lacked the ambition to achieve even minor changes in the organizational structure of the school administration during the postwar period, despite the many urgings to do so from, among others, Stellan Arvidson, the main author of the reform proposal. His criticisms of the methods and structures used to implement the reform were largely ignored by the Ministry of Education.

It is revealing to compare Arvidson's situation to that of the union economist Gösta Rehn, the main architect of the active labor market policy. Rehn had, as shown above, very specific proposals about how to change the organizational structure of the labor market authorities, so as best to ensure the reform's implementation in accordance with the original intentions, and he obtained approval for most of his suggestions. Except for differences in personalities, which might of course have played a role, the main difference between these two men is that, while Rehn could usually mobilize the LO leadership in support of his suggestions, Arvidson had no such power base behind him.

Social power resources thus count, and so does state capacity. The really interesting question is not whether one or the other is most important, but what the logic of the historical interaction between the two has been.

# 9. Epilogue

During the international recession that began in the mid-1970s, the Swedish Social Democrats lost government for the first time in forty-four years. Between 1976 and 1982, five different bourgeois governments ruled Sweden, consisting variously of one, two, and sometimes all three nonsocialist parties. In 1982, the Social Democrats returned to power for a nine-year period. In the "earthquake" election of September 1991, however, the party registered its worst showing since 1928, scoring only 37.6 percent of the votes. The Social Democrats were again replaced by a bourgeois coalition government, consisting this time of four parties yet commanding only a minority of votes in the Riksdag.

Unlike during the previous period of bourgeois rule, the coalition government that took power in 1991 was headed by a Conservative prime minister (Carl Bildt), the first such since 1928. This Conservative-led government has had a more pronounced right-wing profile than any of the bourgeois governments between 1976 and 1982, and it has sought openly to challenge the Social Democratic hegemony in Swedish politics.

The question to be addressed in this chapter is what happened to the active labor market policy and the AMS, and to the comprehensive school reform and the SÖ, during these two periods of bourgeois rule.

The various bourgeois coalition governments ruling between 1976 and 1982 refrained altogether from attacking the AMS and the active labor market policy. Quite the contrary. The bourgeois governments used the AMS, among other means, to wage a very successful fight against unemployment during the recession of the mid- and late 1970s. Indeed, the Swedish bourgeois governments fought unemployment more vigorously than did many of the social democratic governments of other OECD countries during the same period.

By increasing the resources devoted to the AMS, and by other means as well—such as the massive nationalization of declining industries—these governments managed to keep the country's unemployment rate below 3.5 percent throughout this period (Therborn 1986). It was first after the bourgeois parties' defeat in the 1982 election that the AMS and the active labor market policy came under attack. In two reports, a former political aide to the minister of labor accused the agency of inefficiency and waste, and deplored its close collaboration with the Social Democratic union movement (Sjöström 1982, 1985). The political effect of this was next to nil (see below). The reports were instructive, however, in revealing the frustration felt by many within the bourgeois parties at being forced to support a policy with which they basically did not agree.

As Göran Therborn has shown, neither government type nor such economic factors as growth, inflation, wage costs, profits, etc., can account for the great international divergence in unemployment figures between OECD countries from 1973 onward (Therborn 1986, 23, 97; cf. Scharpf 1991). Instead, he argues, the main explanation for this variation lies in whether an "institutionalized commitment" to full employment existed in these countries *before* the crisis began.

Therborn calls particular attention to the Swedish case, and stresses the importance of the active labor market policy and the AMS: "its explicit formulation and establishment of a public policy mechanism for direct intervention into the labour market with a view to maintaining full employment . . . organized by a very powerful administrative agency, the Labour Market Board" (Therborn 1986, 103, 124–36). The AMS's strength and legitimacy made it politically impossible to deny it increased resources to fight unemployment.

This is not to say that the bourgeois governments that ruled Sweden from 1976 to 1982 really wanted to increase unemployment but dared not do so on account of the strength of the AMS. My argument is rather that the existence of an institution known to possess powerful means for fighting unemployment made the other policy option—to fight inflation by increasing unemployment—politically suicidal. When unemployment rose in the early 1970s, no Swedish politician dared deny the AMS additional resources, because the active labor market policy was known to work. In other words, the capacity of the state in this policy area had been firmly established, and this put implacable pressure on politicians, whether Social Democratic or Conservative, to act.

The AMS therefore expanded in this period, in terms of both its finances and the number of its employees (*Arbetsmarknadspolitik i förändring* 1992, 100–20). This again indicates that policy and institutional legacies do not just constrain political agents from acting (cf. Immergut 1992). They can also force political agents to do things they would otherwise not have done.

On the whole, the bourgeois parties that ruled Sweden from 1976 to 1982 did little to undermine the political hegemony of the Social Democrats. One reason for this is that they achieved office by posing as in many respects more social democratic than the Social Democrats themselves—by promising, for instance, even more government measures to create jobs than the Social Democrats did (Bergström 1991; Heclo and Madsen 1987).

When the Social Democrats returned to power in 1982, one of their primary electoral promises was to increase the resources devoted to active labor market policy even further (Prop. 1982–83, no. 100, bil. 12). At that point, however, the party abandoned the overall Rehn-Meidner model (as described in chapter 4) by opting for a more traditional, market-oriented economic policy. Economic growth was to be stimulated by increasing rather than squeezing corporate profits. The reasons for this important policy shift are disputed, but one plausible interpretation is that the combined effects of Swedish capital's internationalization and of post-Fordist changes in production relations was to render two of the model's requirements untenable: (1) keeping corporate profits low, and (2) maintaining the unions' solidaristic wage policy (Pontusson 1992b).

What is important in this context, however, is that the demise of the overall Rehn-Meidner model did not imply a diminishing importance for its third part—the active labor market policy. On the contrary, it became an even more critical asset for the Social Democrats after 1982, both for maintaining flexibility in the labor market and for proving to the electorate that the party was still the main guarantor of full employment in Swedish politics. The political strength of the AMS is also demonstrated by the fact that its director-general, Allan Larsson, became the new Social Democratic minister of finance in 1990. It should also be mentioned that the Social Democrats have made the maintenance of the active labor market policy an absolute condition for their support for Sweden's entry into the EC (*Aktuellt i politiken* 1992, 9).

This strength of the AMS as a political institution was also evident in the 1991 election campaign. Much of the political debate turned on the question of what to do about the rise of unemployment from 1.2 percent to almost twice that, a rise which at the time was reckoned alarming in the Swedish political context. Both the leader of the Conservative party (Carl Bildt, who became prime minister in 1991) and the Liberal leader (Bengt Westerberg, who became the new minister of social affairs) criticized the Social Democratic government for not giving enough resources to the AMS to keep unemployment down.

In his opening speech as prime minister to the Riksdag in October 1991, Carl Bildt said that increased unemployment "demands an active labor market policy. It should mitigate the social consequences of unemployment, but also create a better readiness for the increase in employment that will come. The government intends to make use of every part in the accumulated armory of the labor market policy" (RD 1991–92, no. 6, 6). This was not just loose political talk either, for in its first budget the new bourgeois government did in fact increase the resources allocated to the AMS, in order to fight this dramatic (by Swedish standards) increase in unemployment (Prop. 1991–92, no. 100, bil. 11). This move won the government praise from a most unbourgeois quarter: Villy Bergström, the director of the LO-financed Union Research Institute, and prominent union economist and Social Democrat besides, publicly applauded the new bourgeois government's efforts in the labor market area, and criticized the former Social Democratic government for not having done the same (*DN* 01–05–92).

In the autumn of 1992, the Swedish economy entered its worst recession since the 1930s. Open unemployment—that is, total unemployment minus the number of those taking part in the various labor market programs—rose to a dramatic 5 percent, the highest figure since 1943. Yet the Conservative-led government persisted in its efforts to counter the crisis by increasing funds for the AMS. Indeed, the AMS was allocated so much money that the agency itself started complaining that the limits had been reached for what could be achieved through labor market measures. In a book about changes in the labor market policy recently issued by the AMS, it is claimed that "we are at this moment in a gray zone, close to the limit for what can be done by labor market policy alone" (*Arbetsmarknadspolitik i förändring* 1992, 5; cf. *DN* 11–05–92 and 11–23–92). At that point (November 1992), about 4 percent of the labor force was involved in various active labor market programs, which is probably a world record.

The fate of the SÖ during this period has been the reverse. While there were some conflicts between the SÖ and the different bourgeois ministers of education between 1976 and 1982 (Lindbom 1988), little was changed in the organizational setup. The bourgeois governments tried, however, to move the organization toward greater internal flexibility and decentralization. They also encouraged it to emphasize long-term planning and evaluation rather than short-term details. These efforts to change the SÖ failed, however, largely on account of internal obstruction (ibid., 22–25).

The real difficulties for the SÖ came after 1982, when the Social Democrats returned to power. Briefly, the new Social Democratic government began to strip the SÖ of most of its regulatory powers and cut its personnel by more than half: from 750 to 350 persons. The school system was heavily decentralized, and most of the power was transferred to local school boards appointed by local governments. The result of this was that, instead of a shared responsibility between the state and local governments, the Swedish school system was in operational terms taken over by the local governments. The state would, however, retain the responsibility of setting overall goals for basic education and for evaluating the efforts of local governments to reach these goals.

In line with this, the objective was to change the SÖ from a bureaucratic, rule-governed agency into a bureau for evaluation and information gathering (Prop. 1988–89, no. 4). The SÖ would refrain from detailed direction by rules and would instead concentrate on long-term planning and evaluation (Prop. 1989–90, no. 4). The government commission proposing this change argued that the goal of promoting social, economic, and cultural equality through a reformed educational system had not been attained, because the political direction of the reform process had been too weak. In particular, the desired individualization of the teaching process had not been achieved (Ds. U 1987, no. 1, 181–83). The commission also made the following observation:

The knowledge of school policy history is deficient today. Many teachers, principles . . . lack—judging from the results of various studies—familiarity with the underlying reasons why school reforms have been instituted, and why the school system has been structured in a certain way. This is a serious hindrance to a well-functioning system of management by objectives (ibid., 225).

The commission stressed that, if management by objectives is to work, the staff must know about, understand, and support the political goals of the school system (ibid., 227). The articulation of these goals and policy objectives must be so effective and intense that everyone setting out to implement them has a "conscious, deep, worked-out and active knowledge about them, a knowledge that can be converted into practical action. . . . It requires that the basic and continuing training of teachers and principals is permeated by the basic orientation of which the policy goals and guidelines are expressions" (ibid., 227–28).

One of the major changes introduced by the Social Democrats after 1982 was to strip the SÖ (and its regional school boards) of the right to appoint teachers and principals, and to instead assign this responsibility to local school boards appointed by local governments (Prop. 1989–90, no. 41). This was not just a formal change, because it actually endowed local school boards with much greater discretion in the recruitment of teachers and principals, as well as in the organization of teachers' work.

As one might have expected, the union representing the university-trained teachers protested strongly against this measure, as did the nonsocialist parties in the Riksdag (RD 1989–90, no. 42). In an unprecedented extraparliamentary action, more than five thousand teachers gathered outside the Riksdag to protest the decision (DN 12–09–89). Despite heavy criticism, however, the Social Democratic government did not back down from its determination to strip the SÖ of the power of recruitment.

Despite these changes, however, the SÖ's mode of operation remained largely rule-based and bureaucratic (SOU 1988, no. 20, 9–10). Sensing that this type of incremental change was not enough, the Social Democrats launched a final attack on the SÖ in 1989, when a new minister of education (Göran Persson) was appointed. In 1990, the Social Democratic government decided simply to close down the SÖ. The party justified this move with reference to criticisms of the organization's inflexibility and heavily bureaucratized mode of operation (Prop. 1990–91, no. 18, 111). The government report suggesting the abolition of the SÖ argued that the traditional type of management by rules had become obsolete, and that this had prevented the policy from being implemented in accordance with political intentions (Ds. U 1987, no. 1, 224–26; cf. Prop. 1990–91, no. 4, 18). The government report also called attention to an interesting problem:

A phenomenon, which earlier generations could scarcely foresee—but which has become increasingly urgent as the direction of the school system by objectives has increased—is that *the sum* of all rules may lead to undesired side-effects. When one rule is added to others in a continuous time-flow, it is usually the latest rule that gets attention. It becomes more difficult to foresee its consequences in relation to other rules, or to see if there are other rules which might also come into conflict with one another. If the accumulation of rules becomes too great, the system may become impossible to manage. In the end, those implementing the rules do not know what one to follow. (Ds. U 1987, no. 20)

The Social Democratic minister of education argued, on the one hand, that the detailed rule-based method of management had been successful in the past in changing the organization of the school system. On the other hand, it had not "to the extent one could have expected resulted in education being carried out in the way the Riksdag and the government have prescribed in curricula and other policy documents" (Prop. 1989–90, no. 4, 8). The government declared that the nature of the new school administration's major task—to evaluate how local governments were fulfilling the general goals of the school system—was such that the SÖ had neither the competence nor the type of organization needed (Prop. 1990–91, no. 18, 111) The result of the bill, which on this point was not controversial within the Riksdag, was that all 750 persons employed at the SÖ and the regional school boards were laid off (and in the end some of them were probably taken care of by the AMS!). The severity of this attack must be judged against the fact that such a political measure had never before been used in Sweden. While mergers and reorganizations have been frequent, no national board or agency of such importance has ever been simply abolished (except for the AK 1933, no. 40; cf. chap. 5).

The political symbolism of this decision is evident in the fact that the minister of education first announced his intention to close down the SÖ in a speech at the Social Democratic party convention in September 1990 (SAP-protokoll 1990, C:131). For the SÖ, including its director-general, this decision came as a complete surprise (Gelin et al. 1992). It should be added that, according to newspaper reports, the education minister's announcement was received with great enthusiasm by the party delegates (DN 09–20–90).

The SÖ was to be replaced by a new central educational administration, which would have little power to direct individual schools. The new School Agency (Sw. Skolverket) would instead center its activities on information, research, advice, and the evaluation of educational performance. None of the former school bureaucrats in the SÖ or the regional school boards were guaranteed a job in the new (and much smaller) organization. Instead, they all had to apply for the new positions; in the end, only 61 out of a total of 750 were employed in the new organization (Gelin et al. 1992, 14).

Professor Ulf P. Lundgren was appointed as the new organization's director-general. Lundgren was known as a radical professor of education, a party member, and a close advisor to the Social Democratic minister of education at the time. The Conservative press complained that most top-level positions in the new organization were filled by Social Democrats, and that loyalty to Social Democratic school policy counted as a strong merit in the recruitment process (SvD. 06–04–91; cf. RD 1990–91, no. 125, 78–82). One of the more curious features of the whole episode occurred when Lundgren demanded that the new agency be moved from the old premises of the SÖ, because he was afraid the new organization would otherwise inherit the old bureaucratic way of doing things. "It's in the walls," he said (ibid.). The new organization was duly transferred to new premises.

As mentioned in the preface, I presented the larger part of this book as a Ph.D. thesis in political science in 1986 in Sweden (Rothstein 1986). If good theory is judged by its generation of accurate predictions, I dare say I have come close to hitting a home run. For now, eight years later, the AMS and the active labor market policy are politically stronger and more legitimate than ever in Swedish politics. Nor has the character of the AMS as a Social Democratic cadre organization been changed (cf. Henning and Ramström 1989). The SÖ, for its part, has been closed down by the Social Democrats, who replaced it with a new, more flexible organization designed to evaluate educational goals rather than issue rules.

It seems fair therefore to conclude that the events of the 1980s and early 1990s have confirmed the analysis of this book. For politics is not just about policies, it is also about the administrative and institutional structures by means of which policies are implemented. That is because, to paraphrase the famous German war theorist Carl von Clausewitz, administration is the continuation of politics by other means. The abolition of the SÖ was a logical (but late) step for the Social Democrats. In the same way, the consolidation of the labor market policy (notwithstanding the demise of the Rehn-Meidner model) reflects institutional legitimacy.

**Notes**

**References**

**Index**

# Notes

## 1. Understanding Social Democracy

1. For a somewhat different interpretation, stressing the importance of non–social democratic forces see Baldwin (1990), Castles (1985), and Marklund (1982).

2. For an important exception see Pontusson (1993) in which conditions under which different Social Democratic reforms will fail or succeed are analyzed. In Pontusson's study, the success or failure of reformist strategies is related to factors "external" to the reform put forth, such as appeal to middle class swing voters or confrontation with the interests of capital. This book differs from Pontusson's approach in stressing more "internal" institutional factors as critical for explaining a reform's success or failure.

## 2. State, Class, and Organization

1. In one respect, all three levels may be studied from an institutional perspective. The "general character of the state," for example, can be regarded as an institutional concept, as can microlevel details in the implementation process (cf. Steinmo and Thelen 1992). Another problem is how to distinguish between social norms and formal rules. The problem with a too-broad definition of institutions, however, is that it encompasses almost every kind of political entity;

moreover, *if institutions are everything, maybe they are nothing.* For this reason I prefer the more precise definition of political institutions put forward by Margaret Levi (1990, 405): "formal arrangements for aggregating individuals and regulating their behavior through the use of explicit rules and decision processes enforced by an actor or actors formally recognized as possessing such power."

2. According to George, the selection of cases for this method should be guided not by numbers "but *variety,* that is, cases belonging to the same class that differ from each other. Thus, the investigator in designing the study will either seek cases in which outcome of the dependent variable differed or cases having the same outcome but a different explanation for it. The investigator . . . seeks to identify *the variety of different causal patterns* that can occur for the phenomenon in question" (George 1979, 60).

3. I have not yet seen a single study linking the significant insights of implementation research with the state-centered approach in political history and/or with the class-centered approach in comparative policy analysis.

### 3. Comparing State Apparatuses

1. I want to stress that, while such complaints against bureaucratic organizations might of course be valid, there is also a large literature about patronage and corruption in public life—ills which may be considered to arise from a deficient application of bureaucratic principles. If bureaucracies are understood as government agencies applying explicit, general, and universal rules, and if bureaucratic officials implementing these rules treat citizens in a neutral and objective way (excluding race, political affiliation, etc., from consideration), then the bureaucratic organization appears in a more favorable light (cf. Shefter 1977). The bureaucratic phenomenon is very definitely Janus-faced.

2. See Armstrong 1973; Chester 1981; Evans 1983, 285–91; Fischer and Lundgren 1975; Roy 1981; Skowronek 1982. For a minor study of the Swedish case see Rothstein 1982b.

3. In his classification of organizational types, Mintzberg delineates two types of bureaucratic organization: the machine bureaucracy and the professional bureaucracy. The major difference between these two is that, while the former relies on standardized rules and central control, the latter depends on professional knowledge and standardized skills. The professional bureaucracy is therefore much less centralized, since the "operators" at the bottom of the organization must be granted considerable control over their work, making central control difficult (Mintzberg 1983b, 189–92). The standardization of skills, however, implies that the professional type of organization "is essentially bureaucratic, its coordination—like that of the Machine Bureaucracy—achieved by design, by standards that predetermine what is to be done" (ibid., 191). The problems specific to professional bureaucracies, in particular the power of the professionals and the difficulty of changing their notions of the purpose of their work, are largely similar to those reported in implementation research about "human-processing" agencies; such problems are therefore not treated separately in this chapter.

4. An important exception is Herbert Kaufman's study from 1960 of the

U.S. Forest Service in which he stressed the importance of shared values, commitment, and loyalty of the front personnel to the overall goals of the organization. In Kaufman's words, the organization was such that it "practically merge the individual's identity with the identity of the organization" (1960, 197). Another exception is Amitai Etzioni who in 1961 specified what he called "normative" organizations, in contrast to coercive and utilitarian organizations (12–14).

5. It should be added that structures similar to the cadre organization have been identified in the burgeoning literature about "organizational culture" in the field of modern management.

6. In the literature addressing the relation between political parties and government organizations, patronage and spoils systems often receive attention (cf. Shefter 1977). I want to stress that a cadre organization is very different from a patronage system. The most important differences are that, firstly, while a patronage system is built on the awarding of benefits to followers, recruitment to a cadre organization is based on ideological commitment. Secondly, while a patronage system is intended to promote support for an existing political order, a cadre system is geared to social change.

### 4. Reformist Policies: Success and Failure

1. For example, see Arnman and Jönsson 1983, 149–53; Boucher 1982; Isling 1974; 1980; Marklund 1980, 156–75; and 1982.

2. The primary intentions behind the comprehensive school reform are thus attributable to the Social Democratic party. It is therefore necessary to explain why this party, during its government coalition with the Agrarians from 1951 to 1957, relinquished the education portfolio to an Agrarian, Ivar Persson. The Agrarians held only four of the sixteen posts in the coalition cabinet, and the Social Democrats should have been able, had they so wished, to retain the Ministry of Education. That they did not do so should not be interpreted, however, as a lack of interest in education policy. The school issue had been a source of controversy among the Agrarians for a long time; when the unified school system was approved in principle by the Riksdag in 1950, for instance, a number of leading Agrarians were among the few proposing the direct rejection of the bill (Marklund 1980, 174). Persson, however, belonged to the group of Agrarians who favored the reform and promoted it in their party (cf. his biography in *Svenska Män och Kvinnor* 1949). Tage Erlander, in his memoirs, writes:

> One of my grounds for the coalition was to try to anchor the new school reform among the Agrarians. I was therefore concerned to have Persson from Skabersjö as minister of education (Erlander 1974. 280). . . . As to the composition of the new Ministry, I found strong grounds for having Persson from Skabersjö in the Ministry of Education. He had been an asset on the School Commission, managing among other things to convince his party that the school reform was of major importance for the rural population. Now that the reform was to be implemented, it would be most valuable to have the Agrarians directly involved in the task (Erlander 1974, 259–60; cf. Erlander 1973, 239).

During the coalition negotiations, according to Erlander, the Agrarians hesitated to accept the education portfolio, but were compelled to do so by the Social Democrats (Erlander 1974, 282). The arrangement with Ivar Persson was thus an integral part of the Social Democrats' strategy to gain parliamentary support for the reform. The Social Democrats' parliamentary tactics were successful in that the Agrarians supported their school policy. It is more difficult to assess the administrative outcome—that is, how the Ministry of Education, headed by Ivar Persson, implemented the reform. The appointment of a Social Democrat (Ragnar Edenman) as Persson's under secretary of state at the ministry at least assured Erlander that "our intentions would not be distorted" (Erlander 1974, 260). In Edenman's view, Persson was loyal to the school policy aims of the Social Democrats throughout the coalition years (Edenman, interview). Erlander observed that "the apparent mismatch, Persson and Edenman, came up to my expectations in the implementation of the school reform" (1974, 291). Moreover, the director-general of the National Board of Education from 1948 to 1964, Nils Gustav Rosén, confirmed this assessment of the part played by Persson in school policy (Rosén, interview).

3. Between 1964 and 1974, Gösta Rehn was head of the OECD Manpower and Social Policy Commission. From this position, he tried to export the model to other OECD countries. Conferences between labor and employers' representatives were arranged, reviews of the manpower policy in each OECD country were published, together with policy recommendations for more active measures, etc. (Rhen, interview; Blankenburg 1978). This effort generated some initial responses—in Britain, Germany, France, Austria, and the United States, for example. Despite this, no country has been able to launch an active labor market policy at the same level as Sweden. The setbacks have been dramatic in both Britain and the United States (King and Rothstein 1993; Weir 1992). To explain this, Gösta Rehn has pointed both to a lack of political commitment *and* to faulty institutional arrangements.

4. Even Benny Hjern, who does not usually stress the significance of central power centers in public administration, claims that the National Labor Market Board "has had a dominant position in Swedish policy and administration since the late 1950s" (1982, 76; cf. Hanf, Hjern, and Porter: "In size as well as influence the National Labor Market Board is in the centre of most domestic policy issues in Sweden," 1978, 307; cf. Hjern 1983).

5. See Ragnar Edenman in SAP-protokoll 1956, 297.

6. It is difficult to say exactly when the comprehensive school reform was introduced. Because of the extensive experiments and trials undertaken from 1950 onward, about half of Swedish students already attended some type of comprehensive school in 1962 (Marklund 1981).

7. See Ginsburg 1983; Katzenstein 1985, 119; Mucciaroni 1992 chap. 9; Weir 1992, 8; and Wilensky and Turner 1987.

## 5. Organization and Policy as Historical Structures

1. Compare with the postwar "Swedish model," Rothstein 1982.

2. Previous research has instead pointed more to the formal agreement made in 1938 (the Saltsöbaden-agreement) which regarded the procedures for collective bargaining (Söderpalm 1980). For yet another interpretation, stressing

the distributional intraclass elements behind these cross-class compromises, see Swenson (1991).

3. Thomson emptied his personal archive of everything of political interest save this single document. As a former acting professor of political science, he might have thought it appropriate to give at least one clue to later generations in the profession.

4. See Isling 1980, 131–44, 163–64, 196–98, 230–32, 245–58; Marklund 1984, 131–36; 1985, 264–79; and Wennås 1966.

5. See AK no. 32, 55–70; no. 34, 48–50; no. 35, 61–66, 70, 72, 74–75, 80, 83, 92–97; cf. Herrström 1966, 128, 201.

## 6. Organizational Connection One: The AMS

1. For example, see the AMS archives, Arbetsmarknadsinformation series M 1956, 1 and series A 1957, 4 and 1954, 5; B. Olsson 1954; 1958; 1960; 1963; cf. Furåker 1976, 110–12.

2. See Blankenburg 1978, 280; cf. Showler 1976, 30–35; L. Levine 1969, 17–23, 31; Lewis 1978, 4; and Rehn, interview.

3. For example, see Prop. 1947, no. 239, 236; Prop. 1966, no. 52, 25–26; SOU 1946, no. 51, 45; SOU 1968, no. 61, 58; cf. AK 1962, no. 13, 3–4.

4. Compare with *AB* 08–04–82; *SvD* 08–02–82, 08–03–82, 08–04–82, 08–09–82, 05–07–82, 05–07–82, 05–08–82, 05–10–82, 05–20–82, 05–24–82, and 05–30–82.

5. See Blankenburg et al. 1976; Blankenburg 1978, 292; cf. Scharpf et al. 1982; Hanf et al. 1978; Krautkrämer 1978; Lewis 1978, xv; and O'Toole 1983.

6. See interviews 1, 4, 12, 21, 23, and 30; SOU 1968, no. 61, 68; cf. *Förändring och trygghet* 1967, 36, 49.

## 7. Organizational Connection Two: The SÖ

1. See Isling 1980, 306; Richardson 1983, 152–59; and SOU 1948, no. 27.

2. The reader might be interested to know that the ideas behind this proposal were taken from the educational debate in the United States. One of the most influential persons in the School Commission, Alva Myrda, had been very impressed by the ideas of John Dewey and other progressivists in American education. Although the idea of individualized, nonauthoritarian teaching was neither unknown nor untried in Sweden at the time, it seems to have been the American connection that gave the commission such faith in the possibility of changing teaching methods, and such confidence in the positive implications of such a change.

3. See Isling 1980, 307–11; Marklund 1980, 77–81; and Richardson 1983, 88–89, 152–59.

4. See Stålhammar 1984, 181; Svingby 1977, 27, 56; 1978, 168, 193; cf. Callewaert and Nilsson 1974.

5. For the attitude of the KÖY to the school reform, see Prop. 1950, no. 70, 99, 187–88.

6. Compare with Pincus 1976, 51; Stewart and Bullock 1981; cf. Rodgers and Bullock 1976.

7. Compare with Prop. 1967, no. 4, in particular the submission from the SÖ on p. 36.

8. See Hagelin 1968, 7; Marklund 1982, 66–70; Marklund 1985, 290; cf. Munknäs 1983.

## 8. Summary and Conclusions

1. See Blankenburg et al. 1976; Blankenburg 1978, 292; Janoski 1990; King and Rothstein 1993; L. Levine 1969, 28; Lewis 1978, xv; Scharpf et al. 1982; and Showler 1976.

2. See Bowles and Gintis 1976. For an opposing view see Katznelson and Weir 1985 and Archer 1982.

# References

*AB. Aftonbladet.* Daily newspaper published in Stockholm. Various issues.

Ahrne, G. 1990. *Agency and organization: Towards an organizational theory of society.* London: Sage.

AK. Andra kammarens protokoll. Records from the Swedish Parliament, Second Chamber. Various years.

*Aktiv arbetsmarknadspolitik* 1976. Stockholm: LO

*Aktuellt i Politiken.* 1992. Journal published by the Swedish Social Democratic Party.

Albrow, M. 1970. *Bureaucracy.* London: Pall Mall Press.

Allison. G. T. 1971. *Essence of decision: Explaining the Cuban missile crisis.* Boston: Little Brown.

Amenta. E. 1991. Making the most of a case study: Theories of the welfare state and the American experience. In *Issues and alternatives in comparative social research,* edited by C. S. Ragin. Leiden: E. J. Brill.

AMS archives.

*AMSFS.* 1977. Arbetsmarknadsstyrelsens författningssamling. Stockholm: AMS.

*AMS-handboken.* 1975. Stockholm: Arbetsmarknadsstyrelsen.

Anderson, P. 1979. *Lineages of the absolutist state.* London: Verso.

Andersson, Ivar. 1967. *En man för sig.* Stockholm: Bonniers.

*Arbetarrörelsens efterkrigsprogram.* 1946. Stockholm: SAP.

*Arbetsförmedlingen.* 1952. Stockholm: Kungl. Arbetsmarknadsstyrelsen och Hermods.

*Arbetsförmedlingen.* Journal published by the Swedish Association of Employment Service Officers. Various years.

*Arbetsmarknadspolitik i förändring.* 1992. Stockholm: Liber.

*Arbetsmarknadsservice.* 1967. Stockholm: Arbetsmarknadsstyrelsen.

Archer, M. 1982. The sociology of educational systems. In *Sociology: The state of the art,* edited by M. Archer. Beverly Hills: Sage.

Armstrong, J. A. 1973. *The European administrative elite.* Princeton: Princeton University Press.

Arnestam. L. 1983. Vem bestämmer i AMS. Seminar paper, Department of Political Science, University of Lund.

Arnman, G., and I. Jönsson. 1983. *Segregation och svensk skola.* Lund: Arkiv.

Astley, W. G., and A. H. Van der Ven. 1983. Central perspectives and debates in organizational theory. *Administrative Science Quarterly* 28.

*ASÖ.* Aktuellt från skolöverstyrelsen. Stockholm: SÖ.

Axelsson, A. 1974. Den nuvarande lednings-och beslutsfunktionen i skolan. In *Skolan som arbetsplats.* Stockholm: Allmänna förlaget.

Baldwin, P. 1990. *The politics of social solidarity: Class bases of the European welfare state 1875–1975.* Cambridge: Cambridge University Press.

Balla, B. 1972. *Kaderwervaltung.* Stuttgart.

Barrett, S., and C. Fudge. 1981. Examining the policy-action relationship. In *Policy and action: Essays on the implementation of public policy,* edited by S. Barrett and C. Fudge. London: Methuen.

Beetham, D. 1985. *Max Weber and the theory of modern politics.* London: Allen and Unwin.

———. 1982. A framework for policy analysis. In *Interorganizational coordination: Theory, research, implementation,* edited by D. L. Roger and D. A. Whetter. Ames: Iowa State University Press.

Bergström, Hans. 1991. Sweden's politics and party system at the crossroads. *West European Politics* 14.

Berman, P. 1978. The study of macro- and micro-implementation. *Public Policy* 26.

Bernstein, E. [1899] 1965. *Evolutionary socialism.* New York: Schocken Books.

Berntson, L., and G. Persson. 1979. The Swedish labour market policy. In *Limits of the welfare state: Critical views on post-war Sweden,* edited by J. A. Fry. Farnborough: Saxon House.

Birnbaum, P. 1988. *States and collective action: The European experience.* Cambridge: Cambridge University Press.

Blankenburg, E. 1978. Comparing the incomparable—a study of employment agencies in five countries. In *Organizational functioning in a cross-cultural perspective,* edited by G. W. England, A. R. Negandhi B., and R. Wilpert. Kent, Ohio: Kent State University Press.

Blankenburg, E., G. Schmid, and H. P. Treiber. 1976. "Legitimitäts—und implementierungsprobleme aktiver arbeitsmarktpolitik." In *Bürgerlicher staat und politische legitimation,* edited by R. Ebbighausen. Frankfurt am Main: Suhrkamp.

Blau, P. 1974. *On the nature of organizations.* New York: Wiley.

———. 1987. *Revising state theory.* Philadelphia: Temple University Press.

Boucher, L. 1982. *Tradition and change in Swedish education.* Oxford: Pergamon.
Bowles, S., and H. Gintis. 1976. *Schooling in capitalist America.* New York: Basic Books.
Brand. D. 1988. *Corporatism and the rule of law.* Ithaca, N.Y.: Cornell University Press.
Brevner, E. 1962. Fortbildning av lärare för grundskolan. *Skola och samhälle* 43.
Broady, D. 1982. Den smygande skolreformen. *Kritisk Utbildningstidskrift-KRUT* 23–24.
Bullock, C. S. III. 1981. Implementation of equal education opportunity programs: A comparative analysis. In *Effective policy implementation,* edited by D. A. Mazmanian and P. A. Sabatier. Lexington, Mass.: Lexington Books.
Burrell, G., and G. Morgan. 1979. *Sociological paradigms and organizational analysis.* London: Heineman.
Callewaert, S., and B. A. Nilsson. 1974. *Samhället—skolan och skolans inre arbete.* Lund: Department of Sociology.
———. 1980. *Skolklassen som socialt system.* Lund: Lunds Bok and Tidskrifts AB.
Cameron, D. 1984. Social democracy, corporatism, labor quiescence, and the representation of economic interest in advanced capitalist society. In *Order and conflict in contemporary capitalism,* edited by J. H. Goldthorpe. New York: Oxford University Press.
Carnoy, M. 1984. *The state and political theory.* Princeton: Princeton University Press.
Carnoy, M., and H. M. Levin, eds. 1976. *The limits of educational reform.* New York: Longman.
Castles, F. G. 1985. *The working class and welfare.* Wellington, New Zeeland: Allen and Unwin.
Cawson, A., and P. Saunders. 1983. Corporatism, competitive politics and class struggle. In *Capital and politics,* edited by R. King. London: Routledge and Kegan Paul.
Chester, Sir N. 1981. *The English administrative system 1780–1870.* Oxford: Oxford University Press.
Christofferson, B. 1977. Kan man ha någon nytta av KUL-projekten. *Forskning om utbildning* 4.
Chubb, J. E., and T. M. Moe. 1990. *Politics, markets and American schools.* Washington D.C: Brookings.
Clark, G. L., and M. Dear. 1984. *State apparatuses—structure and language of legitimacy.* Boston: Allen and Unwin.
Clarke, S. 1977. Marxism, sociology and Poulantzas theory of the state. *Capital and Class* 2.
Colignon, R., and D. Cray. 1981. New organizational perspectives: Critiques and critical organizations. In *Complex organizations: Critical perspectives,* edited by M. Zey-Ferrel and M. Aiken. Glenview, Ill.: Scott Foresman.
Collins, H., and Abramsky C. 1965. *Karl Marx and the British labour movement.* London: Macmillan.
Crossman, R.H.S. 1975. *Diaries of a cabinet minister.* London: Jonathan Cape.
Crouch, C. 1986. Sharing public space: States and organized interests in west-

ern Europe. In *States in history,* edited by J. A. Hall. Oxford: Basil Blackwell.

David, P. A. 1985. Clio and the economics of QWERTY. *American Economic Review* 75.

Davidson, A. 1989. *Two models of welfare: The origins and development of the welfare state in Sweden and New Zealand 1888–1988.* Uppsala: Acta Universitatis Upsaliensis.

Dearlove, J., and P. Saunders. 1984. *Introduction to British politics—analyzing a capitalist democracy.* Cambridge: Polity Press.

*Demokrati inom statsförvaltningen.* 1952. Stockholm: SAP.

*DN. Dagens Nyheter.* The leading Swedish daily newspaper, published in Stockholm. Various issues.

Donahue, J. D. 1989. *The privatization decision: Public ends, private means.* New York: Basic Books.

Douglas, M. 1987. *How institutions think.* London: RKP.

*Ds. Departementsserien.* Official reports published by the Swedish Ministries. Various years.

Eisenstadt, S. N. 1965. *Essays on comparative institutions.* New York: Wiley.

Ekholm, M., and N. Lagervall. 1983. Vem blir skolledare. *Skolledaren* 6.

Elander, I. 1978. *Det nödvändiga och det önskvärda: En studie av socialdemokratisk ideologi och regionalpolitik 1914–72.* Lund: Arkiv.

Elmore, R. F. 1978. Organizational models of social program implementation. *Public Policy* 26.

Elster, J. 1982. Marxism, functionalism, and game theory: The case for methodological individualism. *Theory and Society* 11.

———. 1985. *Making sense of Marx.* Cambridge: Cambridge University Press.

Elvander, N. 1972. *Intresseorganisationerna i dagens Sverige.* Lund: Gleerup

———. 1988. *Den svenska modellen.* Stockholm: Allmänna förlaget.

Engvall, M. 1980. *Och så blev det 1939 . . . Glimtar av praktisk arbetsmarknadspolitik.* Stockholm: Korrekt-Repro AB.

Erasmie, T., and S. Marklund. 1977. *Vad blev det av ämneslärarutbildningen.* Stockholm: Skolöverstyrelsen.

Erlander, T. 1973. *1914–1949.* Stockholm: Tiden.

———. 1974. *1949–1954.* Stockholm: Tiden.

———. 1976. *1955–1960.* Stockholm: Tiden.

———. 1982. *1960-talet: Samtal med Arvid Lagercrantz.* Stockholm: Tiden.

Esping-Andersen, G. 1985. *Politics against markets: The social democratic road to power.* Princeton: Princeton University Press.

———. 1990. *The three worlds of welfare capitalism.* Cambridge: Polity Press.

Esping-Andersen, G., R. Friedland, and E. O. Wright. 1976. Modes of class struggle and the capitalist state. *KapitaliState* 4/5.

Ettarp, L. 1980. *Arbetsmarknadspolitiken i teori och praktik.* Vällingby: LiberFörlag.

Etzioni. A. 1961. *A comparative analysis of complex organizations.* New York: Free Press of Glencoe.

Evans, E. J. 1983. *The forging of the modern state 1783–1887.* London: Longman.

*Fackföreningsrörelsen.* 1933. Official journal of the Swedish Trade Union Confederation (LO).

*Fackföreningsrörelsen och arbetsmarknadspolitiken.* 1976. Stockholm: LO.

*Fackläraren.* Journal published by Svenska facklärarförbundet. Various years.

Falkenström, G. 1904. *Redogörelse för arbetsförmedling.* Stockholm: SAF.

Fesler, J. W. 1990. The state and its study: The whole and the parts. In *Public administration: The state of the discipline,* edited by N. B. Lynn and A. Wildavsky. Chatham, N.J.: Chatham House.

Fischer, W., and P. Lundgren. 1975. The recruitment and training of administrative and technical personnel. In *The formation of national states in western Europe,* edited by C. H. Tilly. Princeton, N.J.: Princeton University Press.

FK. Första kammarens protokoll. Records from the Swedish Parliament, First Chamber. Various years.

Fredrikson, V. 1950. *Den svenska folkskolans historia. Femte delen.* Stockholm: Bonniers.

Fudge, C., and S. Barrett. 1981. Reconstructing the field of analysis. In *Policy and action,* edited by S. Barrett and C. Fudge. London: Methuen.

Furåker, B. 1976. *Stat och arbetsmarknad.* Lund: Arkiv.

*Förändring och trygghet.* 1967. Stockholm: AMS.

Gabriel, K. 1981. Organizations and social change. In *An introduction to theories of social change,* edited by H. Strasser and S. C. Randall. London: Routledge and Kegan Paul.

Garrett, G., and P. Lange. 1989. Government partisanship and economic performance: When and how does "who governs" matters? *Journal of Politics* 51.

———. 1991. Political responses to interdependence: What's "left for the left." *International Organization* 45.

Geijer, A. 1969. Fackföreningsrörelsen och det socialdemokratiska partiet. In *Ideerna som drivkraft: En vänbok till Tage Erlander,* edited by L. Andersson. Stockholm: Tiden.

Gelin, G., L. Gonäs, L. Hallsten, and M. Eriksson. 1992. *Statliga myndigheter under avveckling—exemplet Skolöverstyrelsen/ Länsskolnämnderna.* Stockholm: Arbetslivscentrum.

George, A. L. 1979. Case studies and theory development: The method of structured, focused comparison. In *Diplomacy: New approaches in history, theory and policy,* edited by P. G. Lauren. New York: The Free Press.

George, A. L., and T. J. McKeown. 1985. Case studies and theories of organizational change. In *Advances in information processing in organizations.* Vol. 2. Santa Barbara: JAI Press.

Gesser, B. 1985. *Utbildning, jämlikhet, arbetsdelning.* Lund: Arkiv.

Gesser, B., and E. Fasth. 1973. *Gymnasieutbildning och social skiktning.* Stockholm: Universitetskanslerämbetet.

Giddens, A. 1979. *Central problems in social theory.* London: Macmillan.

———. 1981. *A contemporary critique of historical materialism.* London: Macmillan.

———. 1982. *Profiles and critique in social theory.* London: Macmillan.

———. 1984. *The constitution of society.* Cambridge: Polity Press.

Ginsburg, H. 1983. *Full employment and public policy: The United States and Sweden.* Lexington, Mass.: D. C. Heath.

Gough, I. 1979. *The political economy of the welfare state.* London: Macmillan.

Grafstein, R. 1988. The problem of institutional constraint. *Journal of Politics* 50.

Gran, B. 1977. *Lärarutbildning—Svenska erfarenheter och internationella utveck-lingslinjer.* Stockholm: Utbildningsdepartementet.

Grosin, L. 1991. *Skolklimat, prestation och uppförande i åtta högstadieskolor.* Report no. 53, Department of Education, University of Stockholm.

Gustafsson, B. 1976. Den "nya" ekonomisk-historiska forskningen och de kon-trafaktiska förklaringarna: Några synpunkter. *Historisk Tidskrift* 96.

Hadenius, K. 1990. *Jämlikhet och frihet: Politiska mål för den svenska grund-skolan.* Uppsala: Acta Universitatis Upsaliensis.

Hagelin, J. O. 1968. Enhetlighet eller mångfald: Studier i svensk enhetsskolepoli-tik 1950–51. Dissertation, Department of Government, Uppsala University.

Hall, P. 1986. *Governing the economy: The politics of state interventionism in Britain and France.* New York: Oxford University Press.

————. 1989. Conclusion: The politics of keynesian ideas. In *The political power of economic ideas: Keynesianism across nations,* edited by P. Hall. Princeton, N.J.: Princeton University Press.

Ham, C., and M. Hill. 1984. *The policy process in the modern capitalist state.* Brighton: Wheatsheaf.

*Handbok för den offentliga arbetsförmedlingen.* 1936. Stockholm: Socialstyrelsen.

Hanf, K., B. Hjern, and D. O. Porter. 1978. Local networks of manpower training in the federal republic of Germany and Sweden. In *Interorganizational poli-cy making,* edited by K. Hanf and F. W. Scharpf. London: Sage.

Hanf, K., and F. W. Scharpf, eds. 1978. *Interorganizational policy making.* London: Sage.

Hart, H. 1978. *Labour market administration in Sweden.* Report 1978, no. 14a. Berlin, International Institute of Management.

Heckscher, G. 1958. *Svensk statsförvalting i arbete.* Stockholm: SNS.

Heclo, H. 1974. *Modern social policies in Britain and Sweden.* New Haven: Yale University Press.

Heclo, H., and H. Madsen. 1987. *Policy and politics in Sweden: Principled prag-matism.* Philadelphia: Temple University Press.

Hedborg, A., and R. Meidner. 1984. *Folkhemsmodellen.* Stockholm: Raben and Sjögren.

Held, D., and J. Krieger. 1984. Theories of the state: Some competing claims. In *The state in capitalist Europe,* edited by S. Bornstein, D. Held, and J. Krieger. London: Allen and Unwin.

Henning, R., and D. Ramström. 1989. *Förvaltningsförnyelse.* Stockholm: Carlssons.

Herrström, G. 1966. *1927 års skolreform: En studie in svensk skolpolitik 1918–1927.* Stockholm: Svenska Bokförlaget.

Heydebrand, W. 1977. Organizational, contradictions in public bureaucracies: Toward a Marxian theory of organizations. *The Sociological Quarterly* 18.

Hibbs, D. 1977. Political parties and macroeconomic policies. *American Political Science Review* 71.

Hildebrand, S. 1969. *Skola för demokrati.* Stockholm: Sveriges Radios Förlag.

Hill, M. 1981. Unemployment and government manpower policy. In *The work-less state—studies in unemployment,* edited by B. Showler and A. Sinfield. Oxford: Martin Robertson.

Hilton, R. 1984. Feudalism in Europe: Problems for historical materialists. *New Left Review* 147.

Hjern, B. 1982. Arbetsmarknadspolitikens ideer och deras teori-inramning. *Arbetsmarknadspolitik under debatt.* Stockholm: Liberförlag.

——. 1983. Förvaltnings—och implementeringsforskning. *Starsvetenskaplig Tidskrift* 86.

Hjern, B., and C. Hull. 1982. Implementation research as empirical constitutionalism. *European Journal of Political Research* 10.

Hjern, B., and D. O. Porter. 1981. Implementation structures: A new unit of administrative analysis. *Organization Studies* 2.

Hobsbawn, E. 1976. *The age of capital 1848–1875.* London: NAL Dutton.

Husén, T. 1966. *Vad lärarutbildningen gäller—Ett debattinlägg.* Stockholm.

——. 1977. *Jämlikhet genom utbildning.* Stockholm: Natur och Kultur.

Härnqvist, K., and A. Svensson. 1980. *Den sociala selektionen till gymnasiestudier: En forskningsrapport för gymnasieutredningen.* SOU 1980, no. 30. Stockholm: Liber.

Häusserman, H. 1977. *Der Politik der Bürokratie.* Frankfurt: Campus.

Immergut, E. 1992. *The political construction of interests: National health insurance politics in Switzerland, France and Sweden 1930–1970.* New York: Cambridge University Press.

Ingram, H. 1990. Implementation: A review and a suggested framework. In *Public administration: The state of the discipline,* edited by N. B. Lynn and A. Wildavsky. Chatham, N.J.: Chatham House.

Ingram, H., and D. Mann. 1980. Policy failure: An issue deserving analysis. In *Why policies succeed or fail,* edited by H. Ingram and D. Mann. London: Sage.

Isaac, J. 1987. *Power and Marxist theory: A realist view.* Ithaca, N.Y.: Cornell University Press.

Isling, Å. 1974. *Vägen till en demokratisk skola.* Stockholm: Prisma.

——. 1975. MUT:s uppgång och fall. *Arbetet* 1975, March 20, 21, and 24.

——. 1980. *Kampen för och emot en demokratisk skola.* Stockholm: Sober.

Janoski, T. 1990. *The political economy of unemployment: Active labor market policy in West Germany and the United States.* Berkeley and Los Angeles: University of California Press.

Jelinek, M., L. Smircich, and P. Hirsch. 1983. Introduction: A code of many colours. *Administrative Science Quarterly* 28.

Jerneck, M. 1986. *SAF's framtidssyn: Förutsägelser, målsättningar och dilemman.* Stockholm: SAF.

Jessop, B. 1982. *The capitalist state.* Oxford: Martin Robertson.

Johansson, A. L. 1989. *Tillväxt och klassamarbete: En studie i den svenska modellens uppkomst.* Stockholm: Tiden.

Jämlikhet. 1969. Report to the 24th Swedish Social Democratic Party conference 1969.

Katz, E., and B. Danet. 1973. Introduction: Bureaucracy as a problem for sociology and society. In *Bureaucracy and the public,* edited by E. Katz and B. Danet. New York: Basic Books.

Katzenstein, P. 1985. *Small states in world markets: Industrial policy in europe.* Ithaca, N.Y.: Cornell University Press.

Katznelson, I. 1981. Lenin or Weber? Choices in Marxist theory of politics. *Political Studies* 29.

Katznelson, I., and M. Weir. 1985. *Schooling for all: Class, race and the decline of the democratic ideal*. New York: Basic Books.

Kaufman, H. 1960. *The forest ranger*. Baltimore: Johns Hopkins University Press.

———. 1973. *Administrative feedback*. Washington D.C.: The Brookings Institution.

Keegan, J. 1976. *The face of battle*. London: Penguin Books.

Kim, L. 1983. *Att välja eller att väljas: En studie av tillträdesreglerna och övergången frdn gymnasieskola till högskola*. Stockholm: Universitets—och högskoleämbetet.

King, D., and B. Rothstein, B. 1993. Institutional choices and labour market policy: A British-Swedish comparison. *Comparative Political Studies* 25.

Kjellberg, A. 1983. *Facklig organisering i tolv länder*. Lund: Arkiv.

Korpi, W. 1983. *The democratic class struggle*. London: Routledge and Keegan Paul.

Krasner, S. D. 1984. Approaches to the state: Alternative conceptions and historical dynamics. *Comparative Politics* 16.

Krautkrämer, U. 1978. *Labour market administration in the Federal Republic of Germany*. Report 1978, no. 14a. Berlin: International Institute of Management.

Lagreid, P., and J. P. Olsen. 1978. *Byrdkrati og beslutninger*. Oslo: Universitetsforlaget.

Lane, J. E. 1983. The concept of implementation. *Statsvetenskaplig Tidskrift* 86.

Lane, J. E., D. McKay, and K. Newton. 1991. *Political data handbook OECD countries*. Oxford: Oxford University Press.

Lange, P. 1984. Unions, workers and wage regulation: The rational bases of consent. In *Order and conflict in contemporary capitalism*, edited by J. H. Goldthorpe. New York: Oxford University Press.

———. 1987. The institutionalization of concertation. Paper presented at the annual meeting of the American Political Science Association, 3–6 September, at the Palmer House, Chicago.

Lembruch, G. 1991. The organization of society, administrative strategies and policy networks. In *Political choice: Institutions, rules and the limits of rationality*, edited by R. M. Czada and A. Windhoff-Héritier. Boulder, Colo.: Westview Press.

Lenin. V. I. [1907] 1967. *The state and the revolution*. Moscow: Progress Publishers.

Levi, M. 1990. A logic of institutional change. In *The limits of rationality*, edited by K. S. Cook and M. Levi. Chicago: University of Chicago Press.

Levine, L. 1969. *The public employment service in social and economic policy*. Paris: OECD.

Lewin, L. 1967. *Planhushållningsdebatten*. Uppsala: Statsvetenskapliga föreningen.

Lewis, J. 1978. *Labour market administration in the United Kingdom*. Report 1978, no. 14c. Berlin: International Institute of Management.

Lindblom, C. 1977. *Politics and markets: The worlds political-economic systems*. New York: Basic Books.

Lindbom, A. 1988. Vem styr den offentliga sektorn. Seminar paper, Department of Political Science, Uppsala University.

Lindström, R. 1946. Arthur Engbergs gärning. *Tiden* 38.

Lipp, W. 1978. Bürokratische, Partizipative und Kaderorganisation als Instrumente sozialer Steurung. *Die Verwaltung* 11.

Lipset, S. M. 1950. *Agrarian socialism.* Berkeley and Los Angeles: University of California Press.

——. 1983. Radicalism or reformism: The sources of working-class politics. *American Political Science Review* 77.

Lipsky, M. 1978. Standing the study of public policy on its head. In *American politics and public policy,* edited by W. D. Burnham and M. W. Weinberg. Cambridge, Mass.: MIT Press.

——. 1980. *Street-level bureaucracy: Dilemmas of the individual in public services.* New York: Russell Sage Foundation.

LO. 1976. *Utbildning för arbete och demokrati.* Stockholm: LO.

Lukes, S. 1977. *Essays in social theory.* New York: Columbia University Press.

Lundgren. U. P. 1979. *Att organisera omvärlden.* Stockholm: Liber.

Lundquist, L. 1975. *Förvaltningen i det politiska systemet.* Lund: Studentlitteratur.

——. 1985. *Implementation steering.* Lund: Studentlitteratur.

Luxemburg, R. [1899] 1972. *Selected political writings.* London: Jonathan Cape.

March, J. G., and J. P. Olsen. 1989. *Rediscovering institutions: The organizational basis of politics.* New York: The Free Press.

Marklund, S. 1960. *Skolreformen och lärarutbildningen: En undersökning utförd pd uppdrag av 1957 drs skolberedning.* Stockholm: University of Stockholm.

——. 1968. *Lärarlämplighet: Problem och propåer.* Stockholm: Liber.

——. 1979. *Skolöverstyrelsen: Historik oeh nuläge.* Stockholm: Department of International Education.

——. 1980. *Skolsverige 1950–1975: Del 1. 1950 års reformbeslut.* Stockholm: Liber.

——. 1981. *Skolsverige 1950–1975: Del 2. Försöksverksamheten.* Stockholm: Liber.

——. 1982. *Skolsverige 1950–1975: Del 3. Frdn Visbykompromissen till SIA.* Stockholm: Liber.

——. 1982b. *Klass, stat och socialpolitik.* Lund: Arkiv.

——. 1984. *Skolan förr och nu: 50 år av utveckling.* Stockholm: Liber.

——. 1985. *Skolsverige 1950-1975. Del 4. Differentieringsfrågan.* Stockholm: Liber.

Marklund, S. and H. Eklund. 1976. *Innovation and in-service training for teachers: Sweden.* Paris: OECD.

Marks, G. 1989. *Unions in politics: Britain, Germany and the United States in the nineteenth and early twentieth centuries.* Princeton: Princeton University Press.

Marx, K. [1852] 1979. *The Eighteenth Brumaire of Louis Bonaparte.* In *K. Marx and F. Engels: Collected works vol. 11.* London: Lawrence and Wishart.

Mayntz, R. 1972. The study of organizations. In *Statsvitenskap— Mellomfag.* Oslo: Universitetsforlaget.

——. 1975. Legitimacy and the directive capacity of the political system. In

*Stress and contradiction in modern capitalism,* edited by L. N. Lindberg. Lexington, Mass.: D. C. Heath.

———. 1978. *Soziologie der öffentlichen Verwaltung.* Heidelberg: C. F. Müller.

Mazmanian, D. A., and P. A. Sabatier. 1983. *Implementation and public policy.* Glenview, Ill.: Scott Foresman.

Mazmanian, D. A., and P. A. Sabatier, eds. 1981. *Effective policy implementation.* Lexington, Mass.: D. C. Heath.

Meidner. R. 1948. Lönepolitikens dilemma vid full sysselsättning. *Tiden* 40.

———. 1969. Active manpower policy and the inflation unemployment dilemma. *Swedish Journal of Economics* 71.

———. 1978. Arbetsmarknadspolitik inför 70-talets kriser. *Sociologisk Forskning* 15.

Mellbourn, A. 1979. *Byråkratins ansikten. Rolluppfattningar hos svenska högre tjänstemän.* Stockholm: Publica.

Mintzberg, H. 1979. *The structuring of organizations.* Englewood Cliffs. New Jersey: Prentice-Hall.

———. 1983. *Power in and around organizations.* Englewood Cliffs, New Jersey: Prentice-Hall.

Morel, M., and F. Dupuy. 1978. *Labour market administration in France.* Report 1978.14e, Berlin: International Institute of Management.

Mouzelis, N. 1984. On the crisis of Marxist theory. *British Journal of Sociology* 25.

———. 1990. *Post-Marxist alternatives: The construction of social orders.* London: Macmillan.

Mucciaroni, G. 1992. *The political failure of employment policy, 1945–1982.* Pittsburgh: University of Pittsburgh Press.

Muggeridge, M. 1961. *Affairs of the heart.* New York: Walker and Company.

Mukherje, S. 1976. *Government and labour markets.* London: PEP.

Munknäs, S. 1981. *Statlig eller kommunal skola.* Stockholm: Stockholm Studies in Politics.

———. 1983. *Tidningspressen och den nya skolan.* Stockholm: Eget förlag.

Murphy, J. T. 1976. Title V of ESEA: The impact of discretionary funds on state education bureaucracies. In *Social program implementation,* edited by W. Williams and R. F. Elmore. New York: Academic Press.

Murray, M. 1988. *Utbildningsexpansion, jämlikhet och avlänkning.* Gothenburg: Göteborg Acta Universitatis.

Noble, C. 1988. State or class?: Notes on two recent views of the welfare state." Paper presented at the annual meeting of the American Political Science Association, Washington D. C., September 1–4, 1988.

Nordström, G. H. 1944. Arbetslöshetspolitiken. In *Ett Genombrott: Festskrift till Gustav Möller.* Stockholm: Tiden.

North, D. C. 1990. *Institutions, institutional change and economic performance.* Cambridge: Cambridge University Press.

OECD 1989. *Employment outlook.* Paris: OECD.

Offe, C. 1975. The theory of the capitalist state and the problem of policy formation. In *Stress and contradiction in modern capitalism,* edited by L. N. Lindberg. Lexington, Mass: D. C. Heath.

————. 1983. Competitive party democracy and the Keynesian welfare state. *Policy Sciences* 15.

————. 1984. *Contradictions of the welfare state.* London: Hutchinson.

————. 1985. *Disorganized capitalism.* Cambridge: Polity Press.

Offe, C., and H. Wiesenthal. 1980. Two logics of collective action. In *Political power and social theory, vol. 1,* edited by M. Zeitlin. Greenwich, Conn.: JAI Press.

Ohlson, B. 1958. Tillkomsten av arbetarrörelsens efterkrigsprogram. *Statsvetenskaplig tidskrift* 61.

Öhman, B. 1970. *Svensk arbetsmarknadspolitik 1900–1947.* Stockholm: Prisma.

————. 1974. *LO och arbetsmarknadspolitiken efter andra världskriget.* Stockholm: Prisma.

Olofsson, G. 1979. *Mellan klass och stat: Om arbetarrörelse, reformism och socialdemokrati.* Lund: Arkiv.

Olsen, J. P. 1983. *Organized democracy: Political institutions in a welfare state— the case of Norway.* Oslo: Universitetsförlaget.

————. 1983b. De som inte anpassar sig slutar snart. *AdministrationsTema* 12.

Olson, M. C. 1982. *The rise and decline of nations.* New Haven: Yale University Press.

Olsson, B. 1951. Arbetsförmedlingens betydelse i efterkrigsvärlden. *Arbetsförmedlingen* 12.

————. 1953. Hur långt vågar vi gå. *Arbetsförmedlingen* 14.

————. 1954. Arbetsmarknadspolitikens instrument. *Tiden* 46.

————. 1958. Aktiv arbetsmarknadspolitik. *Tiden* 50.

————. 1960. 60-talets arbetsmarknad. *Tiden* 52.

————. 1963. Employment policy in Sweden. *International Labour Review* 87.

————. 1967. *Arbetsmarknadspolitiken.* Stockholm: Stockholms Fackliga Centralorganisation.

Olsson, S. E. 1990. *Social policy and welfare state in Sweden.* Lund: Arkiv.

O'Toole, L. J., Jr. 1983. Interorganizational co-operation and the implementation of labour market training programs. *Organizational Studies* 4.

Ouchi, W. G. 1980. Markets, bureaucracies and clans. *Administrative Science Quarterly* 25.

Palme, M., and B. Östling. 1981. Spjutspets mot framtiden—En intervju med Ulf P. Lundgren. *Kritisk utbildningstidskrift-KRUT* 17.

Palme, O. 1953. Hinder vid startlinjen. *Tiden* 45.

————. 1977. *Med egna ord.* Uppsala: Brombergs.

Palumbo, D. J, and D. J. Calista. 1990. Opening Up the Black Box. Implementation and the Policy Process. In *Implementation and the Policy Process,* edited by D. J. Palumbo and D. J. Calista. New York: Greenwood Press.

Pedersen, M. N. 1977. Om den rette brug af historiske materialer i statskunskaben: Nogle didaktiske overvejelser. In *Festskrift till Erik Rasmussen.* Aarhus: Politica.

Perrow, C. 1979. *Complex organizations—a critical essay.* Sec. ed. Glenview, Ill.: Scott Foresman.

Pfeffer, J. 1982. *Organizations and organization theory.* Boston: Pitman.

Pierson, C. 1986. *Marxist theories and democratic politics.* Cambridge: Polity Press.

Pincus, J. 1976. Incentives for innovation in the public schools. In *Social program implementation,* edited by W. Williams and R. F. Elmore. New York: Academic Press.

Pontusson, J. 1992. *The limits of social democracy.* Ithaca, New York: Cornell University Press.

———. 1992b At the end of the third road: Swedish social democracy in crisis. *Politics and Society* 20.

———. 1993. The comparative politics of labor-initiated reforms: Swedish cases of success and failure. *Comparative Political Studies* 25.

Poulantzas, N. 1968. *Pouvoir politique et classes sociales.* Paris: Maspero.

———. 1978. *State, power, socialism.* London: NLB.

Premfors, R. 1989. *Policyanalys.* Lund: Studentlitteratur.

Pressman, J., and A. Wildavsky. 1979. *Implementation: Or how great expectations in Washington are dashed out in Oakland.* 2nd ed. Berkeley and Los Angeles: University of California Press.

Prop. Proposition till riksdagen. Minutes from the Swedish Parliament, Government Bill. Various years.

Przeworski, A. 1985. *Capitalism and Social Democracy.* Cambridge: Cambridge University Press.

———. 1985b. Marxism and rational choice. *Politics and Society* 14.

Przeworski, A., and J. Sprague. 1986. *Paper stones: A history of electoral socialism.* Chicago: The University of Chicago Press.

Przeworski, A., and M. Wallerstein. 1982. The structure of class conflict in democratic capitalist societies. *American Political Science Review* 76.

Ranson, S., B. Hinings, and G. Royston. 1980. The structuring of organizational structures. *Administrative Science Quarterly* 25.

RD. Riksdagens protokoll. Minutes from the Swedish Parliament. Various years.

Rehn, G. 1957. Hata inflationen. *Tiden* 49.

———. 1977. Finansministrarna, LO-ekonomerna och arbetsmarknadspolitiken. In *Ekonomisk debatt och ekonomisk politik. Nationalekonomiska föreningen 100 år.* Stockholm: Norstedts.

———. 1982. Cooperation between the government and the social partners on labour market policy in Sweden. Manuscript. Department of Social Studies, University of Stockholm.

Rein, M. 1983. *From policy to practice.* London: Macmillan Press.

Rein, M., and F. F. Rabinovitz. 1978. Implementation: A theoretical perspective. In *American politics and public policy,* edited by W. D. Burnham and M. W. Weinberg. Cambridge, Mass.: MIT Press.

*Resultat och reformer.* 1964. Stockholm: SAP.

Richardson, G. 1967. 1950 års enhetsskolebeslut—en politisk nebulosa. *Statsvetenskaplig Tidskrift* 70.

———. 1977. *Svensk utbildningshistoria—Skola och samhälle förr och nu.* Lund: Studentlitteratur.

———. 1978. *Svensk skolpolitik 1940–45.* Stockholm: Liber.

———. 1983. *Drömmen om en ny skola.* Stockholm: Liber.

——. 1984. Folkpartiet och enhetskolefrågan. In *Liberal ideologi och politik*, edited by J. Weibull. Stockholm: Folk and Samhälle.

Ripley, R. B., and G. A. Franklin. 1982. *Bureaucracy and policy implementation*. Homewood: Dorsey Press.

Robbins, J. P. 1983. *Organization theory: The structure and design of organizations*. Englewood Cliffs: Prentice Hall.

Rodgers, H. R., Jr., and C. S. Bullock. 1976. *Coercion to complience*. Lexington, Mass.: Lexington Books.

Rose, R. 1984. The programme approach to the growth of government. *British Journal of Political Studies* 15.

Rosén, N. G. 1958. Att utbilda dem som utbildar—en central uppgift i dagens skola. *Skola och samhälle* 39.

Rothstein, B. 1980. AMS som socialdemokratisk reformbyråkrati. *Arkiv for Studier: Arbetarrörelsens Hisoria* 18.

——. 1982. Fanns det en arbetsmarknadspolitik före AMS?. *Arkiv för Studier i Arbetarrörelsens Historia* 23–24.

——. 1982b. Den svenska byråkratins uppgång . . . och fall. *Häften för Kritiska Studier* 15.

——. 1985. Managing the Welfare State: Lessons from Gustav Möller. *Scandinavian Political Studies* 8.

——. 1986. *Den socialdemokratiska staten: Reformer och förvaltning inom svensk arbetsmarknads—och skolpolitik*. Lund: Arkiv.

——. 1987. Corporatism and reformism: The social democratic institutionalization of class struggle. *Acta Sociologica* 30.

——. 1990. Marxism, institutional analysis and working class strength: The Swedish case" *Politics and Society* 18.

——. 1991. "State structure and variation in corporatism: The Swedish case." *Scandinavian Political Studies* 14.

——. 1992. *Den korporativa staten: Intresseorganisationer och statsförvaltning i svensk politik*. Stockholm. Norstedts.

——. 1992b. State Capacity and Social Justice. *Politics and Society* 20.

Roy, W. G. 1981. From electoral to bureaucratic politics. In *Political power and social theory, vol. 1,* edited by M. Zeitlin. Greenwich, Conn.: JAI Press.

RRV. 1971. *Skolöverstyrelsen: En förvaltningsrevisionell studie*. Stockholm: RRV.

——. 1976. *Grundskolebidraget—budgetering och utfall*. Report (dnr 1972:44). Stockholm RRV.

Ruin, O. 1990. *Tage Erlander: Serving the Welfare State, 1946–1969*. Pittsburgh: University of Pittsburgh Press.

Ruther, M., B. Maughan, P. Monimore, and J. Ouston. 1979. *Fifteen thousand hours—secondary schools and their effects on children*. London: Open Books.

Sabatier, P. A., and D. A. Mazmanian. 1981. The implementation of public policy: A framework of analysis. In *Effective policy implementation*, edited by D. A. Mazmanian and P. A. Sabatier. Lexington, Mass.: Lexington Books.

Sandkull, B. 1981. *Personalutbildning som medel att förverkliga skolans mål*. Stockholm: SÖ.

SAP-protokoll. Minutes from the Swedish Social Democratic Party conference. Various years.

Scharpf, F. W. 1977. Public organization and the waning of the welfare state: A research perspective. *European Journal of Political Research* 5.

———. 1991. *Crisis and choice in European social democracy.* Ithaca: Cornell University Press.

Scharpf, F. W., D. Garlicks, F. Maier, and H. Maier. 1982. *Implementationsprobleme offensiver Arbeitsmarktpolitik.* Frankfurt am Main: Campus.

Schiller, B. 1967. *Storstrejken 1909: Förhistoria och orsaker.* Göteborg: Akademiförlaget.

Schurman, F. 1970. *Ideology and organization in Communist China.* Berkeley and Los Angeles: University of California Press.

Scott, W. 1981. *Organizations: Rational, natural and open systems.* Englewood Cliffs, N.J.: Prentice Hall.

Selznick, P. 1949. *TVA and the grass roots.* Berkeley and Los Angeles: University of California Press.

SFS. Svensk författningssamling. Various years.

Shefter, M. 1977. Party and patronage: Germany, England and Italy. *Politics and Society* 7.

Shepsle, K. 1989. Studying institutions: Some lessons from a rational choice approach. *Journal of Theoretical Politics* 1.

Shonfield, A. 1965. *Modern capitalism.* London: Oxford University Press.

Showler, B. 1976. *The public employment service.* London: Longman.

Sjöblom. G. 1968. *Party strategies in a multiparty system.* Lund: Studentlitteratur.

Sjöström, A. 1982. *Det okända AMS.* Stockholm: Timbro.

———. 1985. *Modellbyte i arbetsmarknadspolitiken.* Stockholm: Timbro.

Skocpol, T. 1985. Bringing the state back in: False leads and promising starts in current theories and research. In *Bringing the state back in,* edited by P. Evans, T. Skocpol, and D. Rueschemeyer. New York: Cambridge University Press.

Skocpol, T. and K. Finegold. 1982. State capacity and economic intervention in the early new deal. *Political Science Quarterly* 97.

Skocpol, T., K. Finegold, and M. Goldfield. 1991. Controversy. *American Political Science Review* 85.

Skog-Östlin, K. 1984. *Pedagogisk kontroll och auktoritet.* Malmö: Liber.

Skogh, S. 1963. *Arbetets marknad.* Uppsala: Almqvist & Wiksell.

*Skola för jämlikhet.* 1971. Stockholm: SAP.

*Skollag och skolstadga.* 1971. Stockholm: Kungl. Skolöverstyrelsen.

*Skolledaren.* Journal published by Svenska Skolledarförbundet. Stockholm. Various years.

*Skolvärlden.* Journal published by Lärarnas Riksförbund. Stockholm. Various years.

*Skolöverstyrelsens författningsbok.* 1969–70. Stockholm: Kungl. Skolöverstyrelsen.

*Skolöverstyrelsens skriftserie.* Stockholm: Skolöverstyrelsen. Various years.

Skowronek, S. 1982. *Building a new American state.* Cambridge: Cambridge University Press.

Smith, S. 1991. If politics matters: Implications for a new institutionalism. Paper presented at the annual meeting of the American Political Science Association, Washington D. C.

SNA. Swedish National Archives. Stockholm. (Riksarkivet, Stockholm).

SOU. Statens Offentliga Utredningar. Official reports published by the Swedish government. Various years.

*Skolledare i dag.* Stockholm: Bonniers.

Statskontoret. 1985. *Erfarenheter av stora omorganisationer.* Stockholm: Statskontoret.

*Statsliggaren.* Stockholm: Swedish National Archives. Budget directives from the Swedish Ministries.

Steinmo, S., and K. Thelen. 1992. Historical institutionalism in comparative politics. In *Structuring politics: Historical institutionalism in comparative politics,* edited by S. Steinmo, K. Thelen, and F. Longstreth. New York: Cambridge University Press.

Stephens, J. 1979. *The transition from capitalism to socialism.* London: Macmillan.

Stewart, J., Jr., and C. H. Bullock III. 1981. Implementing equal education opportunity policy. *Administration and Society* 12.

Streeck, W., and P. C. Schmitter. 1985. Community, market, state—and associations: The prospective contribution of interest governance to social order. In *Private Interest Government,* edited by W. Streeck, and P. C. Schmitter. London: Sage.

*SvD. Svenska Dagbladet.* The leading conservative daily newspaper in Sweden, published in Stockholm. Various issues.

*Svenska Män och Kvinnor.* 1949. Stockholm: Bonniers.

Svensson, T. 1994. Socialdemokratins dominans. Dissertation, Uppsala: Acta Universitatis Upsaliensis.

Svingby, G. 1977. Mål för lärarutbildningen. Report for the committee on the education of teachers. Stockholm: Ministry of Education.

———. 1978. *Läroplaner som styrmedel.* Göteborg: Acta Universitatis Gothoburgensis.

———. 1981. Läroplan för 80-talet. In *Från Lgr 69 till Lgr 80,* edited by U. P Lundgren, G. Svingby, and G. Wallin. Stockholm: The College for Teachers' Education.

Swenson, P. 1991. Labor and the limits of the welfare state. *Comparative Politics* 24.

von Sydow, H. 1907. *Om arbetarstatistik och arbetsförmedling inom arbetsgifvarorganisationer.* Stockholm: SAF.

Söderpalm, S. A. 1980. *Arbetsgivarna och Saltsjöbadspolitiken.* Stockholm: SAF.

Tegborg, L. 1969. *Folkskolans sekularisering 1895–1909.* Uppsala: Almqvist & Wiksell.

Therborn, G. 1980. *What does the ruling class do when it rules?* London: NLB.

———. 1986. *Why some peoples are more unemployed than others?* London: Verso.

Therborn, G., A. Kjellberg, S. Marklund, and U. Öhlund. 1978. Sweden before and after social democracy. *Acta Sociologica* (supplement) 21.

Thomson, A. 1944. Gammal och ny arbetslöshetspolitik." *Ett Genombrott: Festskrift till Gustav Möller.* Stockholm: Tiden.

Tilton, T. 1990. *The political theory of Swedish social democracy*. Oxford: Clarendon.

Torper, U. 1982. *Tidsramar, tidsanvändning och kunskapsutveckling i den svenska grundskolan*. Diss.

Tsebelis, G. 1990. *Nested games: Rational choice in comparative politics*. Berkeley and Los Angeles: University of California Press.

Unga, N. 1976. *Socialdemokratin och arbetslöshetsfrågan 1912–32*. Lund: Arkiv.

Ussing, P. O. 1982. *Skolestyrets udvikling*. Vejle, Denmark: Dafolo forlag.

Vedung, E. 1991. *Utvärdering i politik och förvaltning*. Lund: Studentlitteratur.

Vincent, A. 1987. *Theories of the state*. Oxford: Basil Blackwell.

Waldo, D. 1990. A theory of public administration means in our time a theory of politics also. In *Public administration: The state of the discipline*, edited by N. B. Lynn and A Wildavsky. Chatham, N.J.: Chatham House.

Weber, M. [1922] 1971. *Makt och Byråkrati*. Oslo: Gyldendal.

———. [1922]. 1947. *The theory of social and economic organization*. New York: The Free Press.

———. 1968. *Economy and society: Volumes one and two*, edited by G. Roth and C. Wittich. Berkeley and Los Angeles: University of California Press.

Weir, M. 1992. *Politics and jobs: The boundaries of employment policy in the United States*. Princeton: Princeton University Press.

Weir, M., and T. Skocpol. 1985. State structures and the possibilities for "Keynesian" responses to the Great Depression in Sweden, Britain, and the United States. In *Bringing the state back in*, edited by P. Evans, T. Skocpol, and D. Rueschemeyer. New York: Cambridge University Press.

Wennås. O. 1966. *Striden om latinväldet*. Uppsala: Almqvist & Wiksell.

Wilensky, H. 1990. Active labor market policy: Its content, effectiveness, and odd relation to evaluation research. Working paper no. 21, the Institute of Industrial Relations, University of California at Berkeley.

Wilensky, H. L., and L. Turner. 1987. *Democratic corporatism and policy linkages*. Berkeley: JJS.

Williams, W. 1971. *Social policy research and analysis*. New York: Elsevier.

Wingborg, M. 1982. Grundskoleelever utan grundskola. *Kritisk Utbildningstidskrift-KRUT 23–24*.

Wittrock, B. 1983. Governance in crisis and withering of the welfare state: The legacy of the policy sciences." *Policy Sciences* 15.

Wolfe, A. 1977. *The limits of legitimacy: Political contradictions of late capitalism*. New York: Free Press.

Wolman, H. 1980. The determinants of program success and failure. *Journal of Public Policy* 1.

Wright, E. O. 1978. *Class, crisis and the state*. London: NLB.

Yin, R. K. 1982. Studying the implementation of public programs. In *Studying implementation: Methodological and administrative Issues*, edited by W. Williams. Chatham, N.J.: Chatham House.

Zald, M. N. 1981. Trends in policy making and implementation in the welfare state. In *Organizations and the human services*, edited by H. D. Stein. Philadelphia: Temple University Press.

# Interviews

0. Arvidson, Stellan. Member of the 1946 School Commission and member of Parliament 1957–68.

1. Bergom-Larsson, Matts. Director of the SAF, member of the AMS board 1960–75 and the SÖ board 1964–72.

2. Edenman, Ragnar. Under secretary of state 1951–57 and minister of ecclesiastical affairs 1957–67.

3. Eldridge, Clarence. Deputy director of the United States Department of Labor.

4. Engvall, Martin. Director of the Regional Labor Market Board 1957–76.

5. Erlander, Tage. Prime minister 1946–67 (telephone interview).

6. Fiander, Winston. Director, executive secretariat, at the Employment and Immigration Department, Canada.

7. Forster, Richard. Labour market attaché at the British Embassy in Stockholm.

8. Hofsten, Greta. Senior administrative officer 1966–68, AMS.

9. Iloonen, Matti. Senior administrative officer of the Department of Labor, Helsinki, Finland.

10. Isling, Åke. Member of the SÖ board 1964–71 and senior administrative officer at the SÖ 1972–75.

11. Jönsson, Ove. Head of Personnel Division at the AMS 1960–65.

12. Karlson, Tore. LO-representative, member of the SÖ board 1964–76 and of the AMS board 1963–75.

13. Lindström, G. SAF-representative and member of the AMS board 1962–82.

14. Lundberg, Arne. Chairman of the investigation on democracy in the public administration (Sw. *Demokrati inom statsförvaltningen*) presented at the SAP convention 1952.

15. Löwbeer, Hans. Under secretary of state 1957–64 and director general of the SÖ 1964–68.

16. Östergren, Bertil. Director of the SACO, member of the AMS board 1967–71 and of the SÖ board 1964–67.

17. Marklund, Sixten. Senior administrative officer of the SÖ 1961–65.

18. Moberg, Sven. Director general of the National Agency for Administrative Development 1968–82.

19. Molin, Karl. Senior administrative officer, the AMS Division of Personnel 1961–.

20. Nilsson, Gunnar. Chairman of the LO 1973–83.

21. Nyström, Per. Under secretary of state, Department of Social Affairs 1945–50.

22. Olsson, Bertil. Director general of the AMS 1957–72.

23. Olsson, Tryggve. Senior administrative officer in the Division of Personnel, AMS 1951–83.

24. Rehn, Gösta. Economist at the LO 1941–52 and 1958–59 and head of Division of Manpower and Social Affairs of the OECD 1962–74.

25. Rehnberg, Bertil. Director general of the AMS 1972–83.

26. Rosén, Nils-Gustav. Director general of the SÖ 1947–64.

27. Sträng, Gunnar. Minister of finance 1955–76.

28. Tobisson, Lars. Director of SACO, member of the AMS board 1971–74 and of the SÖ board 1970–74.

29. Ulvhammar, Birgitta. Director general of the SÖ 1977–81.

30. Wittrock, Jan. Senior administrative officer of the AMS.

# Index

of bureaucracy in, 35; Forest Service, 172–73, 205n4; labor market policy in, 17–18, 176, 180, 206n3; welfare state expansion in, 38

Vahlberg, Gustav, 119
Van der Ven, A. H., 35
Veblen, Thorstein, 48
Verein für Sozialpolitik (German Society for Social Policy), 10
vocational education, administration of, 103–04
Von Sydow, Hjalmar, 82–83

Wallentheim, Adolf, 69
Wallerstein, Michael, 29

Weber, Max, 10–12, 18, 44–45, 48, 79, 107, 125, 133, 173–74, 180, 183
Weijene, Josef, 69
Weir, Margaret, 29, 62, 176, 180, 184
welfare state, 5; labor movement and, 32; mode of intervention of, 14–15
Westerberg, Bengt, 194
Wildavsky, A., 36–37
Wilensky, Harold, 17
Williams, Walter, 175
Wolfe, Alan, 21
Wolman, Harold, 38–39, 137
World War II, 81, 104, 109, 186
Wright, Eric, 22, 43–44

Zald, Meyer, 177